GREENBERG'S GUIDE TO MARX TOYS

Volume I: 1923-1950

By
Maxine A. Pinsky

Edited by
MaryAnn S. Suehle

Cover photograph by **Robert Grubb**

Greenberg Publishing Company, Inc.
7566 Main Street
Sykesville, MD 21784
(301) 795-7447

First Edition

Manufactured in the United States of America

Greenberg Publishing Company, Inc. offers the world's largest selection of Lionel, American Flyer, LGB, Ives, and other toy train publications as well as a selection of books on model and prototype railroading, dollhouse miniatures, and toys. For a copy of our current catalogue, please send a large self-addressed stamped envelope to Greenberg Publishing Company, Inc. at the above address.

Greenberg Shows, Inc. sponsors the world's largest public train, dollhouse, and toy shows. They feature extravagant operating model railroads for N, HO, O, Standard, and 1 Gauges as well as a huge marketplace for buying and selling nearly all model railroad equipment. The shows also feature, a large selection of dollhouses and dollhouse furnishings. Shows are currently offered in metropolitan Baltimore, Boston, Ft. Lauderdale, Cherry Hill and Wayne in New Jersey, Long Island in New York, Norfolk, Philadelphia, Pittsburgh, and Tampa. To receive our current show listing, please send a self-addressed stamped envelope marked "Train Show Schedule" to the address above.

ISBN: 0-89778-027-2

Library of Congress Cataloging-in-Publication Data

Pinsky, Maxine A.
    Greenberg's guide to Marx toys / by Maxine A.
Pinsky ; edited by MaryAnn S. Suehle.
        p.   cm.
    Includes index.
    Contents: v. 1: 1923-1950
    ISBN 0-89778-027-2 : $40.00
    1. Toys. 2. Louis Marx & Co. I. Title.
II. Title: Guide to Marx toys.
TS2301.T7P48 1987
688.7'2'0973—dc19   87-30250
                                    CIP

DEDICATION

This book is dedicated to my dear husband, **Edward,** who, except for the actual research and writing, helped in every conceivable way. I could not have written this book without his assistance and support.

ACKNOWLEDGMENTS

It is a pleasure to thank the following people whose contributions were truly extraordinary.

Special Contributors
The following people deserve special recognition for their considerable help: **Dr. Malcolm Kates, Walt Maeder, John** and **Philip Ritter, Philip Rolin, Paul** and **Stephanie Sadagursky,** and **Charles** and **Cheryl Weber.** They allowed the study of their collections, answered numerous questions, and provided comprehensive toy listings. They always showed considerable interest and caring concern. I am extremely appreciative of their contributions.

It is hardly possible to contribute more generously than **John Fox.** John worked as hard on the Honeymoon Express chapter as I did, revising his information several times. He also provided information about other toys and detailed drawings. I am deeply grateful to him.

Charles Cox, Eric J. Matzke, and **Trip Riley** deserve special mention for contributing detailed toy listings and other information.

Ken Pfirman kindly devoted much essential information, including newspaper clippings, and was helpful in many important ways.

Collectors
The following collectors graciously allowed their collections to be photographed: **Tom Croyts, Mike Dency, John Fox, Dr. Malcolm Kates, Bob Liebno, Walt Maeder, John S. Newbraugh, Frances** and **James Nichols, Ed Owens, Trip Riley, John** and **Philip Ritter, Philip Rolin, Stephanie** and **Paul Sadagursky, Elaine** and **Larry Schafle, W. Spencer Stoughton,** and **Cheryl** and **Charles Weber.**

Interviewees
The following former Marx employees generously shared their extensive knowledge and unique experiences at Marx: **Richard Carver, Cal Cook, Edmond Galloway, C. Edward Hjelte, Kenneth L. Johnson, William J. Kalsch, Leroy "Chippy" Martin,** and **Lawrence Passick. Philip Zacks** also provided invaluable information. It was a privilege to share information with them. **Ralph L. Carver** arranged for the interview with his brother, Richard Carver.

Researchers
Hal R. Ashley sought information from a Scarsdale, New York newspaper office and different libraries. He sent obituaries and articles, including one from **Life** magazine.

Gerrit Beverwyck and **Peter Fritz,** the former and present editors of the **Marx Toy Collector Newsletter,** graciously allowed the use of the newsletter as a resource and offered many helpful suggestions.

Lillian B. Gottschalk permitted me to use information from her fine book, **American Toy Cars & Trucks.** Ms. Gottschalk also supplied information about the Marx Company and offered helpful suggestions.

Rev. Carl H. Kruelle, Jr. contributed interesting information and newspaper clippings.

Barbara Seidler authored a helpful article which appeared in the Girard, Pennsylvania **Cosmopolite Herald Newspaper.** Ms. Seidler kindly gave me access to her personal notes.

Gary T. Shoup, editor of the **Erie Story Magazine,** sent information and photocopied articles at the Erie Historical Society.

Information Contributors

Edward G. Carter shared information concerning his father's toy company, the C. E. Carter Company, and details about the Climbing Monkey Toy.

Ralph Kaufman provided interesting information about Louis Marx and the Jaymar Specialty Company. **Donald Kaufman** permitted slide copies of Marx toys to be used for this book.

Francoise Milder, my sister-in-law in England, donated information gleaned from her research in various British libraries. She wrote letters to solicit further information.

Lawrence P. Orr graciously shared information, supplied photographs, and answered questions.

Anne D. Williams gave detailed information about Marx jigsaw puzzles.

The following also contributed invaluable information presented in this book: **the Erie Historical Society, Edward L. Kelly, Al Marwick,** and **Harry Naffin.**

Catalog Contributors

The late **William Clapper** permitted me to have a valuable Marx catalog.

Hillel Don Lazarus, D.D.S., past National President of T.T.O.S., was the first person to help me. He voluntarily put together a book of catalogs. He sent patents, information, and advice. Throughout the years of writing this book, "Hilly" showed great warmth, interest, concern, and support.

John S. Newbraugh sent numerous catalog copies, loaned me original catalogs, answered questions, and provided encouragement and support.

Lloyd W. Ralston allowed me to use his helpful auction catalogs as a reference.

Richard L. Stafford loaned me an important Marx catalog and sent a Marx winding key. He was always supportive.

Lenore Swoiskin, Chief Archivist at Sears, Roebuck and Co., and her assistant, **Victoria Cwiok,** gave access to essential **Sears** catalogs and went out of their way to be helpful.

Keith Wills supplied catalog pages with information.

Readers

Not only did the reviewers point out errors and omissions, but sometimes they read large sections of the manuscript under tight deadlines. Special thanks go to **Bert Adair, Gary Anderson, David Ashworth, Bill Berresford, John Breslin, Mike Dency, Georges Denzene, Ron Fink, John Fox, Paul Kruska, Eric J. Matzke, Dan McLain, John S. Newbraugh, Frances Nichols, James Nichols, Lawrence P. Orr, Fred Pauling, Trip Riley, John Ritter, Charles Sharp, I. D. Smith, Ken Starke, Len Warner, Charles Weber, Anne D. Williams,** and **Keith Wills.** Their patience and continued enthusiasm were very much appreciated.

While some of the values were collected from the readers, the following collectors shared their expertise with us by supplying many of the values that appear in this book: **Stewart Bearn, John Fox, Stephen Leonard, Pete Levine, Eric Matzke, Ronald Moss, Frances** and **James Nichols,** and **Len Warner.**

Publisher and Staff

Heartfelt thanks to my Publishers, **Bruce** and **Linda Greenberg** for their enthusiasm, helpfulness, sensitivity to my feelings, and for giving me the opportunity to write this book.

This book in its final form was made possible by **MaryAnn S. Suehle.** MaryAnn re-wrote large sections of a complicated manuscript. She streamlined, organized, and clarified each section and carefully researched a myriad of details.

Samuel Baum helped to design the front cover, the text layout, and organized and placed the photographs. **Steve Kimball** sorted through the patents, researched and collected values, and added them to the manuscript.

Other Greenberg staff provided logistical support. **Marsha Davis, Judith Davidson,** and **Jerry Kiley** typed the manuscript into the word processor. **Donna Price** proofread the book for consistency and style. **Maureen Crum** assisted with page design and did the paste-up for the book.

The photographs were produced largely through the painstaking efforts of **Robert Grubb.** Other photographers that contributed to the project are **Maury Feinstein, Cary Myers, Tim Parrish, George Stern,** and **Paul Summers.**

Maxine Pinsky
November 1987

TABLE OF CONTENTS

PREFACE

In order to present first-hand information in the Marx toy guide, I conducted several interviews with former Marx personnel. This information is based on the memory of those interviewed and some of the events belong to another time, so the reader is cautioned that slight inaccuracies may occur in the text. However, I believe that these interviews do give a truer sense of the Marx company, and what it was like to work there.

The former employees that I interviewed were creative and dedicated people. They loved their jobs at Marx, had pride in the company and its work, and thought of themselves as a family. Most of these employees started to work at the company shortly after high school and stayed 20, 30, or even 40 years. Many of them said that if the company were still in business, they would be working there today. Without exception, all were sincerely willing to help with the research required for the writing of this book. Admittedly, probably not all Marx workers were like those interviewed, but I believe that much of the greatness of Louis Marx was due to his employees.

Leroy "Chippy" Martin was one of the first people to help in the research of this book. I was in contact with Mr. Martin by telephone and letter. He was most pleasant and willingly provided information. He was born and raised in Platea, Pennsylvania, a small town situated between Albion and Girard. He started to work at the Girard Model Works in 1931 at the invitation of his friend, Wayne Dickey.

When the Girard Model Works went bankrupt, Louis Marx bought the company and Mr. Martin became an administrative director at the the new Girard Manufacturing Company. Leroy Martin believed: "We had a different class of people at Girard...who came with us and stayed for ages. It was a very fine place to work." Mr. Martin remained with the Marx company until his retirement in 1974.

The next person interviewed was **Philip Zacks,** president of the Erisco Wire Company. Mr. Zacks was a bright, energetic, affable person who went out of his way to help with this book. The Erisco company began to manufacture steel wire and wire parts for the Marx company in the mid-1960s, when Marx developed the Big Wheel tricycle. Now Erisco manufactures and fabricates steel wire and makes custom components.

Kenneth Johnson, a former Marx employee for 31 years, now works for the Erisco Company as a production foreman. He started at the Erie plant in 1948, and at its close he was transferred to the Girard plant until 1979. He originally started as a toolmaker, then moved to tool engineering, and went to Girard as a tool and manufacturing engineer. Mr. Johnson was a charming, modest, and very knowledgeable person.

Philip Zacks authorized a tour of the factory, formerly Marx's main Erie plant, with Ken Johnson as guide. I had a mixture of feelings seeing the factory, somewhat akin to a movie fan touring Hollywood. It was easy to imagine the great Marx toys going down the line. Easy to imagine, but to see in reality—what a sight it must have been! Mr. Johnson, who still works in the building that was once owned by Marx, said: "This is a Marx building and (when) I'm back in one of the offices...I think maybe I'm still there."

The next person interviewed was **Richard Carver** who had been design foreman for the Research and Development department at Marx and head of that department during World War II. He was a naturally gracious and modest person whose interview was very informative. He kindly loaned me his personal set of patents for study.

Jobs were difficult to find in the early 1930s, but a friend told Mr. Carver of an opening at the "Monkey Works," as the Carter Toy Works was locally known in tribute to the popularity of the Climbing Monkey toy. Richard Carver started at Marx as a model maker and toy designer, inventing and developing many of Marx's well-known toys. He was with the company for 42 years until Dunbee-Combex bought it in 1976.

Mr. Carver described the experience of seeing a toy he had designed in a store. "Many times I worked so hard on...(a toy, and) got into so many details, that I tended to get tired of it....Later, when the toy was finished and I saw it on a store counter all brightly colored...it's funny, but I got...a charge out of the toy." "I used to get satisfaction if I made a toy that was a success, and we sold enough of them so that the company made money. I felt that I was earning my pay."

Surprisingly, Mr. Carver said that he did not have any personal favorite toy. "People ask if I still stay interested in toys, but I don't....I don't even know what's out besides video games and electronic toys. It would be nice if they could produce some of the old toys again, but I don't suppose they'd sell."

The next interviewee was **Edmund Galloway,** a production worker for over 30 years at the Marx company. Mr. Galloway was most agreeable and helpful. Spending the evening with him and his wife was almost like being with old friends.

Born and raised in Albion, Pennsylvania, Mr. Galloway graduated from high school in 1948 and went to work at the Girard plant shortly thereafter. He was still with the company when it declared bankruptcy in 1979. Mr. Galloway thought that perhaps half the people who lived in Albion, including his mother and father, worked at the Marx plant.

Mr. Galloway worked on the assembly line, putting together transformer laminations used inside the copper coils. (Laminations are multiple thin layers of iron or steel which form the frame for mounting the primary and secondary coil.) The metal case was placed over the assembly and run through a press. He had a collection of some postwar toys from which he was kind enough to give me a few plastic items.

The next interview was with **Cal Cook,** a dynamic and confident person. Mr. Cook was one of the pioneers in blow-molding for plastics. With partner Phil Lantzy, Mr. Cook now owns a toy development company which designs toys for major companies such as Mattel and Milton Bradley. In addition, the company designs products for household goods.

At age 17, Mr. Cook and his family moved to the Erie area from the coal-mining region between Wilkes-Barre and Scranton. His mother opened a beauty shop and one of her customers was a Floor Lady at the Marx plant. The Floor Lady got Mr. Cook a job at the Marx company in 1946. He started in the maintenance department, became a foreman who ran two or three production lines, then was put in charge of an entire building. After the Korean War, he continued for a short time as a foreman before getting into the Research and Development department, where he worked from 1956 to 1979. Having been blessed with an inventive mind and the ability to profit by his experience, his background on the line gave him good insight into what was necessary to design a toy. In product development, Mr. Cook worked as part of a team that included Richard Carver under the direction of Raymond Lohr. Mr. Cook was involved with most of the ride-on toys that were developed at Marx.

Like other former Marx employees, Mr. Cook did not feel the need to keep the toys he had made. "It is nice to look at a catalog and say, yes, I did that. But by the same token, up over the hill, there are 33 other things waiting to get done."

Although Mr. Cook thought that the benefits could have been better, he enjoyed working at the Marx company. "I used to love the challenge. I couldn't wait to get there in the morning and didn't want to leave at night. We would work sometimes 70 to 80 hours a week. We would go home to eat and come back. It was just the gratification of doing something with your hands and then—all of a sudden—it's painted, it's working, it's in the box. Then...there are thousands of toys jumping off the line."

The next interview was with **William Kalsch,** who had been head of the lithography department and later was production superintendent. Mr. Kalsch, a capable and interesting person, is still vigorous and youthful after a serious illness.

He came to Erie at age 17 and worked with the Marx company from 1937 to 1974. Mr. Kalsch started in the Lithography department where a laborer was needed to handle the steel sheets. Roy Hitchcock, head of the Lithography department, taught Mr. Kalsch the entire lithography trade in one year, a considerably shorter time than usual. After running the second shift for 2-1/2 years, Mr. Kalsch was promoted to the head of the Lithography department. "I ran that lithograph and was in charge of it right up until I retired, but I broke in men...to take my place on the machine so I could run the department...." Much of the information about lithography in Chapter III: Making A Marx Toy was supplied by Mr. Kalsch.

When Erie's lithograph machines were shut down in 1966, Mr. Kalsch became a troubleshooter at the plant, then General Foreman responsible for pressing, painting, and spraying toys. Later, he became Plant Superintendent, responsible for every department except the Model Room, Toolroom, and plastic manufacturing.

Mr. Kalsch recalled, "I used to love to run that lithography machine. I used to make improvements on it and really get it humming. I could get 63 to 65 sheets a minute through it. I made a record run one night, working on the 'Honeymoon Express'...we put (almost) 35,000...sheets through that machine in eight hours." "After I retired, I used to go back once a month to visit....They were just like a family to me, all the years I was there. I grew up with them."

Like many of the other employees interviewed, Mr. Kalsch did not have the toys on which he had worked. He had kept the toys as he made them, but eventually disposed of them. Mr. Kalsch particularly regretted not keeping the "Climbing Monkey" toy since it was the first that he had lithographed.

An interview with **C. Edward Hjelte** was conducted by telephone. Mr. Hjelte was born in Warren, Pennsylvania and worked for Abraham & Strauss as a sporting goods buyer in 1935 and a toy buyer in 1936. He joined the Marx company in 1948 and remained until 1972 when Marx sold the business to the Quaker Oats Company. Mr. Hjelte stayed an additional year at the company to assist the new management.

Mr. Hjelte acted as Director of Marketing at the Marx company and eventually worked with the Research and Development department. "The first toy item that I had my hand in was the metal dollhouse which had a complete set of plastic furniture. It retailed at $3.98 in 1949 or 1950...we sold almost a million dollhouses."

One of the last interviews was with **Lawrence Passick** who was born in Brooklyn, New York and joined the Marx company in 1953 as an office clerk for Joe Pastore, assistant to Louis Marx. Mr. Passick advanced to a position in which he provided world-wide licensing and technical support to companies that borrowed Marx tooling. Later, Mr. Passick, along with Roy Farge, operated Marx's Canadian subsidiary. Passick handled production and outside contracting and Farge handled sales. When the Marx company was bought in 1972, Mr. Passick worked at the Quaker Oats Company for 1-1/2 years until it moved to Connecticut. He subsequently rejoined Marx under Dunbee-Combex-Marx as Manager of International Operations.

At Dunbee-Combex-Marx, Mr. Passick was responsible for closing down the Marx facilities, turning assets into liquid cash, and locating and recording all of the Marx tooling that could be leased or sold. When the Erie and Glendale facilities were closed down, Mr. Passick was involved with the auctions to dispose of the toys.

Of his many years at the company, Mr. Passick commented, "I enjoyed immensely the years I worked for Marx and the number of associations made. I still maintain many friendships. Friendships made at Marx lasted a long time." [1]

The final interview was held with a former Marx employee who wished to remain anonymous in order to preserve his privacy. This gentleman generously spent a considerable amount of time in order to share much information. He was a gracious and fascinating man of boundless energy with a wealth of knowledge and a sincere love of children and toys. He worked on a host of toys through the years.

He was a former draftsman and designer in the research and development department at the Marx company from 1952 to 1976. He began work at the plant when he was asked: "Would you like to come out and draw monkeys?"

He pointed out that, in the toy business, "you have to have a youthful mind and attitude. You can't be a stiff old slide rule jockey; you have to blend into the style." He considered his job to have been "more fun than labor."

It is my hope that these 10 interviews will add a more personal perspective to the history and listing of Marx toys. Quotes from these interviews appear liberally throughout the text sections and are footnoted in order to identify the speaker.

---

[1] **Marx Toy Collector Newsletter,** Vol. 3, No. 2, p. 13.

INTRODUCTION

INTRODUCTION TO TOY LISTINGS

Marx toys were described in the January 1927 issue of **Playthings** magazine as follows: "The Marx Mechanical Toys are famous for their mechanical ingenuity, bright colors, and foolproof construction. They are popularly priced, and show a very wide range of vehicle and novelty mechanical playthings." Marx made almost every type of toy which performed almost every kind of action. His toys range from fanciful to realistic, but, in general, Marx believed that children liked toys which reflected what was familiar to them.

The innovative design, amusing action, outstanding artwork, and rich, vibrant colors give an immediacy to Marx toys that makes them almost able to leap from the shelves. Marx toys often have a whimsical sense of humor that is continued in the illustrations on the toy's box.

How does one cover such a range and multitude of toys? Unfortunately, it is impossible to cover all of them. Unknown toys and different variations are always being discovered by the author, who quickly learned never to assume a Marx toy or variation did not exist just because it had not been seen. Then there are toys that appear to have been made by Marx, but, because of the lack of proper identification, this can not be proven.

Since catalogs are mentioned frequently in the toy listings, a few words about them are in order. Early Marx catalogs are rare and it is believed that Marx did not regularly issue catalogs for his toys until later years.[1] The catalogs of chain stores and mail order houses help in the research of early toys. However, frequently a number of unidentified toys not produced by Marx appear on a page with the Marx name and other Marx toys. This understandably leads to incorrect identification of these toys as being manufactured by Marx. There may indeed have been a connection between the toy and the Marx company because sometimes manufacturers shared dies, parts, or patents.

Catalogs of the same year differ from city to city, and some toys in one city's catalog do not appear in another city's catalog. The **Sears** catalog was used extensively for dating and describing many of the toys in this volume. None of the toys mentioned in this book are currently available through Sears.

The reader may not be familiar with the **PB 84** auction catalog from which the catalog numbers for most of the toys are taken. Sotheby Parke Bernet is a leading auction house in New York and other countries. **PB 84** refers to the smaller auction gallery located on 84th Street which is a division of Sotheby Parke Bernet, Inc., New York.

It only remains to be said that it is the author's earnest wish that the toy listings will be interesting and of help to the reader.

DETERMINING VALUES

The author has not provided any of the market values shown in this book. She has provided the detailed descriptions and variations of the Marx toys, highlighting their historical significance and technical development. The toy prices were supplied by Greenberg Publishing Company staff with the assistance of several Marx Toy collectors.

The toy prices shown in this guide may vary somewhat with the prices at auctions and shows for several reasons. Marx toy prices are sometimes influenced by events completely outside of the toy industry. For example, Cinderella toys sold at higher prices during the 50th anniversary of that film. In addition, prices do not necessarily reflect the availability of a particular toy, and this information has been added to the listings when known. Finally, prices fluctuate between regions, such as the East and West coast, with higher prices usually expected in the West. While we have attempted to compile toy prices from several collectors in different regions, buyers should be aware that the prices in this book serve as a guide only. **It is recommend that the novice consult with experienced collectors for large purchases.**

Condition:

Good — scratches, small dents, dirty.

Excellent — minute scratches or nicks, no dents or rust.

NRS — **N**o **R**eported **S**ales; information is insufficient to determine price.

These standards are descriptive of the condition of the finish, and in no way describe the operation of the toy. Prices will be higher for a toy sold in its original box.

EDITOR'S NOTE

The toys in this book are organized in chapters either by theme or type. While some toys were discussed according to theme, it was as important that other toys of the same type could be compared. I have cross-referenced toys that fell into both categories as much as possible, but the most direct way to find an item is to use the alphabetical index at the back of the book.

The pre-1950s toys are covered in Volumes I and II. Volume II contains the vehicular toys and a miscellaneous chapter. Third and fourth volumes are planned for the Marx post-1950s toys.

---

[1] A Marx catalog is mentioned in an ad from the June 1921 issue of **Playthings** magazine.

CHAPTER I: THE STORY OF LOUIS MARX

Louis Marx became a millionaire in his twenties, an age at which most young men are just beginning in the business world. He received fame as well as fortune, and became known by such glowing superlatives as the "Toy King" and the "Henry Ford of Toys." Marx was the friend of a president, top generals, show business celebrities, and other luminaries of his time. At one time, he was the largest toy manufacturer in the world.

Beginnings

Louis Marx was born on August 11, 1896 in Brooklyn, New York to parents of German origin, Jacob, who worked as a tailor, and Clara Lou Marx.[1] Because of his German background, it was later said that Marx spoke English in a gutteral manner. His siblings included an older sister, Rose, and a younger brother, David. Louis attended Public School 11 and Fort Hamilton High School in Brooklyn, graduating at the age of 15.

In a childhood incident, young Marx gave early "promise" of his daring. As if they were part of the shipping department, Marx and an accomplice picked up a canoe, put it over their heads, and walked out the delivery door of Abraham & Strauss, a department store. What a prank for a nine-year-old! Perhaps this incident was an early indication of the cunning that would serve Marx in his future daring sales policies.

In 1912, sixteen-year-old Marx worked for Ferdinand Strauss, whose Zippo the Climbing Monkey and Alabama Coon Jigger, a clockwork minstrel, were two of the first lithographed tinplate, mechanical toys mass-produced in America. In four years Marx was managing the company's New Jersey plant and subsequently became a company director.

Strauss remembered Marx as a boy with the mind of a man. Marx was not satisfied "just to stand behind a counter and sell...he wanted volume, even then." Eventually, Marx and Strauss differed in establishing the company's production policy. Marx thought the company should concentrate on volume production. Strauss and the Board of Directors voted against Marx's policy and he was fired.

Marx then entered the Army in 1917 as a private and, characteristic of his ambitious nature, attained the rank of sergeant before resuming civilian life in 1918.

Marx next worked as a salesman for a Vermont wood products company. Just as he had done for Strauss, Marx increased the profits at the company. According to an article in the December 12, 1955 issue of *Time* magazine, "...Marx redesigned a line of wooden toys, and sales soared from 15,000 to 1,500,000 in two years."

Louis Marx & Company

The outcome of World War I signaled the end of the competitive German toy manufacturers who had all but closed the American toy market. After the war the toy market was open, especially to U.S. manufacturers, and notably to an enterprising, young U.S. salesman.

With the help of his brother, David, Marx turned his talents to his own company. The two became middlemen between chain stores and manufacturers. They would determine how to cut costs on a toy, then get orders for the toys that they could produce at a lesser cost. Marx paid other

June 1921 **Playthings** *magazine ad.*

manufacturers to produce the toys for them, since the Marx company had no manufacturing facilities at this time.

While Louis Marx remained at the helm of the young company, brother David played a major role in keeping the company afloat. David Marx was reported to have had a lively and cheerful disposition. Undoubtedly, he was quite successful at handling the social contacts needed for the business and often entertained the buyers.[2] Leroy Martin, a former Marx employee, said of David Marx: "he was never one to stand in the front line and wave his hand."

In 1919, Louis Marx & Company incorporated and Marx set up an office in New York's Fifth Avenue Building, sometimes referred to as the headquarters of the toys of the world where many other toy manufacturers were located. The brothers shared an office so small that one of them had to leave when a visitor entered.[3] The company's central offices remained at 200 Fifth Avenue throughout Louis Marx's ownership of the company.

By 1921, Marx acquired manufacturing facilities. When Marx's former employer, Ferdinand Strauss, sold his business, Marx purchased the dies for the two toys that sold so well for Strauss, the Climbing Monkey and the Alabama Coon Jigger, mentioned previously. "The monkey and minstrel had been on the market for more than twenty years, but Marx gave them bright new colors, brought out bigger models, and sold 8,000,000 of each."[4] Due largely to the success of these toys, Marx was a millionaire at age 26. In the late 1920s, Marx took note of a Filipino toy that later became known as the yo-yo. He sold more than 100 million of them.[5]

In the mid-1920s Marx was nationally known. He acquired what was to become the three major manufacturing plants for the Marx company by the 1930s. These were the Erie and Girard plants in Pennsylvania and the Glendale plant in West Virginia. However, production at all three plants practically shut down between January and April until the 1940s, when increased sales warranted continued production year-round. By the 1950s, Marx was licensing to factories in foreign countries.

Marx In Business

While Marx was an extraordinary and successful businessman, he rarely visited the plants that produced his toys. In the late 1930s and into the 1940s, Marx would visit the Erie plant several weeks before the production of Christmas toys. The toys were displayed on the assembly tables so that Marx could walk up and down the assembly line to decide how many of each toy would be produced. It is believed that Marx's last visit to the Erie plant was in 1950. Still, Marx maintained control over which toys would be manufactured at the plants because he was close to buyers who told him what they would buy.

One of Marx's visits to the Girard plant was in the early 1950s. He was accompanied by his second wife, Idella. But many employees at the Marx company, even those who worked there for over thirty years, never saw Louis Marx. After World War II, he often sent Vice-president Archie Marcus in his place to review the plants' budgets and other manufacturing procedures. Chippy Martin, a former Marx executive, said that Archie Marcus had the ability to put his finger on a weak spot in any argument. His mind churned out answers like a machine. It appears that Marx never hesitated to spend money on anything that Archie Marcus approved.[6]

Marx depended on trusted and able employees, sent numerous memos, and kept constant telephone contact with the plants. The Erie plant had a direct telephone line that was open 24 hours a day. According to former employee Richard Carver: "...you couldn't get on that phone as there was somebody on it all the time. I think he felt he didn't need to be here." Chippy Martin remembered: He "was always calling up to say what we

January 1922 **Playthings** *magazine ad.*

should have or what we could make...." He seemed to allow the plants to run with little outside control. "Yet," Martin continued, "from time to time he came up with some little thing that indicated he knew a little more than showed on the surface."

For as seldom as Marx visited the plants, "in general, he was liked," said Richard Carver. "We were kind of in awe of Louis in the early days, but he was friendly and I think he treated people right. If he hadn't I would not have stayed there for forty-two years, and I know a good many others who stayed there—all of them liked Marx." Former Marx executive Larry Passick described Marx as "an extremely decisive, quick-moving man who made fast judgments and decisions." *The Wall Street Journal* reported that Marx was "driving and stern but also as charming and generous."[7]

Marx aggressively cultivated ideas for toys. From a warehouse full of all kinds of toys, he extracted the best features as inspiration for the company's production. Even Marx himself said of the toy business, "When they copy you, it's piracy... When you copy them, it's competition." But when Marx "competed," he did make small improvements on the toys and sold them at lower prices.[8]

Another way in which Marx "competed" with toy companies that produced a similar product was to buy the company. In the 1950s, Marx bought the Unique Arts Company and Wyandotte Toys. Similarly, in the early 1960s, Marx owned LOJO Trucks located in New Jersey.[9]

At the close of World War II, General Eisenhower, later to become President of the United States, asked Marx to visit Germany to determine which toy factories could safely be allowed to operate without developing into munitions plants.[10] Some people believe that Marx may have had his own interests at heart, namely, finding ideas for toys. Although his German heritage had prompted Marx to visit Germany on his own, he could have been serving his own interests in agreeing to tour the factories, especially since Marx kept such a keen awareness of the toy market.

No matter how successful Marx became, he always wanted to do better and continued to be interested in self-improvement. For example, instead of eating lunch, he was known to study notes on vocabulary while running for exercise around the top of the Fifth Avenue Building.[11] Regardless of his healthful efforts, he was in the habit of smoking large cigars. In addition, later photographs of the toy manufacturer show that he was somewhat overweight, a characteristic which was not lost on publishers who saw his resemblance to Santa Claus.

From the 1931 **Sears** *catalog.*

A Louis Marx Close-up

Marx did not belong to the various toy organizations that some of the other manufacturers did, but he relished the company of the prominent and famous.[12] He was known as the "Cafe Society Santa" at the "21" nightclub in Manhattan where he handed out, from the extra-large pockets of his expensive suits, a stream of toys for his friends. These included such notables as ventriloquist Edgar Bergen, boxer Gene Tunney, Prince Bernhard of the Netherlands, and Lieutenant General Emmett O'Donnell. In fact, Marx held generals in such high esteem that he named some of the children from his second marriage after them.

Though it was a commonly held attitude at the time, Marx seemed somewhat of a chauvinist toward women by today's standards. When General Gruenther met Marx's attractive wife, Idella, he jokingly asked her why she had married Marx. Marx answered for her saying, "...I'm the one with the brains." Marx seems often to have preferred the company of male celebrities. "Go to dinner with Fred Allen," he revealed, "and you can discuss the world situation. An actress would think it's a line."

Marx was a man who worked hard and played hard. His favorite expression was said to be "Dum vivimus, vivamus" which roughly means "Live it up." As befitted a man with such a motto, Marx's home was lavish. The largest privately-owned estate in Scarsdale, New York, the Marx 25-room Georgian mansion was situated on 20-1/2 acres. The house had nine fireplaces and fourteen baths and was fenced to enclose Marx's thirteen dogs. In addition, there was a swimming pool, tennis court, paddle court, and a four-car garage, above which was a seven-room caretaker's quarters. Two paintings by President Eisenhower, who painted Marx's portrait, hung on the walls. According to an article that appeared in the *New York Times* on April 3, 1982, the property was sold to a developer who planned to build on the estate.

Marx was a solicitous father who enjoyed playing with his eight children, four from each of his two marriages. Marx liked to roughhouse with the children, playfully pummeling and chasing them around the house. They were allowed to squirt water guns and smash toys in order, Marx believed, to rid them of their aggressive energy. Marx told the children horror stories in an effort to teach them courage, while Idella read them digests of the classics. They were given French and word-building lessons during the day, while at bedtime classical music was piped into their rooms. Although Marx was an agnostic, the children from both marriages, who were referred to as the first and second shifts, belonged to the Episcopal Church. Marx did not attend services with his children, but contributed toys to the Church.

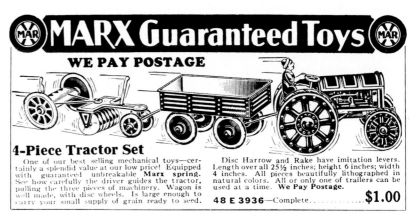

A Marx toy ad from the 1929 **Montgomery Wards** *catalog.*

Although fond of his children, Marx showed remarkable forgiveness to a woman who threatened to kidnap one of them. Marion Harris, the Marx's nursemaid, demanded $20,000 from Marx under the threat that she would kidnap one of his two young children, Barbara or Louis Jr. When Marx spoke in her defense, Judge Rosalsky replied: "Your plea for mercy for this woman must be disregarded...I shall not permit myself to be moved by maudlin sentimentality...."[13]

Marx was also known for his generosity. For example, he donated as many as one million gift toys each year to children.[14] He gave freely to charities, particularly those interested in fighting cancer, because his first wife Renee died of the disease in the mid-1940s.

Marx's generosity extended to his family members as well. Marx gave his 21-year-old son, Louis Marx, Jr., prominent in his own right, almost one million dollars.[15] In the 1920s, Marx financed a new toy company for his father, Jacob, known as the Jaymar Specialty Company, the name of which was derived from Jacob Marx. Louis Marx's older sister, Rose, helped run Jaymar.

According to a top executive at Jaymar, Ralph Kaufman, the new company was restricted to offer products made of cardboard or wood to avoid competition with the Marx company which made metal and plastic toys. But Jaymar displayed products in the Marx showroom for nine years. People from the Marx organization were also available to Jaymar for free advice and information.

Paradoxically, Louis Marx & Company is out of business, while Jaymar, still located at the Fifth Avenue Building in New York, continues to manufacture toy pianos and jigsaw puzzles and import miscellaneous toys. Jaymar is thought to be the second oldest Disney licensee in the toy industry. The Jaymar Specialty Company is now owned by Jacob Marx's grandchildren and great-grandchildren, though not by any members of Louis Marx's immediate family.

Although quite generous to most family members, there was one of whom he was not so fond, Dr. Daniel Ellsberg, husband of his daughter Patricia. Marx and Ellsberg did not share a good relationship and when Ellsberg was accused of stealing the Pentagon Papers in the late 1960s, Marx reportedly did not contribute any funds toward Ellsberg's exorbitant legal fees.

Former Chief Domestic Affairs Adviser John D. Ehrlichman claimed that the White House was justified in condoning the break-in at the office of Ellsberg's psychiatrist. Apparently, Ehrlichman believed that there was vital information to be found in the psychiatrist's office, the disclosure of which FBI director J. Edgar Hoover was blocking because of Hoover's close relationship with Louis Marx.[16]

A Toy King's Ideas About Toys

It was Marx's belief that, above all, toys should be fun. Marx's own humor, as well as his interest in novel ideas, is evident from a number of toys that are less suited to children. For example, Marx manufactured a poodle and bartender that drank liquor. There was also the "Lucky Louie" figure of Louis Marx which sat in the Buddha posture and, like all figures of this type, had a large belly.

Strangely, for a man so interested in education, Marx generally did not believe in educational toys for children. He felt that "the ones who buy them are the spinster aunts and spinster uncles and hermetically-sealed parents who wash their children 1,000 times a day."[17] In an article that appeared in the January 1955 issue of the *Reader's Digest*, Marx was quoted as saying: "It's true that children can learn as they play. But I don't go along with psychologists who want to sneak up on them and...jam education into them through toys. The few short years of childhood are precious...." Regardless of his opinions on educational toys, he did make some toys of this type. One example is the 1950s "Presidents of the United States" set consisting of 36 hard plastic figures, each three inches high. The Marx company even published a booklet in conjunction with this set entitled "American Presidents in Miniature" giving the history of all of the presidents up to Eisenhower. The Electric Question and Answer Toy, listed in the Games chapter, is another educational toy.

To Marx, the gift of a toy to a child represented love and reassurance. An article in the November 23, 1959 issue of *Life* magazine called "Top Toy Maker's Buying Guide" quoted Marx as saying: "Toys should be given regularly rather than expensively. A 29 cent toy thoughtfully bestowed once a week does more for youthful security and happiness than $20 worth of toys at Christmas or on a birthday."

The *Life* article outlined the six categories Marx used to judge a toy:
1. *Familiarity:* "The toy must reflect the life around the child."
2. *Surprise:* "Toys should offer the child something he does not expect."

From the 1929 **Montgomery Wards** *catalog.*

3. *Skill:* "A toy that requires a child to practice a little is good, because children like to develop skills and be able to display them."

4. *Play Value:* "This is what keeps the child occupied for hours in an entertaining or creative way."

5. *Comprehensibility:* "A child does not like toys that are too hard to understand."

6. *Sturdiness:* "Not only do (toys) get rough treatment, but a child senses shoddiness." For years, the Louis Marx & Company slogan was "Mechanical Toys That Are Durable And Mechanically Perfect."

In addition to the above qualities Marx said, "A toy should also be safe. There should be no sharp points or cutting edges."[18] This particular point of view may have eventually been forced on Marx by government regulations. In the early years, many of the tin toys did have sharp edges. For example, the six-inch, four-wheel, tin lithographed train cars were sold for 40 years. A victim of OSHA regulations, the toy trains appeared in the *Sears* Christmas catalog for the last time in 1972. While granting that no one would ever wish to risk a child's safety, many children played with the early Marx toys without mishap.

Louis Marx was Louis Marx & Company. Though others tried to run the company after him, none had Marx's gifted touch and the company suffered a decline to the end. On February 5, 1982 at White Plains, New York, Louis Marx died at the age of 85. There was only one Louis Marx; there will never be another like him.

Real Tractor With Chain Pull $1.49

Constructed on the same mechanical principle as the steel tanks used during the war. This Tractor will climb almost anything that is not at complete right angles with the floor. Make piles of books or dig holes in the sand and watch her go over the top!

Sturdy Construction

Fitted with guaranteed **Marx unbreakable spring.** All metal parts are aluminum except driver at the wheel. Stop and start lever gives you opportunity of stopping tractor though spring is not completely unwound. About 7½ inches long, 3¾ inches wide and 6 inches high over driver's head. Chains that run over wheels are of heavy black rubber with suction cups that hold tractor to its course in steep ascents. Runs slowly with strong pulling power for quite a distance. **We Pay Postage.**

48 E 4021---Aluminum tractor... **$1.49**

From the 1929 **Montgomery Wards** *catalog.*

1 The factual information about Louis Marx's early life was originally reported in "The Little King" **Time,** December 12, 1955 and "Louis Marx: Toy King" **Fortune,** January 1946.

2 "Louis Marx: Toy King," p. 125.

3 J. P. and Peggy McEvoy, "Talk With a Toy King" **Reader's Digest,** January 1955, p. 126.

4 "The Little King," p. 96.

5 "The Little King," p. 94.

6 Barbara Seidler, "Marx Toys and Girard A Good Team for 50 Years" **Cosmopolite-Herald,** Girard, Pennsylvania, February 12, 1982, p. 1.

7 Cynthia Saltzman, **Wall Street Journal,** February 8, 1980, p. 6.

8 "The Little King," p. 94.

9 **Marx Toy Collector Newsletter,** Vol. 3, No. 2, p. 13. Information contributed to newsletter by L. Passick.

10 "Louis Marx: Toy King," p. 125.

11 "Louis Marx: Toy King," p. 125.

12 Much of the information in this section about Marx's personal life, including his quotations, was reported in "The Little King" **Time,** December 12, 1955 and "Louis Marx: Toy King" **Fortune,** January 1946.

13 **New York Times,** July 15, 1933, p. 28.

14 Obituary, **Time,** February, 15, 1982, p. 65.

15 "Dan Lufkin's Partner—Whatsisname?" **Forbes,** April 1, 1974, p. 58.

16 Wolfgang Saxon, **New York Times,** February 6, 1982, p. 16.

17 "The Little King," p. 93.

18 Herbert Brean, "Top Toy Maker's Buying Guide" **Life,** November 23, 1959, p. 120.

CHAPTER II: THE RISE OF THE FACTORIES

Early Manufacturing Capabilities

Marx's enterprise as a cost-cutting middleman between chain stores and manufacturers was a quick success. He incorporated in 1919; continued as a sales representative for manufacturers in the early 1920s, notably the Strauss and C. E. Carter companies; and set up his own manufacturing facilities in 1921. At first, Marx rented space in a building owned by C. E. (Nick) Carter at 19th and Cascade Streets in Erie. But as early as 1922, Marx needed increased manufacturing capabilities, and contracted the C. E. Carter Company to produce mechanical toys for him at the 19th Street plant.

According to Edward Carter, son of the now deceased C. E. Carter, the Carter company produced the Climbing Monkey for Marx in the late 1920s. As a tribute to the popularity of the toy, and indicative of Marx's success, the Carter factory was locally known as the "Monkey Works." In the early 1940s, Marx purchased the Carter Company and incorporated it under the name of Louis Marx & Company, Inc. of Pennsylvania.

The Marx Facilities

In the 1930s Marx expanded, acquiring plants in Erie and Girard, Pennsylvania and in Glendale, West Virginia which were to become the three main factories of the company. With the increase in manufacturing capabilities, Marx was selling millions of toys to volume buyers, which enabled him to continually expand and modernize his American factories. The last published balance sheet for the company and its U.S. subsidiaries revealed, as of December 31, 1937, current assets of $3,218,428; current debts of $524,358; and tangible net worth in excess of $2 million.[1] In 1955, the company's gross income was over $50 million and net income was $5 million.[2]

While all three facilities were owned by the same company, each of the plants had its own system of doing things. For example, some of the specification sheets, which listed the materials needed to produce a toy, were different at each plant for the same toy. Each plant bought its own supplies and managed its own budget. A central purchasing office for the Marx company did not even exist at a time when, for instance, needed steel could have been bought in bulk quantity for all of the plants. It was not until later, when the company was manufacturing in plastic, that a centralized purchasing office bought bulk quantities of plastic and distributed it to the plants.

According to Ken Johnson, a former Marx employee, "The feeling between the plants was competitive, too...." Philip Zacks, President of the Erisco Wire Company, explained that each plant would bid on the toys to be produced. Whichever plant could manufacture the item at the lowest price got the job. No matter what each plant produced, all of the toys were funneled through corporate sales in New York.

Erie, Pennsylvania

While Marx was renting factory facilities from the C. E. Carter company, he continued to offer commissions to toy manufacturers and use salvageable dies in order to avoid large plant investments. But by the mid-1920s, when Louis Marx & Company became nationally known, Marx acquired an interest in the Erie plant.[3]

Carter's Climbing Monkey.

SELLS ON SIGHT

KNOWN AND SOLD EVERY-WHERE

The most staple, most popular and biggest selling mechanical toy in the world. Brightly lithographed and perfectly constructed. The action is startlingly realistic and delightfully amusing.

April 1921 **Playthings** *magazine ad.*

In September 1933, the Erie factory was incorporated as the Louis Marx & Company, Inc. of Pennsylvania with an authorized capital of $250,000. In 1935, this subsidiary of the Marx company purchased the plant of the defunct Eriez Stove Company, also located in Erie. Later, the Pennsylvania-based subsidiary leased and then bought the Fokker aircraft plant at Glendale, West Virginia.

Marx's first building in Erie, located on 19th Street, was brick with two stories. The later Erie plant, located at 1816 Raspberry Street, was about 1,000 feet long. This larger factory actually covered one city block and was bordered by 18th and 19th Streets on one side, and Raspberry and Cranberry Streets on the other.

The Erie plant made mechanical windup toys, even mechanical trains that ran on a formed, sheet metal base. According to the June 1981 issue of the *Marx Toy Collector Newsletter*, in 1950 one million cars, and as many tanks and tractors, were produced on the assembly line in Erie. The Erie plant progressed from metal toy production to blow-molding plastics, which marked the development of a child's tricycle called the Big Wheel. Much of the research and development work for the world of Marx—both United States and, later, foreign factories—came from the Erie plant.

Eventually, the Erie facility was comprised of three buildings on 12th Street, with an estimated capacity of 180,000; 140,000; and 25,000 square feet respectively. At the close of the Erie plant in 1975, wire equipment was bought from the Erisco Wire Company in order to continue supplying the wire components for the remaining Glendale and Girard plants. Many of the workers at the Erie plant then went to work at Girard.

Late in 1976, the Erisco Wire Company purchased the plant and the equipment that it had previously leased from Marx. Presently, the Erisco Wire Company manufactures and fabricates steel wire and produces custom components. The Bucyrus-Erie Company, which manufactures construction and mining machinery, owns one of the other Erie buildings.

Girard, Pennsylvania

Toy manufacturing began in Girard with Frank Wood who made mechanical toys in a garage on Penn Avenue in the 1920s. About 1925, Fred Ziesenheim and Stan Connell bought Wood's toy patents and started the Girard Model Works. In the late 1920s, Marx acted as a salesman in New York for Ziesenheim and Connell. The business experienced financial difficulties in 1931 and, in order to avoid paying Marx's eight or ten percent commission, the company terminated his position. But Marx, always thinking ahead, had already bought the plant in Glendale, West Virginia.

In 1934, Ziesenheim declared bankruptcy.[4] At the bankruptcy proceedings, Marx, who had been a stockholder in the Girard Model Works, bought

Moon Mullins Hand Car
6 in. long. Brightly colored. Strong Marx spring motor. They pump the handle up and down and race along. Shpg. wt., 9 oz.
49 K 5772......25c

From the 1935 Sears catalog.

A 1976 photograph of the Marx Girard factory, formerly the Girard Model Works, courtesy of **The Cosmopolite Herald,** *Girard, Pennsylvania, February 19, 1976.*

the company and renamed it the Girard Manufacturing Company, sharing ownership of the plant with S. Boyd Gunnison, former president of the company and owner of the Union Bank and the Tannery. The company went into receivership until 1936 when it was re-opened.

Although other toys were manufactured at Girard, the plant was manufacturing trains in the early 1930s and became known as the "train factory." In the 1960s, the popular speedways accounted for as much as 50 percent of the Girard plant's production. But according to Ed Galloway, a former Marx employee at Girard, while Marx tried other items at the plant, "like everything else, they did a few and that would be the end of them. They went back to trains...."

Some of the other toys made at Girard, besides trains and train accessories, were roller skates (some are believed to have only two wheels), pens, play-sets, bowling games, and pinball games. When Quaker Oats owned the company, even a T.V. Tennis game was produced!

The Girard factory, still located on 227 East Hathaway Street, is presently being converted into an industrial complex. At one point, the Marx Company had planned to move its corporate headquarters to Girard and built new offices and a large warehouse. According to an article in the *Erie Daily Times*, February 1, 1979, the Marx company announced that it would move its corporate offices from Stamford, Connecticut to Girard, Pennsylvania in a newly built 25,000 square foot addition. About 20 executives and their families were expected to make the move. A later article from the same newspaper, April 11, 1979, stated that several offices would not be moving to Girard as previously announced in order to remain close to the New York City area.

Glendale, West Virginia

The Glendale plant, formerly an aircraft factory, was approximately one-quarter of a mile long before Marx added to it. Because of its size, the Glendale plant could manufacture a larger volume of toys than Erie. In 1946, Glendale was so busy that the automatic paint line dipped and baked about 3,500,000 toys each month. Still expanding, the company purchased a warehouse a short distance away.[5]

In the early years, the Glendale plant made the simpler, heavy gauge toys that consisted of, perhaps, two pieces and four wheels, but no mechanisms. The Glendale plant manufactured the larger toys, for example, dollhouses, stagecoach toys, tin buildings, pinball games, and the Big Wheel. However, some of the smaller toys such as the Johnny West figures, Western and Battle sets, and the Presidents sets were manufactured there as well.

Although the Girard and Erie plants both had their own wire-producing capabilities, the Erisco Wire Company helped to supply these plants as well as all of the wire needs of the Glendale plant. Steel wire and wire parts were needed in the mid- to late 1960s for riding toys, notably the Big Wheel tricycle.

The Labor Force

In the early 1960s, at the height of the Marx company production, the Girard plant employed over 1,000 people; Erie employed 1,700; Glendale more than 2,000. Marx's peak employment in the United States reached 8,000.[6]

The Marx company was described as a very close-knit organization by several former employees. "Everyone knew everyone and they knew how the other person thought and what you were expected to do almost automatically," said Cal Cook, a former Marx product development employee. In fact, it has been suggested that the very cohesiveness of the work force at Marx contributed to Quaker Oats' failure to keep the company alive under its new management.

Because women ordinarily worked on assembly lines, Marx employed more women than men at an estimated ratio of ten to one. According to former Marx employee William Kalsch, "On (an assembly) table, there would be maybe ninety women and five men." Usually, men set up the assembly line, brought the work to the assembly tables, and sealed cartons.

An October 1937 photograph of the Honeymoon Express assembly line at one of Marx's Pennsylvania plants. The photograph was provided by William Kalsch.

Unlike most jobs at that time women did piecework and made more money per hour than men, who were given a day rate. To compensate, men were allowed to work overtime. Although some companies paid higher wages than Louis Marx & Company, in general, Marx employees believed that they were paid fair wages and tended to stay with the company for many years. Before World War II, model makers earned the modest sum of 30 cents an hour, a fair wage for the times, while tool and die makers earned about 85 cents an hour.

The factories ran their production schedules based on the sales of an item. But sometimes for a popular toy, the plants, Erie in particular, would produce beyond the schedule and rent warehouse space in which to store the toys. As might be expected of a toy manufacturer, the work was geared to Christmas time. Peak production was between July and December, when 1,500 workers were employed at one plant, which operated around the clock. Production stopped at all of the Marx plants about two or three weeks before Christmas. According to Richard Carver, a former Marx employee: "We wouldn't bother to make any items that couldn't be shipped to the stores in time for Christmas."

In the 1930s, the factory practically shut down between January and April. But the research and development department, then called the experimental department, as well as the toolroom and model room employees, worked year-round in order to develop new toys. When production was resumed in April or May, some 900 workers came back on the job. It was not until the 1940s that the production employees worked more steadily throughout the year. With the addition of Easter toys, the factory could provide work year-round.[7]

In the late 1940s, an independent union charged Marx employees a monthly fee of 50 cents for dues. About 1960, the Retail, Wholesale Department Store Union took the place of the independent one. But the workers did not appear to have done badly without the larger union because in 1951 Boyd Gunnison, former President of the Girard plant, had put a cost of living clause in the labor contracts.

Workers at the Girard plant went on strike only once or twice. Girard had few labor problems perhaps because it was a farming community and many of the plant's employees worked part-time. Since toy production and agriculture were at opposite ends of the calendar, employees were able to work both at the factory and on the farms.

The Erie facility seems to have had the most labor unrest. In the mid-1960s one long strike and some shorter ones may have figured in the decision to move Big Wheel production to the Glendale plant. As a safeguard for the company, labor contracts were staggered to expire at different times so that a strike at one plant could not shut down the whole company.

The Marx company did offer an unusual benefit, especially for the times, but only to its New York employees. Due to Marx's interest in education, in 1947 the New York University held classes at the company's office on Fifth Avenue called "How To Read And Think" for executives and clerks. This was one of the first times that a college course was brought directly to the student. The company paid half the tuition.

Other benefits for workers at Marx increased with time. For example, in 1954, breaks were increased from ten minutes in the morning and again in the afternoon, to 30 minutes in the morning and additional breaks in the afternoon. In later years, the company paid for employees' health insurance, although then it was an expense of only about $5.00 per month.

Perhaps owing to Louis Marx's extravagance, company employees enjoyed another benefit. Louis Marx owned a country club at French Creek in Pennsylvania. The club was open for the enjoyment of all Marx emplyees.

Expansion to Foreign Countries

Business expanded until Marx operated six U.S. factories and was licensing to factories around the globe.[8] His first factory outside the United States was in England, but eventually, Louis Marx & Company was to have manufacturing interests in many parts of the world.[9] In 1955, Marx's overseas factories included France, South Africa, Australia, Japan, Wales, and Mexico.[10]

Eric Matzke, in his excellent book, *Greenberg's Guide To Marx Trains*, said that in 1952 the company stationery listed (in addition to many of the above) plants in England, Canada, and Brazil, though the Sao Paulo, Brazil facility did not survive into the next decade. At one time, a second plant was located in England as well as one in Germany. But, according to Mr. Matzke, eventually the number of foreign plants decreased to include only those in Wales, Mexico, and, in 1960, Japan. Later, there was a Hong Kong facility.

Marx had different arrangements with the foreign plants. A Canadian plant in Toronto received the toy parts from Glendale and Erie, assembled the toy, and finished painting it. Marx's Japanese operation, Linemar, produced mechanical toys for U.S. and foreign markets. Marx also had work done by plants other than those he owned. These were located in Germany, Holland, and Australia.

Still another arrangement was made with a plant in Mexico. The management at the Mexican plant would choose what they would produce from the assembly lines at the United States factories. Due to importation

Orphan Annie-Skipping Rope
New, Unique and Clever
When mechanism is wound Orphan Annie skips rope. If she falls she gets up herself to an upright position, never stopping her rope jumping, regardless of whether she falls on her back or on her face. This toy is just as full of pep and action as the Orphan Annie you see in the comics. Height about 5 in. Shpg. wt., 1 lb.
49F5776 . . . . **25c**

From the 1931 Sears catalog.

regulations, none of the products made at the Mexican plant were brought into the United States.

Manufacturing toys in foreign countries did not always work out as well as Marx hoped. According to an article written in the January, 1946 issue of *Fortune* magazine: "On staple items, it was a simple matter to lend his English factories the dies to run off a few million, and then take the dies back to resume U.S. production. On novelty items, it was equally simple to keep the dies until the toy had outlived its U.S. popularity, then send them to England." In this way, Marx hoped to save the cost of duplicating expensive dies and, at the same time, stretch the dollars used for the original developmental work on such toys. The article reported that the plan did not work out as well as Marx expected due to the differences between the English and American tastes.

When asked in 1955 whether he thought foreign toys were a threat to the United States toy industry, Marx replied, "We should complement what they do best abroad rather than try to compete with them. I have a factory in Germany where the Germans make small mechanized things better than we can. I have one in Japan where the Japanese lead the world in small hand-made toys."[11]

A Marx toy ad from the 1932 Sears catalog.

The Marx Company Decline

Since none of his children was interested in managing the company, Marx decided to sell it when he grew older because he believed that "toys are a young man's business."[12] Louis Marx & Company was sold to the Quaker Oats Company for $51,000,000 in April 1972.

Quaker Oats lost money and sold Marx in April 1976 to Dunbee-Combex Ltd., an international trading firm located in London. Quaker's loss in the company was evident in the Marx company's sale price of only $15,000,000.[13] The Quaker Oats Company retained only Marx's Mexican plant.

Dunbee-Combex, renamed Dunbee-Combex-Marx, had a similar lack of success and the company filed for bankruptcy in February 1980, which began the dissolution of the Marx company. Apparently, the corporate identity of the Marx company was sold a number of times to subsidiaries of Dunbee-Combex-Marx. Each time it was sold to a subsidiary, one asset stayed with that subsidiary. For example, one Dunbee-Combex-Marx subsidiary might own the right to produce the toys, another one owns the toys' trade name, still another owns the tools to make the toys.

The Marx product line was sold to different companies. Aurora Product Toys, previously manufactured at the Girard plant, was sold to Aurora of

Canada Ltd. Similarly, the Empire of Carolina Company bought all of the production equipment at the Glendale plant as well as the rights to manufacture 90 percent of the ride-on products.

A profitable company named Leslie Fay, which manufactures women's clothing, bought the Marx company's corporate stock for tax purposes. Leslie Fay issued shares to Marx creditors which could not be sold for several years.

What Happened to All of Those Toys?

At the close of the Marx company, an astounding variety of antique toys were gathered, evaluated, and subsequently offered for sale through the large auction houses. All of the toys for auction were sorted by motif and variation, then photographed and catalogued. Current toys were stored for reference and used in the sale of duplicate tooling. Profits from many of the sales went to Dunbee-Combex-Marx which later went bankrupt in 1980.

Some of the auctioned toys landed safely in museums. For example, Dunbee-Combex-Marx gave one full set of every antique toy to a museum which was to be established in England through the efforts of Dennis Carter. A museum in Nuremberg, Germany under the direction of Dr. Lydia Boyer purchased a large number of tin toys.[14] However, in a nightmare come true for collectors, Dunbee-Combex-Marx cleaned one of the warehouses in Erie by throwing hundreds of toys out of the windows into waiting semi-trailers, loading them like garbage. What became of the toys after that is unknown.

Balking Mule 48¢
Poor old Si is having his troubles with balky Maude! He just can't make any headway with the stubborn critter. She goes backwards, rears up on her hind legs, sideways and stops and balks. Made of metal lithographed in bright colors that make a big appeal to little folks. Marx guaranteed unbreakable spring. Length over all 10½ inches. Height 5¼ inches.
We Pay Postage.
48 E 3983.............. 48¢

From the 1929 Montgomery Wards catalog.

1 Eric Matzke, **Greenberg's Guide to Marx Trains** (Sykesville, Maryland: Greenberg Publishing Co., 1985), p. 16.

2 "The Little King" **Time**, December 12, 1955, p. 92.

3 Matzke, p. 19.

4 Barbara Seidler, "Marx Toys and Girard A Good Team for 50 Years" **Cosmopolite-Herald**, Girard, Pennsylvania, October 12, 1982, p. 1.

5 "Louis Marx: Toy King" **Fortune**, January 1946, p. 163.

6 Gerritt Beverwyk, ed., **Marx Toy Collector Newsletter**, Vol. 1, No. 1, June 1981.

7 Beverwyk.

8 Beverwyk.

9 "Louis Marx: Toy King" **Fortune**, January 1946, p. 163.

10 J. P. and Peggy McEvoy, "Talk With a Toy King" **Reader's Digest**, January 1955, p. 127.

11 McEvoy, p. 129.

12 Cynthia Saltzman, "Successors Couldn't Match His Genius, So Louis Marx's Toy Empire Crumbled" **Wall Street Journal**, February 8, 1980, p. 6.

13 "Quaker Oats / Dunbee Dialectical Yo-Yo" **The Economist**, April 24, 1976, p. 108.

14 Larry Passick, **Marx Toy Collector Newsletter**, Vol. 3, No. 2, p. 13.

CHAPTER III: MAKING A MARX TOY

As the plants expanded, labor became more specialized, and the factory was divided into departments. Not all of the plants had the same departments for toy making, but most of them did have the following divisions: research and development, art, drafting, toolmaking, die-cast molding, lithography, automatic press, plastics division, blow-molding, plating, stamping, painting, assembly line, and quality control and inspection. Other departments not directly involved in the manufacturing process were engineering, machine maintenance, and time study.

RESEARCH AND DEVELOPMENT

Ideas—The Spark of Louis Marx & Company

At the Marx company, the spark of an idea came from several sources. Some toys were developed from completely new ideas. According to Richard Carver, a former Marx toy designer, "it was part of the job to come up with ideas."

Apparently it was also part of Louis Marx's job to come up with new ideas. One former employee, Chippy Martin, said that Marx had the ability to know that an idea from an ordinary discussion would be valuable to the toy industry in the future. He would tell his development personnel to prepare for the manufacture of the toy, and perhaps one year later, Marx would have something entirely new on the market. Apparently, Marx "had a great feel for the market."[1]

According to one former Marx draftsman, not too many ideas were spontaneous. In order to help cultivate toy ideas, the Erie plant had a room called the "morgue" which was filled with hundreds of old toys. These toys, some manufactured by companies other than Marx, were analyzed to see if an old toy would give a new idea. Sometimes a toy could be modernized or changed in some way and then produced and marketed. Even Louis Marx looked at these old toys when he visited the plant to fuel his own toy ideas.

Similarly, ideas came from seeing toys in trade magazines as well as from the trends that were created by the sale of popular toys. As former Marx employee Cal Cook explained, "You keep looking through these periodicals and think, wouldn't it be nice if this did that...."

While in the earlier years most of the ideas for toys came out of the model room and experimental department, later, some ideas were bought from professional toy designers.[2] One example is the "Rock'em, Sock'em Boxing Toy." Wherever the ideas came from, the Marx company always developed the toy in order for the parts to be molded and assembled by the millions.

Toy Development

The research and development department communicated with marketing, which helped determine the amount of resources that the company should spend to develop a toy. Small complicated toys would perhaps be allocated one thousand hours for development. Items were categorized as speculative and non-speculative. For example, ride-on toys were considered a speculative item. As Cal Cook pointed out: "Whoever heard of ride-ons before? It was the beginning of an industry."

Whoopee Cowboy Driver
Watch this Whoopee Cowboy perform side-splitting antics with his broncho-like auto when spring is wound!. Lithographed metal. Size, 9x6½x3 in. Not Prepaid. Shpg. wt., 1 lb.
49 D 5706........ 47c

From the 1933 Sears catalog.

"People who have not researched toy manufacture do not know what a big engineering project it is.... Toy manufacturing is much more technical than anyone would guess," said one former Marx toy designer.

In the 1930s, the model making staff consisted of three employees, who had to form a model by hand without the help of artists or sculptors. The first body for the Scottie Dog, for example, was made of small metal pieces soldered together. Later, an artist was able to improve on the toy's shape. Without drawings and specification sheets, model makers drew their own rough sketches. For the climbing monkey, model makers gave the draftsman a tracing with a few lines and some notes in order that a blueprint could be made.

The first model was made for appearance and mechanical operation only. Then, the model would be sent to New York for Louis Marx's personal approval. If Marx believed that the model was worthwhile, the model maker proceeded to make a development model, for which the parts were redesigned so that they could be fabricated on tools and assembled properly. At this stage, the production cost of the tooled toy was estimated.

The parts for the development model, which were also made by hand, were given to the toolmaker who built the steel die that would reproduce that part. According to one toy designer, in the absence of specification sheets:

One toolmaker would get one part and another toolmaker a different part, (but in the end) these parts were supposed to match....one toolmaker would shout over to the other, "How big are you making your lugs?" The other would say, "I'm making them 1/4" wide." The first would reply, "All right, I'll make the slots big enough so they'll fit."[3]

It was not until 1936 that the company hired draftsmen who made drawings of parts that were already being manufactured. Previously, the company did not have accurate records, prints, or dimensions. Thereafter, every part was drawn and dimensioned and had a complete development folder. One former Marx draftsman revealed that 50 to 52 hours per week was usually required to get the work finished. The Glendale plant did not have a drafting department. The designers and model makers simply worked from an old model to make a new one. For most of their vehicles and other toys, there were no formal drawings.

In addition to a drafting department, the company expanded to include an art department to do all of the art work and sculpting. This gave rise later to a pattern-making department which made wood patterns. Eventually cast cavities, a new process developed by the Marx company, allowed molded sculptures to be cast in beryllium copper, instead of being machined from a sculptor's model.

In later years, the engineering of a toy still began in much the same way: a model maker would sketch the toy mechanism in order to produce the prototype. In a few instances the toy had been developed first and the model maker, using the toy already produced, simply made improvements on it. Then the sample would go to the drafting department with notes for the dimensions of the toy from which a working drawing or blueprint was made for the mold maker.

Marx model makers specialized in certain toys. For example, one model maker handled ships and guns; another, pinball machines; still another, ride-on toys. In this way, a model maker could develop skill in modeling a toy.

While in some factories items are developed strictly on a drawing or drafting board in the engineering department, the Marx company worked differently. Louis Marx or Ray Lohr, who was manager of the research and development department at Erie, discussed their toy ideas with the model makers. Then the model makers would rough sketch it for size and make a working model of the toy. After it was perfected and approved, the pieces

Comical Monkey Cyclist
Push down lever and see Jocko ride his cycle in realistic fashion. Monkey may be detached. Made of metal 5⅞ in. long.
Not Prepaid. Shpg. wt., 10 oz.
49 D 5748.....19c

From the 1933 **Sears** *catalog.*

would finally reach the drafting room where commercial drawings were made for the mold makers.

The cost of a die or mold varied depending on the item. Wire dies, for example, could cost as low as $250 or as much as $7,000 or $8,000. Molds were known to cost between $30,000 or $40,000 and as much as $100,000 for one set. The differences in the cost of dies and molds were due to the varying complexity and detail of the toys. The cost to develop a toy could add up rather quickly since the company usually needed at least two sets of molds for production, and even more for popular toys. Some of the Marx molds, since purchased by other toy companies, are still in usable condition.

The Marx company strove to use what is known as open-and-shut molding for toys. This technique allowed a form to be extracted from the mold without suspending or hanging it. In order for the technique to work, the width and thickness of the toy parts were designed to taper inward. When detail was essential to the toy, as on the sides of plastic railroad cars and locomotives, the center or core of the mold was made to open automatically. These molds were even more expensive because they had springs and slides that helped pull the sides of the toy part out of the mold.

Usually the Marx company tried to do all of the work needed to produce a toy in its own factories, but occasionally the company subcontracted work. While it is possible that the company made its own molds in earlier years, by 1952, the Marx company was so busy that it normally subcontracted small molding companies in Erie to make the molds. Philip Zacks, president of the Erisco Wire Company which supplied parts for Marx, observed that there were probably more molding companies in Erie, per capita, than any place in the country—because of Marx. Nevertheless, the Marx company always retained the capacity to repair and alter the molds used.

A two-page ad that appeared in the January 1930 **Playthings** *magazine.*

In the later stages of toy development, a list of materials was compiled, the costs to produce the toy computed, an assembly sheet for the assembly line written, and the superintendent of production was instructed concerning how the toy should be assembled.

When the Marx company moved the employees in Erie's research and development department to West 12th Street, separating them from the rest of the plant, the employees generally believed that the move put them at a disadvantage. Design and development personnel continually needed to redesign toys in order to troubleshoot production problems. "One of our responsibilities whenever a new product came out," explained Cal Cook, "was to actually go down on the line and help the foremen, supervisors, and operators...tell them to do it this way or that in order to have a better product."

The development staff continued to be responsible for improvements on the toy, especially in mechanical engineering, even as late as a toy's assembly on the line. In later years, the company conducted tests on the toys before full production. For one of the tests, a large group of children was brought into the plant. The children were given the toy and would "kick it around, jump on it, move it, (and do) whatever it was designed to do."[4] Improvements were made based on the test and then the toy was tested again.

The responsibility of the manufacturer to produce safe toys increased in recent years, so toys also needed to be tested to meet safety regulations. A piece of steel tubing 3" long with a hole 1-1/4" in diameter cut at an angle served as a tester to determine if a piece from a toy could get lodged in a child's throat. Sharp edges needed to be eliminated from existing toys and from the design of new toys which further induced the company to use plastic because it was less expensive.

If a toy did not sell on the market, it was brought back to the development department to be re-evaluated and improved in order to increase its saleability.

The model room of the company's youth became the experimental room, then, with increased sophistication, it became research and development. Research and development had regular meetings every two weeks so that toys could be presented to department personnel who decided which toys would continue to be developed. Ideas concerning the design and pricing of the toys were also discussed.

Each plant had its own research and development division which designed new toys. Girard and Erie each employed about forty people in this division; Glendale had about twenty-five. At Erie, six or seven of the forty employees were draftsmen and about eighteen were model makers. Erie's department, headed by Ray Lohr, provided much of the toy development work for the entire Marx company.

LITHOGRAPHY

Before the plant became automated, mostly sheet metal toys were made.[5] Almost all of the toys were mechanical, lithographed steel with spring-wound motors. Lithography is the method by which a design is painted onto a flat, metal surface. Since none of the plants had a lithograph machine until after 1936, the company bought the steel for the toys already lithographed with artwork provided by Marx.

Marx eventually set up lithograph departments at Glendale and Erie. The Glendale plant had two single-color presses with which they lithographed the sheets needed for dollhouses. The dollhouses were more intricate as compared to other lithographed toys and required printing on both sides. The

From the 1929 **Montgomery Wards** *catalog.*

Erie plant supplied all of Girard's lithographed steel.   When business increased just before World War II, a second shift ran Erie's lithography machine. At the peak production of metal toys, Erie's lithograph department grew from five employees to fifty.

Materials

Most metal toys are made of steel. Although popularly referred to as tin, the shiny tinplate is actually plated steel.   While the Marx company economized in the early years by trying to use the seconds from can factories, later prosperity and volume production allowed the company to purchase prime tin.

The steel sheets came in different sizes, weights, gauges, and thicknesses. The Marx company used sheets from .012 to .032 inches thick. The latter were the heaviest sheets that the plant's equipment could handle.

While a steel toy was much heavier, aluminum, which was also used for toys, could be lithographed in the same way as steel. After World War II, leftover sheets of aluminum from sections of airplanes were used to make toys.

An October 1937 photograph of a lithography machine with Marx Erie employees (from left to right) Roy Hitchcock, William Kalsch, Jack Quirk, Andy Marchionna, and Nick Marchionna. Photograph was provided by William Kalsch.

The Lithographic Process

About 1936, a new way of laying out the lithography was developed. In the development phase, a grid with 1/8" squares was scratched on a flat sheet of metal before being placed into the forming die. The distortion of the lines after the metal was formed gave the artist a guide for doing the art work. Columns and rows of the grid were labeled with numbers and letters in order for the paint color to be laid out properly on the flat sheet for each separation in the lithographic process.

Although the image on the flat sheet was often distorted, when the metal was stretched into the desired shape, the colors ended up in the proper place. Then a litho plate was produced with lines so that the grids were no longer needed for that toy. Before this new process was discovered, toolmakers had painstakingly scribed the lines onto the lithographed steel in order to produce the litho plate.

A sheet of steel was run through a machine that coated it before the sheet could be lithographed. Next, the steel was run through the lithography machine which put the ink on the sheet. The machine had four rollers: two in front to mix the ink; one on top, the composition roller; and one on the bottom, a steel roller with a blade that kept the bottom side of the sheet dry. The litho plate, which had the design on it, was placed in the lithography machine so that the inks would travel through the front rollers and onto the plate.

Another consideration when making the lithographic pattern was that tabs were needed to put a toy together. The tab needed to be colored to blend in with the section that joined it. Depending on which way the tab was bent, sometimes the back of the steel sheet was colored so that the tab would be the same color as the metal background.

Most of the sheets were white on one side and gray, black, or red on the back. Although multiple-color presses were available, Marx only had one-color presses. One at a time, the colors were applied, starting with yellow, then red, blue, and black. While the black ink was still wet on the sheet, the lithographed steel was varnished in another machine to protect the ink. The ink did not blur even when wet because the color was not absorbed by the steel sheet, but lay on top of it. Eleven minutes in ovens, each ninety feet in length, dried the sheets at 250 to 350 degrees.

Even though lithography might seem a long and complicated process to explain, in reality it was a speedy operation. A machine could lithograph as many as 63 to 65 sheets of steel per minute! A thin coating of wax prevented the lithographed sheet from sticking during the stamping process in which the pieces were cut out. In addition, a special coating, developed over several years, allowed the lithographed ink to stretch into form with the metal when the toy was assembled. Otherwise, like spray-painted metal, the paint would crack at the seam when the metal was bent.

The Colors of Steel

A process called overlapping allowed two colors painted over each other to produce a third color. With overlapping, four lithographed colors could produce as many as nine different colors. For example, to produce orange, first yellow ink was lithographed to the steel, then red ink was applied over the yellow. Using the screening technique, in which colors of ink are applied in so many dots per inch, the resulting orange color would be light or dark depending upon the density of the yellow and red dots. With overlapping and screening, Marx was able to produce the khaki color for army items.

All of the colors reproduced equally well through the lithographic process, even silver and gold ink. The toy was manufactured in whatever color the artist chose, no matter how difficult that color was to produce. The ink companies were willing to work with Marx's lithographers in order to meet artistic demands.

The color of a toy also depended upon the buyer. Marx often produced a toy in the colors that a buyer chose. Because only the ink colors changed and the lithographic plates remained the same, Marx could cater to the buyers' requests. For this reason, some variations of Marx toys are actually the same toy with different lithography.

Lithography in a Plastics Toy Market

The Marx company was able to do superior lithographic work because Louis Marx used the best machinery and materials. The toys were also well designed so that careful application of the colors would yield only the best results.

But regardless of the lithographic quality of steel toys, eventually, the plastic toys drove the steel ones right out of the market. Following market

*From the 1929 **Montgomery Wards** catalog.*

A Marx toy ad from the 1926 Sears catalog.

demand, the plant "phased over" into molds for plastic after World War II. Although at first metal was preferred to plastic because plastic was considered cheap material, from the standpoint of the toolmaker, plastic allowed the manufacture of a better product with fewer tools.

The need for metal parts was never eliminated because metal was used to make motor frames, axles, and various other parts. As late as 1962, lithography was still in great demand at the Marx plants. The only lithography machine at the Erie plant continued to run two twelve-hour shifts every day. It was not until 1963 that the need for lithographed steel was on the decline, and in 1966, Erie's lithography machine was finally shut down.

WORLD WAR II BOMBS TOY PRODUCTION

Toy manufacturing during the war was difficult because manufacturers were allowed to make toys that were only 10 percent metal. Instead, materials not needed in the war effort were used, such as paper, cardboard, and wood. Eventually, the Marx plants shut down toy production completely and manufactured items for the war effort.

Toy production at Marx was stopped for four years during the war. At Erie all of the machinery was disassembled so that the Air Corps could use the plant as a depot to dispatch supplies. Since the Air Corps did not need all of the space, the tool and press rooms were kept open. Other employees at the Erie plant helped the Girard plant fulfill its large government contract.

During the war, the Marx company made fuses, lock nuts, and other parts for bombs; pull pins for hand grenades; and wind elevators for machine guns. A bombshell four to six feet long was mounted on the wall of the Girard plant's cafeteria—a grim reminder of the war era.

Just as the war broke out, it was believed that manufacturers could use materials in stock to continue production. The Marx company bought enough inks, steel, and aluminum to last the Erie plant ten years. After Marx had already bought these additional supplies, the government allowed very little manufacturing to continue. When the war was over, and the entire country experienced a shortage of materials, the Marx company was able to gear up for toy production immediately. Some of the supplies at Erie were even sent to the Glendale plant so that production there could also begin.

At Marx, toy production reached its greatest level after World War II due to the previous scarcity of toys and rapid recovery of the economy. Toy production soared again in the 1960s as a result of the baby boom. The company proved more versatile after the war, producing many other items besides toys such as ball-point pens, jewelry, and cosmetics. As Richard Carver, a former Marx employee explained, "Louis Marx was great for looking into all sides, (at) every angle."

THE TRIUMPH OF PLASTIC TOYS

Although the Marx company was quick to recognize the possibilities of manufacturing in plastic, Marx was not the first to use plastic. In order to remain competitive, "all of us (toy manufacturers) had to do the same things at the same time," particularly after World War II.[6]

Techniques for handling plastic in production evolved slowly in the industry, but the Marx company was able to begin working with plastics in the early 1950s. At first, only toys like the eccentric car figures were partially manufactured in plastic. Full production with plastic started about 1952.

The Good and Bad News About Plastics

Certainly, manufacturing toys in plastic had its advantages. So much more could be done with plastic than with sheet metal. For example, a man's head made out of sheet metal was shaped with lithographed metal and lugged together. The result was a razor sharp figure in front and back. With plastic, a full, three-dimensional figure could be produced.

In addition, plastic toys were less expensive to manufacture than metal ones. One-half of a plastic toy could be made in one operation. In comparison, five operations might be needed to produce the same half in metal. The more handlings needed to produce a toy, the more expensive the toy.

Not only could plastic toys be produced, but so too could plastic molds. The master molds needed in toy production, previously made from wood, were much more easily made from plastic.

So why wouldn't toy companies abandon metal and jump into plastic production? According to Richard Carver of the Erie plant, "Nobody knew what you could do with plastic and what you couldn't do with it."

The first plastics at the Marx plants were in two blocks measuring 14" square and 3" thick. The blocks were known as Tenite 1 and Tenite 2; one was acetate, and the other was butyrate. Initially, Marx had four or five plastics machines that made plastic which broke easily. It was not until later improvements that a stronger plastic was developed. Further problems arose concerning the proper temperatures for molding and cooling.

In 1945-1946, when the Marx company started designing toys with plastic, the designers had no knowledge of draft angles. Through trial and error, the development staff discovered the amount of space needed for the plastic to come out of the mold. Nothing was known about by-pass cores which fit together and fell apart to produce the desired holes in the molded plastic.

*From the 1931 **Sears** catalog.*

Marx contracted other shops to build the molds needed for plastic toys. Except for the material backing the cavities, the molds for plastic were made roughly the same as those for die casting. Molds made for a particular piece were not guaranteed to work and sometimes, at an additional cost, the molds had to be re-worked.

The experimentation with plastic led to scrap toys. Marx's scrap toys were bought by the The Erisco Plastic Company, later to become the Erisco Wire Company. Erisco dismantled the toy's metal parts and melted the plastic in order to sell it back to Marx.

Great Strides in Plastic Pay Off — At First

Through the persistence of the development personnel, the correct procedures for manufacturing in plastic were discovered. The Marx company developed a way to weld plastics by using a process called sonic welding and pioneered the use of air drills for blow-molding.

Blow-molding became popular in the production of toys in 1958 or 1959. The plastic was melted above the machine, then molten plastic was fed through a nozzle. The machine closed on the plastic and air was forced into the tube of plastic, blowing it into the desired shape. Then the air escaped from the molding through blow-hole cavities. The resulting blow-molded plastic was strong and needed few secondary operations.

Prior to the oil shortage of the early 1970s, blow-molding plastic was one of the most inexpensive ways to manufacture any item. Unfortunately, just before Marx sold his company, the status of the plastics market made it increasingly difficult to purchase plastic.

THE ASSEMBLY LINE: AN ARMY OF WORKERS

Rough Assembly

After its development, all of a toy's parts were produced in the rough assembly section of the factory. The production of a steel toy required several operations. After the steel had been lithographed, the printed sheet was then run through a machine that stamped or cut out the individual parts of the toy.

The Tower Aeroplane assembly line at the Marx Erie plant. This October 1937 photograph was provided courtesy of William Kalsch.

In the press room, the pieces were put into presses that formed them to the desired shape.

By 1936, Marx began his own die-cast department in Erie, which started with one small machine and gradually increased to a dozen. Although not many toys were made from die casting, like the Tootsietoys, components such as gears, wheels, brackets, and parts of mechanisms were produced.

Assembly

When the Erie plant was located on 19th Street, between Cascade and Raspberry Streets (not to be confused with the later one on 18th and Raspberry Streets) the assembly line was not yet automated. Toys were assembled by hand on wooden tables between which parts were carried. Finished toys went down a chute and into Marx trucks below.

In 1936, when the Marx Erie facility was moved to the building formerly occupied by the Eriez Stove Company, the moving belt assembly line was started, which greatly increased production efficiency. According to Ken Johnson, a former Marx employee: "The parts started down this end of the assembly line, (workers) kept putting things (on) all the way down, you get to the end, it was finished. Everything at Marx was time-studied. It was very efficient. Fewest number of people on a line, get it down to the end, package it."

A moving belt carried the toys from assembly line to testing, and were finally boxed at the end of the line. In assembling the toys, the wheels, motor, light, and other accessories were put on the vehicles. Toy gun production at Marx reached 10,000 to 20,000 a day. Women workers assembled the guns on tables and hung them on a conveyor belt. The spray department painted the guns and put them back on conveyors which moved them to the packing tables. In 1952-1953, even the packing lines were speeded up with the addition of automatic sealers.

Marx's production lines were among the smoothest and most automated to be found. To cut waste, Marx continually studied the efficiency of his equipment. He once said, "When we find a machine that will do a thirty-second job in twenty-five, we'll scrap the old one, even if it's new."[7] The advance of more sophisticated machinery eventually helped Marx reduce labor costs. Since improved manufacturing capabilities meant increased production, the Marx factories were often at the forefront of manufacturing technology.

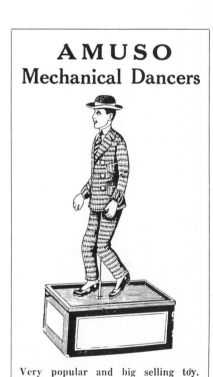

AMUSO
Mechanical Dancers

Very popular and big selling toy. Dances like a real comedian. Substantially constructed of lithographed steel, measuring 11½ inches high, 3¼ inches wide and 4⅝ inches long.

April 1921 **Playthings** *magazine ad.*

---

[1] Leroy Martin, telephone interview, July 25, 1983.

[2] Richard Carver, interview, October 29, 1983.

[3] Carver.

[4] Cal Cook, interview, October 29, 1983.

[5] Most of the information in the Lithography section was supplied in an interview with William Kalsch, November 1, 1983.

[6] Martin.

[7] "The Little King" **Time**, December 12, 1955, p. 94.

CHAPTER IV: LOUIS MARX & COMPANY MARKETS TOYS

COMMERCIAL ADVERTISING

From the 1920s to about 1930, the young Marx company bought full-page advertisements in trade magazines. A June 1921 *Playthings* ad even offered a Marx catalog and free samples for interested buyers. In subsequent years, full-page ads became rare. Instead, Marx ads reverted to just a few lines of text. For example, in *Playthings* magazine, one large-sized Marx ad appeared in 1941, and another appeared in 1946. These two ads were discreet, nearly blank pages compared to other ads, with the Marx logo in the corner of the earlier ad and in the center of the later one.

The early Marx logo was a large, circled "X" with the smaller letters "M A R" printed over the "X". A newer trademark was published in the *Official Gazette* on February 14, 1939. It retained the design of the early logo but the words "Made in United States of America" were added around the outside of the circle.

From the 1934 **Sears** *catalog.*

The company usually bought one or two pages in the annual toy fair catalog. Like the other early ads, however, these pages were also simple with only the Marx logo and no other text. While Sears or Montgomery Wards mail order catalogs featured Marx toys, unfortunately most of the toys were not identified as being manufactured by Louis Marx & Company. In fact, the Marx logo did not appear in the toy section of the *Sears* catalog until 1926.

Former Marx employee Cal Cook said that since Louis Marx knew everyone at the stores, neither advertising nor catalogs were needed. Marx telephoned the major chain stores throughout the country and met the stores' buyers over lunch. Volume buyers could visit the large permanent showroom at the company's office in the Fifth Avenue Building. "There was not much pressure for salesmen to go out for additional orders," said former Marx executive Larry Passick. As a general rule, Marx salesmen did not travel to make sales.

Although the Marx company did a limited amount of advertising, it sometimes used other strategies to woo buyers. Complimentary cigarette lighters and letter openers were among such tactics.

Former Marx employee Richard Carver believes that "the company lost out" by keeping commercial advertising to a bare minimum before the 1950s and also with the advent of television. But perhaps, as Mr. Carver explained, Marx "was selling all he could produce anyway."

In the 1950s, Marx's attitude about advertising began to change. The company produced annual catalogs that featured the new toys for that year.[1] One 1950s catalog, actually a small booklet, was devoted to the Marx line of small, hard plastic figures.

Still, the belief that advertising was not cost-effective lingered into 1955, when the nationally known Marx company spent the small sum of $312.00 for commercial advertising.[2] The amount of advertising could have been minimized because the Marx name was already so well-known. Besides, with a small advertising budget, Marx could offer his toys at a lower price.

In 1956, the entire toy industry and notably Mattel had extensive advertising campaigns which included television commercials. From 1956 to 1959, Marx contracted the Ted Bates Agency, a professional advertising company, to launch Marx's own advertising campaign.

In the August 1959 issue of *Toys and Novelties* magazine, Marx had an elaborate, pull-out color advertisement of twelve pages which introduced the Magic Marxie symbol. Magic Marxie was an elfin figure whose middle was the circled "Marx Toys" logo. The ad promised "The Biggest, the Most Powerful TV Advertising Barrage the Toy Industry Has Ever Known." True to the ad's words, 30- and 60-second commercials for Marx toys began to appear on television.

MARKETING KEYS TO MARX'S SUCCESS

Cost-Cutting Strategies

Despite the company's scant advertising, other policies enabled Marx to offer the public quality toys at reasonable prices, often under-selling competitors. Generally, the research and development department was not only concerned with a new toy's design, but its cost as well, because the cost was directly related to a toy's eventual marketability.

Marx paid close attention to the toy market, and reportedly had people observing the market all over the country. New toys were bought and sent to one of the Marx factories to see if the toy could be improved upon and produced more cheaply. According to Richard Carver: "Somebody makes a toy, you look at it and think it's a good toy, but it could be made better and, in most cases cheaper, so we did it."

Marx found several ways to produce toys more economically than other companies. For example, he attempted to improve the design of a competitor's mechanism so that the toy worked as well, but did not require as many parts or operations, and was therefore less expensive to produce. Production costs could also be cut by simplifying a toy. Marx could extract the toy's best features, sometimes eliminate details, and sell the toy for less money. Although the toy was made more economically, its durability was often improved. The idea was to sell good quality toys at a low price. Marx toys were made with extra-strong springs, sometimes said to be unbreakable by winding.[3] For years the company's slogan was "Mechanical Toys That Are Durable and Mechanically Perfect."

December 1924 **Playthings** magazine ad.

Marx was keenly aware of the price factor in the sale of most toys. The toys of the 1930s sold for 10, 29, or 39 cents, with some toys on the market costing up to 59 cents. The most expensive toy of that time sold for as much as one dollar, but "this amount seemed to be...like the sound barrier."[4] Toys over one dollar did not sell. Sometimes Marx would even sacrifice quality for price. For instance, in later years, although a Tonka toy was better in quality, the Marx toy would cost as much as 25 cents less.[5]

While in the 1920s and 1930s, Marx packaged toys in very colorful boxes with scenic backgrounds; in the 1940s, he returned to the plain boxes labelled in blue or black ink. The less expensive packaging gave the customer more value for their money. According to C. Edward Hjelte, former Director of Marketing at Marx, "roller skates (were) wrapped up in (plain) paper with a string around them." Less wrapping meant the same toy at a better price. Christmas train cars were sold loose in store bins with no packaging at all for 10 to 15 cents each. Later, in the 1960s or 1970s, Marx returned to the brightly-colored packaging.

Large-Volume Sales

By the 1940s and 1950s, Louis Marx had become the largest toy manufacturer in the world earning the title, "Toy King." Marx's success was due, in part, to his large-volume sales policy. In 1951, "with sales estimated at around $45,000,000...Marx's thousands of low-priced...toys captured some 15 percent of the wholesale market."[6]

In a January 1946 *Fortune* magazine article Marx's volume sales policy was described as follows:

Marx manufactures about 275 different items each year. Of these, some 45 are already selling so well that he does not dare touch them. The others are also selling, but require perhaps a "face-lifting job," such as new color, to keep them up to the volume Marx would like. Twelve are usually brand-new Marx items, and it is his skill at landing an average of 7 of these 12 in what he calls "the red-hot hit class" that gives him his position of leadership in the industry.

Because those 12 new toys could cost as much as $100,000 each to develop, it was essential that Marx sell a large volume of the toys.[7] According to an article in the November 5, 1951 issue of *Time* magazine, "On some items, Marx must sell half a million (toys) before he makes a profit." In later years, Marx produced one quarter of a million of each toy when it was introduced on the market.

Part of Marx's volume sales policy meant that toys were sold to stores in carload lots. Only large chain stores such as J. C. Penney, Montgomery Ward, Murphy, Sears, and Woolworth could buy products in large volumes. Because there were no discount stores, Marx toys were made available to the public only through these department stores and mail order houses.

Marx catered to the department stores, often making special variations of a toy for a particular store. For example, Marx would offer to make a toy with added features, in different colors, with the Sears name printed on it, and sell that toy exclusively to Sears stores. This was especially common for the Marx train sets which Sears marketed under the names "Happi-time" and "Allstate." In addition to having its name stamped on the box, Sears usually specified the items that were to be included in the train set. Sometimes the colors of the same trains varied for each buyer. But at other times, the only difference between the sets were the covers on the boxes. Other manufacturers of the time were much less flexible, setting up the production of a toy once, then offering the same toy to all of the stores.

From the 1931 **Sears** *catalog.*

An ad that appeared in the 1932 **Sears** *catalog.*

Marx's belief in volume selling to chain stores, where he sold 90 percent of his products, created problems for smaller stores that wanted Marx toys.[8] The smaller establishments, such as drugstores, could not purchase a large quantity of Marx toys to sell in their stores. Harry Naffin, of Meissner and Hess, supplied the solution. His firm and other stores in the area formed a buying group called "Standard Syndicate and Stores" to purchase toys in a large volume like the department stores. According to Mr. Naffin, at first only a few stores were part of the group, but at its height, 30 stores in the Eastern Pennsylvania area were members.

Mr. Naffin pointed out another problem for buyers. Marx required buyers to purchase a quantity of the less popular toys in order to get the more desirable ones. Other manufacturers continue to adopt a similar policy, even at the present time. In dealing with Marx, Mr. Naffin said that it was "either his way or no way." But Marx, then one of the biggest toy manufacturers in the world, could afford to implement the policy.

Gearing-Up For Fast Production

Not only did he market a large volume of toys, but Marx could produce the toys quickly as well. The Marx company was thought to be more efficient than others because it was a privately-owned company in which key people made the decisions. According to former Director of Marketing C. Edward Hjelte: "We could move in one day what it took other people weeks and months to move."

The Marx company had the facilities, the resources, and the manpower to bring a toy to the market faster than any other company. Whereas other toy companies often subcontracted work, the Marx company had its own die casting, lithography, and tooling departments. Often, Marx was known to duplicate the tooling of popular toys so that, with the help of other plants, the volume of toy production could be further increased.

Marx's plants were able to tool up quickly for new items as well as for the buying trends of popular toys. Sometimes, Marx was said to have a "feel" for what would sell. Kenneth Johnson, who worked as a tool engineer at Marx said, "He'd give orders for full speed ahead—tool up for (a toy) and try to (produce) it before Christmas..." Marx was decisive, affirmed Marx's former marketing director, Mr. Hjelte. "He was very quick. If something started selling in our field, he would make a toy similar to it, but priced lower."

While Marx was often described as having a knack of knowing what would sell, sometimes even he made mistakes. For instance, Marx was ahead of his time in bringing a toy airport onto the market. Similarly, he introduced the Amos 'n' Andy Fresh Air Taxicab in the spring instead of at Christmas time and incorrectly gauged the number that would sell.[9]

But even with Marx's early neglect of commercial advertising; his hard-nosed, high volume policy which disadvantaged the smaller stores; and his periodic miscalculation of the toy market, the Louis Marx & Company became a leader in the toy industry. They were able to market a large volume of sturdy, reasonably priced toys that delighted the hearts of children world-wide.

Acrobatic Monkey! Wind the spring— see monkey do lots of cute tricks. Lithographed metal. Toy, 6¾ in. high. Not Prepaid. Shpg. wt., 10 oz. **49 D 5722 19c**

From the 1933 Sears catalog.

[1] "The Little King" **Time,** December 12, 1955, p. 92.

[2] "The Little King," p. 92.

[3] Gerritt Beverwyk, "Why Marx" The Marx Toy Collector Newsletter, Vol. 1, No. 1, June 1981, p. 11.

[4] Richard Carver, interview, October 29, 1983.

[5] "Louis Marx: Toy King" **Fortune,** January 1946, p. 124.

[6] "Toys & The King" **Time,** November 5, 1951, p. 110.

[7] "Louis Marx: Toy King," p. 123.

[8] Gerritt Beverwyk, **Marx Toy Collector Newsletter,** Vol. 1, No. 1, June 1981.

[9] "Louis Marx: Toy King," p. 124.

CHAPTER V: ANIMAL TOYS

INTRODUCTION

Louis Marx and Company made a wide range of animal toys such as dogs, cats, monkeys, geese, fish, and even a butterfly. Some of the best known and most popular Marx toys feature animals. For toys of famous animals, see chapters entitled: Comic Strip Character Toys; Walt Disney Toys; and Film, Radio, and Television Toys.

All of the toys in this section are lithographed tin windups, unless otherwise noted.

BEAR CYCLIST: 1934. 5-3/4" x 5-3/4". The costumed, trick bear rides a tricycle with a yellow frame, red wheels, and imitation rubber tires. In the September 1934 **Butler Brothers** catalog, the Bear Cyclist sold for $2.00 per dozen.

The **Marx Toy Collector Newsletter** featured an advertisement for an all-tin Bear Cyclist which is almost identical to earlier 1933 ads for the Monkey Cyclist. This variation of the Bear Cyclist resembles a version of the actual monkey toy and box. The ears are the most noticeable difference between the two toys: the Bear Cyclist has rounded ears, and the Monkey Cyclist has flat ears.[1] To change the Monkey Cyclist into a Bear Cyclist, Marx altered the ears of the toy, possibly some of the lithography, and the type and color of the cycles. (The Monkey Cyclist is listed under "Monkeys" in this chapter.)

Add $70 to the price of the toy with box.   30   80

BUTTERFLY

It is believed that Marx made only one butterfly toy which he called "Flutterfly."

Unusual Flutterfly with metal body and fluttering celluloid wings powered by a spring motor. The toy has a rubber suction cup to enable it to be placed in many locations. This toy measures 3" long with a 5" wingspan. W. Maeder Collection. R. Grubb photograph.

FLUTTERFLY: 1929.   3" long x 5" wide (wingspan). Flutterfly has multicolored celluloid wings and a red, tin body with black, white, and yellow stripes. A rubber suction cup allows the toy to be placed almost anywhere. The suction cup is often unusable after so many years because rubber hardens with time. The wings flutter when the spring motor is wound.

According to the 1929 Fall/Winter **Sears** catalog, this "new" toy "looks and acts like a real butterfly." In 1929, Flutterfly sold for 25 cents.

The butterfly comes in an attractively illustrated box which is possibly more desirable than the toy. The orange and dark blue box shows a detailed drawing of the Flutterfly on a boy's forehead, a hand, the window of a car, and a baby's stroller. Add $10 to the price of the toy with box.   **15   50**

CATS

MYSTERY CAT: 1931.   8-1/2" x 3-3/4" x 4-1/2".   The crouching Mystery Cat holds a wooden ball between its two front paws. Its back legs are partially hidden by two large wheels. The cat wears a collar around its neck. Mystery Cat came in a variety of colors and styles of lithography.

The word "mystery" in the title of the toy refers to how it works. Instead of a key, the Mystery Cat's tail acts as a lever which, when pressed down, winds the spring inside the toy. According to the ad in the 1931 Fall/Winter **Sears** catalog, the "new simplified mechanism...(enables) the tiniest tot to play with...(this) action toy." The toy sold for 47 cents.

By 1933, the price of the Mystery Cat dropped to 25 cents. In 1937, rubber ears were added to the cat, but unfortunately, the ears are often missing from the toy today. A lithographed collar with a bow was added to the 1942 Mystery Cat, and the price was then 35 cents. Mystery Cat continued to appear in catalogs into the 1950s and sold then for 94 cents.

Several Marx toys are similar to the Mystery Cat. The most popular of these is the dog Sandy from the Little Orphan Annie comic strip (see Little Orphan Annie section, Comic Strip Character Toys chapter). Except for the lithography, Sandy is the same toy as the Mystery Cat. Also similar to Mystery Cat is Marx's Pluto toy modeled after the Walt Disney character

This variation of the Flippo dog has differently lithographed fur.   Mr. and Mrs. C. Weber Collection.   T. Parrish photograph.

(see Pluto section, Walt Disney Toys chapter).   Pluto's head is low to the ground, he does not play with a ball, and his legs are lithographed instead of separate appendages.

The Mystery Cat is an available and reasonably priced toy. Add $5 to the price of the toy with box.   **30   40**

ROLL-OVER CAT: 1951. 5-1/4" long. The Roll-over Cat was made of metal and came in at least four different varieties of

The Snappy toy was manufactured in 1931 and measures 3-1/2" x 2-1/2". His dog house measures 4-1/2" x 4-1/2" x 3-1/3". When the dog is pressed against the spring action inside the house, he runs out.   E. Owens Collection.   G. Stern photograph.

lithographed styles and colors. Its rubber ears are frequently missing on the toy today. The cat holds a ball between its front paws. According to the 1951 Fall/Winter **Sears** catalog, a keywound, clockspring motor powered the cat's "natural action" which is interrupted so that the cat can roll on one side. Then the cat rolls to return to its upright position and continues on its way. The cat's curved tail turns to facilitate the toy's roll-over action.

The patent for this toy, number 2,189,759, is entitled Reversing Roll-over Toy and was filed June 3, 1939 (see Patents appendix). Despite the patent date, a 1951 ad for the Roll-over Cat describes the toy as "new." Richard Carver, an Erie design foreman interviewed by the author, is one of the inventors of the toy (see Introduction).

Marx used roll-over action with the earlier Figaro toy, modeled from the cat character in the Walt Disney film **Pinocchio**. Figaro was manufactured about 1940 and is essentially the same as the later Roll-over Cat. One Figaro version has lithographed rather than separate front legs, and does not clutch a ball between his paws; another version of Figaro exists with separate front legs and a ball. Whether the latter was a prototype or another production variation is unknown. (For information on Figaro, see Walt Disney Toys chapter.)

The Roll-over Cat is commonly available and reasonably priced. Add $5 to the price of the toy with box.   **25   45**

DOGS

FLIPPO: 1940. 3" high. An appealing little dog, the Flippo toy somersaults and returns to a sitting position. Flippo is white with brown and black patches. Curiously, the dog has nicely lithographed blue-green fur. He wears a red collar and a red coat with a yellow border. Lettering on the coat reads "Watch Me Jump Flippo". Flippo came in a less common variation with different lithography which excluded his collar. Another variation has fur with more prominent brown and black patches. Marx's Dumbo toy (see Walt Disney chapter) is similar to Flippo.

The Flippo toy sold for 47 cents in 1940. By 1950, the price of the toy was 94 cents. Strangely, Flippo's name was sometimes spelled with a single "p," as in the 1940 **Sears** catalog. As late as 1950, catalogs use the double "p" spelling, which is seen most often.

Flippo's box is black and tan and entitled "Flippo the Jumping Dog". The dog is shown jumping and lettering reads "WHE-E-E-E-E". The toy is commonly available and inexpensive. Add $20 to the price of the toy with box.   **15   50**

RUNNING SCOTTIE: 1938. 12-1/2" long x 3-1/2" wide x 6-1/2" high. Just about the size of an actual Scottie Dog, the metal Running Scottie is black with rubber ears and wagging rubber tail. He wears a harness and coat with lettering that reads "Scottie". According to the 1938 **Sears** Christmas catalog, the Running Scottie was powered by a clockwork motor and could be guided in any direction by tightening or slackening the string in his leash. The toy sold for 89 cents.

The patent for the Running Scottie was filed January 3, 1938 by Richard Carver, Erie design foreman, and Raymond Lohr, head of Erie's research and development department. The patent is particularly interesting because two designs were submitted for the same concept and mechanism. One was a car, and the other was a dog later produced as the Scottie dog. (See Patents appendix.)

Add $10 to the price of the toy with box.   **25   50**

RUNNING SPANIEL: 1938. 12-1/2". The Running Spaniel is similar to the Running Scottie but moves by friction. The Spaniel has the same wagging tail and lithographed harness as the Scottie, but longer rubber ears. The toy came in an illustrated box.

The June 1977 **PB 84** catalog lists 1188 as the catalog number for the Running Spaniel. Add $10 to the price of the toy with box.   **25   50**

SNAPPY THE MIRACLE DOG: 1931. 3-1/2" x 2-1/2". The uncommon Snappy is a white bull terrior with brown patches and a red collar. He came with a lithographed steel dog house which measures 4-1/2" x 4-1/4" x 3-1/3". The house is

The 1940 Flippo dog and box. The dog measures 3" high and performs somersaults. E. Owens Collection. G. Stern photograph.

colorfully lithographed with shingles on the roof and animals on the sides. Lettering reads "Snappy" above the arch-shaped opening of the house. Lettering on one side of the opening reads "Beware of the Dog" and, on the other side, "Snappy the Miracle Dog". Ed Owens Collection.

According to the October 1931 **Butler Brothers** catalog, Snappy runs out of his dog house when he is pressed against the spring action inside. Snappy the Miracle Dog is also listed in **Kovel's Antiques and Collectibles Price List.**[2]

In 1931, Snappy the Miracle Dog sold for $2.15 a dozen wholesale.

The patent for this toy is number 1,514,216, and was filed January 5, 1924. The patent and toy are basically the same except that the patent illustration shows a platform under the house and the dog house roof slopes backwards rather than from the center to each side. (See Patents appendix.)

Add $20 to the price of the toy with box.   **40   70**

WEE RUNNING SCOTTIE: 1930s. 5-1/2" long. The Wee Running Scottie is a cheerful little black dog that comes in a variety of lithographed styles. The earliest Wee Scottie wears a lithographed blue and yellow coat with a lithographed tassel. When the key is wound, the little dog's front paws move rapidly as he runs in a large circle.

Lettering on the coat reads "Wee Scottie" and "Made in United States of America". The older Marx logo and patent number "1,959,493" also appear on the coat. The patent was filed on January 26, 1933 by Heinrich Müller of Nuremberg, Germany. (See Patents appendix.)

Like the Scotties to follow, the Wee Scottie has rubber ears and tail. Two large, steel wheels on the toy's base are connected to the front paws, and two small, wooden wheels on the back of the toy help the dog to run on the ground. This Scottie has wooden front paws, while later Scotties have metal ones.

Add $10 to the price of the toy with box.   **30   50**

WEE RUNNING SCOTTIE (VARIATION): 1952. 5-1/2" long. Just as if there had never been an earlier Scottie dog, an ad in the 1952 Fall/Winter **Sears** catalog stated: "New! Wee Running Scottie Dog. Watch his front paws work realistically

This 1952 variation of the Wee Running Scottie measures a "wee" 5-1/2" long. E. Owens Collection. G. Stern photograph.

as he scoots across floor on concealed wheels." The toy sold for 79 cents.

The Scottie has metal paws and wears a red and yellow coat with red lettering that reads "Wee Scottie". This coat differs from that of the earlier Scottie in that it has the new Marx logo which was filed November 1938 and has lettering that reads "Made in United States of America" around the edge of the logo. The Wee Scottie variation, and probably the earlier variation as well, came in an illustrated box. Add $10 to the price of the toy with box.   **20   40**

WEE RUNNING SCOTTIE (BRITISH VERSION): Made by Marx's British plant, this Wee Running Scottie variation is tan with blue eyes. The dog has metal legs and wears a red and black coat with a window-frame design and blue border. Lettering on the coat reads "Wee Scottie". The lettering around the Marx logo reads "Made in Great Britain". Mr. and Mrs. C. Weber Collection.

Add $20 to the price of the toy with box.   **30   40**

DONKEYS: See Horses, Donkeys, and Mules.

FISH

POOR FISH: 1936. 8-1/2" long x 2-3/4" high. Poor Fish is a tin, windup toy with lithographed scales. The fish body is made from separate sections of sheet steel joined together. Wheels are situated just below the back of its head.

The Poor Fish sold in the 1936 catalog of the **Blackwell Wielandy Company**, located in St. Louis, at $4 per dozen wholesale. The fish was described as follows: "Mechanical Poor Fish...New and novel idea in mechanical action toy. Crawls along in wobbly fashion and wavy motion of its body as if walking out of water, very amusing action...lithographed in natural colors."

The prototype for this toy is painted gray without lithographed scales and has blue wheels. Instead of the mouth being closed as in the production toy, the prototype reveals shark-like teeth.

In the box illustration for the toy, Poor Fish, pictured with its mouth open, is quite large and looks as if it might devour a bather standing nearby.

The Marx Poor Fish is not commonly found. Other manufacturers made similar toys. Add $5 to the price of the toy with box.   **35   50**

HORSES, DONKEYS, AND MULES

BALKY MULE: 1925. 10-3/4" long x 5" high. The metal Balky Mule toy consists of a mule-drawn cart with a driver and dog. The mule is gray with a yellow, red, and black blanket, although a variation has a red and blue blanket. The driver is dressed in a burgundy shirt and hat and tan overalls. The dog is brown and white.

The driver and dog sit on the cart's burgundy seat. The cart's curved sides have a wood-grained, burgundy exterior and a blue interior. Six milk cans are attached in the back of the cart. The wheels are green with lithographed yellow spokes and edges, and the variation has pale gray or white wheels edged with red but without the lithographed spokes. A small balance wheel is at the front of the cart. Lettering on the back of the cart reads "Hee Haw, Louis Marx & Co., New York, USA, PAT's PEND'G".

Two variations of Wee Scotties. The 1930s toy (left) has wooden paws, and the later toy (right) has metal paws and was made by Marx's British factory. Mr. and Mrs. C. Weber Collection. T. Parrish photograph.

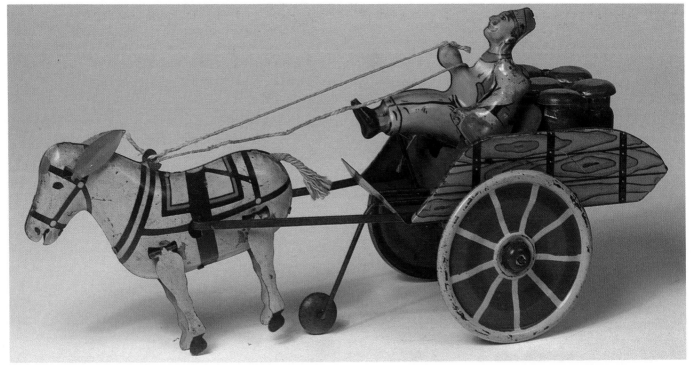

The earliest version of the Balky Mule, manufactured in the mid-1920s, measures 10-1/4" long x 5" high. All of the figures on the toy move. W. Maeder Collection. R. Grubb photograph.

The windup mechanism is between the wheels with the key underneath the toy. As the cart rolls forward, the man moves rapidly up and down on a pivot. The mule's ears and legs and the dog are also movable. The 1926 Fall/Winter **Sears** advertisement further describes the action as follows: "Mule backs up when he should go forward and rears up on his hind legs so that the poor driver doesn't know what to do."

The Balky Mule was also advertised in the 1925 Fall/Winter **Sears** catalog. But the cart in the advertisement drawing differs from the actual toy. In addition, the ad describes the driver as "old," though the driver does not appear to be aged.

In the 1926 Fall/Winter **Sears** catalog, the advertisement drawing is much more realistic and the word "old" has been dropped from the ad copy. The toy sold for 43 cents in 1926. Ads for the Balky Mule toy continued until 1940 when it disappeared from catalogs until 1948.

Except for the hat and lithography, the Balky Mule driver is the same as that of the Marx Snoopy Gus eccentric car and the American Tractor toy (see Greenberg's Guide to Marx Toys, Volume II). The large wheels of the cart are also the same as some of those on the early eccentric cars, but with different lithography. The dog is also found on the early eccentric cars, except in the Balky Mule toy he has shorter, lithographed ears.

The Donkey Cart was made in the late 1940s or early 1950s, has two donkeys, and measures approximately 10-1/4" long. One of the donkeys was used in a later version of the Balky Mule toy. W. Maeder Collection. R. Grubb photograph.

The Horse and Cart with Driver measures 9-1/2" long x 3-1/4" wide x 5-1/2" high and was probably made in the late 1940s or early 1950s. Parts of this toy were later used to make other toys. W. Maeder Collection. R. Grubb photograph.

The patent for the Balky Mule is number 2,095,646. The patent was not filed until 1936, quite some time after the toy was marketed (see Patents appendix). The patent drawing differs from the actual toy, showing a differently-shaped mechanism on the underside of the cart and an extra piece under the mule's neck. It is possible that the patent was intended to be an updated version of the toy. Marx did, in fact, produce a version of the Balky Mule in the late 1940s, but the patent described above clearly resembles the earlier toy.

Marx was not the only manufacturer of toys like the Balky Mule. Both the Ferdinand Strauss Corporation and the Unique Art Manufacturing Company advertised a similar toy called Jenny the Balky Mule. (For additional information on the Marx-Strauss-Berger relationship, see Black Toys chapter, Charleston Trio.) Jenny the Balky Mule was advertised in the early 1920s and has action similar to the Marx toy. The driver figure has a beard and a larger hat than the Marx toy. Jenny's cart has straight sides with a railing around the top.

The Lehmann Balky Mule, introduced in the late 19th century, has action similar to the Marx toy, but a different appearance. The donkey's skin is textured and the clown driver wears a cloth shirt. The clown figure rises up and down like an accordion, while the Marx driver pivots up and down.

The early version of the Marx Balky Mule toy is reasonably priced. Add $15 to the price of the toy with box.   **30   85**

(LATER) BALKY MULE: 1948. 8-3/4" long. This later version of the Balky Mule toy has a brown mule with a red and yellow ornate bridle. The mule has an angry, caricatured expression. He does not have movable ears or legs. There are two small, wooden wheels attached to the mule's front legs. The driver is dressed in a yellow, wide-brimmed hat; blue or yellow shirt; red neckerchief; and brown overalls. The toy came in an illustrated box and sold for 94 cents in 1948. The later Bulky Mule continued to appear in catalogs at least until 1952.

The later Bulky Mule toy came in at least two variations with different carts. One variation has a wood-grained pattern on the cart and wheels, while the other lacks the pattern and has a contrasting color around the wheels.

In comparison to the earlier Balky Mule, the later version has a cart with straight sides, no milk cans, and no dog. The driver of the later toy has a larger hat and his legs do not stick out as do those of the earlier driver.

Add $20 to the price of the toy with box.   **35   80**

DONKEY CART: Late 1940s or early 1950s. 10-1/4" long. The Donkey Cart toy has two donkeys identical to the mule of the Balky Mule toy. The donkeys pull a different cart with the same Bulky Mule driver. The driver is perched on the edge of the cart with a metal piece through his legs which fits into a slot of the wagon, allowing the figure to be removed. The figure is therefore sometimes missing from the toy today. Very small Marx logos are printed on the underside of the donkeys.

The donkey cart has curved sides which have a wood-grained pattern on the exterior. Three barrels are lithographed on each side of the cart and a container of oats is pictured on one side. A lithographed rope ties the barrels together, adding to the three-dimensional effect of the lithography. Tankards are lithographed on the front and back of the cart. The windup mechanism is between the wheels, and the key is underneath the toy.

Illustrations on Marx boxes occasionally differ from the actual toy. The box shows a decorative design with hearts and

a bag on the side of the cart. The box also has instructions for fastening the driver to the cart.

A minor difference between the Donkey Cart and the Balky Mule toys is the steel rods which attach the carts to the animals. The Donkey Cart has red rods and an extra piece, while the Balky Mule toy has uncolored rods only.

Catalog advertisements for the Donkey Cart have not been found. The June 1977 **PB 84** auction catalog lists this toy under number 142.

Add $15 to the price of the toy with box.   **35   70**

FARM WAGON: c. 1940s. 10" long x 4-1/4" high. A gray horse with a white mane and tail, pulls the orange, wood-patterned Farm Wagon toy. The horse can be detached from the cart. The Farm Wagon has a driver with unusual, blue skin; a blue shirt; red pants; and yellow and red boots and hat. White lettering reads "Farm Wagon" on the top sides of the wagon. "Made in Canada" is rubber-stamped on the green inner floor of the wagon. Although there is no Marx logo, the toy must have come from Marx's Toronto factory. Black lettering reads "Low Pressure" and "8.00 x 14" on the white tin wheels.

Add $10 to the price of the toy with box.   **30   60**

HORSE AND CART: 1934. 7" long x 3" high. This Horse and Cart toy has a black and white horse and a red-enameled cart with yellow wheels. The key for the windup mechanism is on the side of the toy. In the 1934 Fall/Winter **Montgomery Ward** catalog, the toy sold for 10 cents.

The same horse and cart was marketed with the celluloid figures of either Popeye or Bluto. While it is possible that the wheels came in a variety of colors, the Popeye and Bluto Horse and Cart have black wheels.

The toy is not commonly available. Add $10 to the price of the toy with box.   **30   75**

HORSE AND CART WITH CLOWN DRIVER: 1923. 7-5/8" long x 5" high. This rarely seen toy consists of a clown in a cart pulled by a small horse. The clown wears a pointed cap and a costume with a circular pattern. The cart body, excluding the disc-style wheels, is covered with a circular pattern which differs from the costume.

The Horse and Cart with Clown Driver appeared in a 1923 **Sears** catalog advertisement. It is believed to be the first year that a Marx item was shown in a catalog, although Marx ads did appear at that time in toy magazines. The ad did not mention the name of the manufacturer and the illustration differs from the actual toy in a number of ways. While the actual toy has a large Marx logo on its pointed cap, the ad shows the cap with a star design. The ad shows the clown's costume with a crescent pattern. No pattern is shown on the cart and the wheels are open-spoked in the illustration. A few years later, other catalogs showed the wheels in disc-style as on the actual toy.

In the 1925 **Sears** catalog, the Horse and Cart with Clown Driver appeared on a page with other toys. Some of the toys were made by Marx, but others were from different manufacturers. The Marx Horse and Cart toy sold for 21 cents and is described as follows: "Pony trots around in a circle as clown driver moves in his seat."

The horse and cart appeared in catalogs without the clown driver as early as 1920. The toy is on a page with some Strauss toys, which suggests that Marx may have acquired the horse and cart from Strauss. In fact, even with the addition of the clown driver, the toy may have originally come from a Strauss die which would explain the toy's appearance in catalogs as early as 1923.

A picture of the Horse and Cart with Clown Driver can be found in the interesting book by Don Cranmer, **Cast Iron & Tin Toys of Yesteryear.** [3]

The cart and horse of the toy resembles the 1930s Popeye Horse and Cart. The length of the two toys is approximately the same, but since there is a different figure in both toys, the height of each toy differs.

Add $25 to the price of the toy with box.   **50   100**

HORSE AND CART WITH DRIVER: c. late 1940s or early 1950s. 9-1/2" long x 3-1/4" wide x 5-1/2" high. The driver wears a wide-brimmed hat, red shirt, and blue overalls. He is removable and fits into the seat with a metal piece attached to his hips. The horse is dappled gray-brown with a blonde mane. He wears a red, yellow, and black bridle. One wooden wheel is on his left front foot. The horse is attached to the cart by steel rods. The cart has a coil of rope near its back, at its top, and on its right wheel.

This horse and cart toy is a good example of how Marx used parts of other toys to make a new toy. Both the cart and driver of this toy are similar to the wood-patterned variation of the Balky Mule. The Horse and Cart toy has a cart with a straight front which has an extra curled piece on the top. The horse is the same as the one that pulls the Milk Wagon and Horse toy described later in this chapter. The wood-patterned lithography on the cart and wheels is the same as that on the roof of the 1930s Marx Popeye and Olive Oyl Jigger, even to the use of the same coil of rope which appears on the back of the wagon and on its right front wheel. (For Popeye listings, see Comic

Strip Character Toys chapter.) Marx was known to let nothing go to waste, and it is very possible that leftover lithographed sheets from the Popeye toy were used on the Horse and Cart toy.

A variation of the Horse and Cart with Driver has a differently-shaped, dark tan horse. A horse of this shape in black, and possibly in tan, also pulled the Milk Wagon and Horse toy. The Horse and Cart variation has a differently-colored cart which is blue with a yellow interior and yellow wheels edged in black. The cart in the variation lacks the extra curved piece of the first variation. [4] The base of the cart is red with the mechanism on the underside. The farmer driver is dressed in tan overalls.

The toy came in a plain box entitled "Mech. Horse & Cart With Driver". Add $10 to the price of the toy with box.

30   70

MILK WAGON AND HORSE

This toy came in at least two main variations with the same wagon differently lithographed. The wagons are pulled by one of two horses both of which are shaped and lithographed differently. The horse is attached to the wagon by steel rods.

In the 1931 Fall/Winter **Sears** catalog, the toy sold for the surprisingly high amount, for the times, of $1.39. The ad incorrectly describes the toy with a driver and a horse with jointed legs, but the Milk Wagon has never been seen with tabs for a driver. The 1932 ad was corrected and the illustration portrayed the toy as it was actually produced. In the 1932 Fall/Winter **Sears** catalog, the price of the Milk Wagon had plummeted, and the toy was sold with a group of other Marx toys at five for one dollar. Through the 1930s, ads for the Milk Wagon remained the same.

This variation of the Horse and Cart with Driver has a horse with a different shape which was also used to pull a milk wagon. T. Riley Collection. C. Myers photograph.

First manufactured in the early 1930s, the Milk Wagon and Horse measures 10" long x 4-1/4" high. The version shown was manufactured in the late 1930s. W. Maeder Collection. R. Grubb photograph.

One variation of the Milk Wagon and Horse with a different horse pulling the wagon. Mr. and Mrs. C. Weber Collection. T. Parrish photograph.

EARLY MILK WAGON: 1931. 10" long x 4-1/4" high. The wagon is white with a red roof. Its white balloon tires have red and black centers. A scene with cows grazing in a meadow is shown on the right side of the door. Above this scene, blue-green lettering reads "Toyland's", and below the picture, lettering reads "Farm Products". "Milk & Cream" appears on the front side of the door in red lettering and on the back of the

wagon in blue-green lettering. The Marx logo appears on the back of the wagon. An ad in the September 1934 **Butler Brothers** catalog describes a color variation of this wagon with orange wheels and orange roof.

LATER MILK WAGON: Although the date is uncertain, it is known that this variation was manufactured later than the Milk Wagon previously described. The later Milk Wagon is the

A later Milk Wagon and Horse toy. Dr. M. Kates Collection. R. Grubb photograph.

Shown is a British version of the Musical Circus Horse. An American version was made with different lithography c. 1939. The toy measures 10-1/2" long and 4-1/4" high. W. Maeder Collection. R. Grubb photograph.

same shape as the earlier wagon, but predominantly yellow, red, and white with either a red or white front.

Red lettering reads "Toytown Dairy" on the top of the wagon, behind the driver's door. Beneath "Toytown Dairy" lettering reads "Cheese". Under the front side window lettering reads "Cream", and beneath that, "Grade 'A'". The rear of the body has two lithographed doors with handles.

Lettering reads "Farm Products" beneath the doors. The Marx logo appears on the rear of the toy at the bottom. Footsteps are beneath the driver's door on either side.[5] This wagon comes with the white wheels of the earlier wagon and also with red-centered, black wheels.

The box for the later Milk Wagon and Horse is not illustrated but has black lettering that reads "New Milk Wagon

& Horse". The Marx name, address, and logo are also on the box. The Milk Wagon and Horse, especially the later version, is commonly available. Add $25 to the price of the toy with box.   35   75

EARLY MILK WAGON HORSE: The early horse's left front leg is bent slightly above the ground. It comes in black with a light-colored mane and a red and white bridle. The horse also came in white and tan, but the latter was used for the Horse and Cart with Driver toy, listed previously in this chapter. Ads mention that the horse also came in a dappled design.

The early Milk Wagon horse was marketed pulling both the early and late variation wagons.

LATER MILK WAGON HORSE: c. 1939. The later horse has an arched neck and a front and back leg raised from the ground. It comes in black and is dappled beige-gray. The later horse was sold with both the early and late variation wagons.

The dappled version pulls a wood-grained open cart with a driver (see Horse and Cart with Driver, earlier in this chapter). A solid gray version of this horse pulls the orange Farm Wagon (see Farm Wagon, listed previously in this chapter).

MUSICAL CIRCUS HORSE: 1939. 10-1/2" long x 4-1/4" high. 4-1/4" diameter drum. The Musical Circus Horse is a pull toy with a gray, dappled horse which has a blonde mane. The horse wears a red, yellow, and black bridle and pulls a musical drum. Its left front foot has two wooden wheels, and its right front and left back leg are raised from the ground. The circus horse has sometimes been seen with a cloth plume on its head. The horse also came in brown and perhaps other color combinations. The same horse was used on the toy Horse and Cart with Driver, previously described.

The revolving musical drum is attached to the horse with steel rods. The white drum has yellow sides and is lithographed with elephants, bears, and clowns. Lettering reads "Musical Circus" on the sides.

The toy sold for 25 cents in 1939. Add $15 to the price of the toy with box.   45   80

MUSICAL CIRCUS HORSE (BRITISH VERSION): 10-1/2" long x 4-1/4" high. The British version of the Musical Circus Horse is from the same dies but has different lithography. Although the horse is still dappled, it is a different tone of gray. It has a more elaborate saddle with decorative edge and tassels. Ribbon is wound through the horse's mane.

Each side of the drum features the figure of a clown with arms and legs outstretched. The clown's face is cleverly lithographed to coincide with one of the four holes in the drum through which the musical sound comes out. The hole makes the clown's mouth look as if it is open. Lettering around the clown reads "Musical Circus Horse". The edge of the drum is lithographed with a lion wearing a red soldier's jacket and a crown, an elephant playing the cymbals, a seal playing an instrument, a monkey in a blue and white jacket and hat playing an accordion, and a snake charmer with a snake. Colors used are red, white, blue, yellow, brown, and black.

Two different logos appear on this toy. On the drum edge, there is a logo which resembles the old Marx logo with a large "X" and the letters "MAR". On the horse's stomach, the new logo filed November 4, 1938 reads "Made in Gt. Britain". At one time, Marx had plants in both London and Swansea, Wales.

The Musical Circus Horse is not commonly available. Add $25 to the price of the toy with box.   45   125

WAGON WITH TWO-HORSE TEAM: Late 1940s. This toy consists of two horses pulling a four-wheel trailer. The set includes a spade, pitchfork, wheelbarrow, wooden barrel, milk case, and pail.

The 1950 Wagon with Two-Horse Team has two black metal horses with arched necks which pull a plastic wagon with removable sides. The wagon came as a stake or panel wagon. It is possible that the horses were available in different colors.

Add $10 to the price of the 1940s toy with box and $20 to the price of the 1950s toy with box.

Late 1940s	30	50
1950	20	40

GEESE

As with the Black Toys, different manufacturers produced geese toys which have similar characteristics.

GERTIE THE GALLOPING GOOSE: Gertie is a cheerful-looking goose with a flowered shawl. She appears to have been made from the same dies as the Golden Goose. Gertie is frequently thought to have been manufactured by Unique Art, although the toy has also been attributed to Marx as well. Possibly, the toy was sold under both of the manufacturers names. Marx often sold toys for Samuel Berger of Unique Art and purchased Unique toys to resell. It was not uncommon for tools and dies for toy parts to be exchanged.[6] Samuel Berger also submitted patents used by both companies.

GOLDEN GOOSE: 1929. 9-1/2" long. As its name implies, the Golden Goose toy is metallic gold with red and black accents and large black feet. A cavity in its back carries five gold-painted, wooden eggs. The Golden Goose hops rapidly along and lays eggs. Its body moves up and down while it

Goblo the Gobbling Goose was manufactured by the Girard Model Works in the mid-1920s and the Golden Goose was manufactured by Marx in 1929. Both geese measure approximately 9" long and are similar, but not identical. W. Maeder Collection. T. Parrish photograph.

seems to peck at the ground. Catalog number 87 is listed for this toy in the June 1977 **PB 84** catalog.

The Golden Goose was first advertised in the 1929 Fall/Winter **Sears** catalog. The toy shown in the ad actually resembles a white goose called Goblo the Gobbling Goose made by the Girard Model Works as early as 1925. Before Marx had his own manufacturing facilities, other factories such as the Girard Model Works manufactured toys for him, which explains the similarities between the two geese. By 1931, some catalogs had corrected the ad illustration so that it resembled the actual Golden Goose toy.

The 1924 patent for the toy, number 1,500,590, was submitted by Louis Marx, but probably not designed by him (see Patents appendix). The patent refers to the movement of both toys. Girard's Goblo did not lay eggs and this feature was added in a later Marx patent, number 1,783,511, which was filed March 15, 1929. The date of the later patent coincides with the Golden Goose's appearance in catalogs and would seem to indicate that the actual toy was produced in 1929. The 1924 date refers to the patent with the toy's mechanism only. Although there are a number of differences between the two toys, the later patent drawing resembles the earlier Girard goose.

Marx's Golden Goose is 1/2" longer than the 9" long Goblo. The Marx toy has a jointed neck and straight tail, while Goblo's neck is not jointed and his tail turns up at the end. An extra piece strengthens and joins the Marx toy's thicker legs which makes the toy harder to wind. The Marx goose has a wider back piece in the foot. Both of the toys have the same hopping action, but Goblo cannot lay eggs. Both geese have the following lettering but in different places: "Patented July 8, 1924. Other Patents Pending". Additional lettering on Marx's Golden Goose reads "Louis Marx & Co., New York, U.S.A." near the legs.

A plastic goose which lays golden eggs is advertised in the 1950 **Montgomery Ward** Christmas catalog for 94 cents. The toy is not credited to Marx, but it appears to be the same as the Marx Golden Goose and is advertised on the same page as some other Marx toys.

The Golden Goose is readily available, reasonably priced, and comes in a blue and yellow illustrated box. Several children are pictured admiring the Goose which is shown as large as the children. Add $10 to the price of the toy with box.

                                                                                      40   70

MOTHER GOOSE: c. 1920s. 7-1/2" high. Mother Goose is white and has a woman in a pointed hat seated on its back. A striped cat stands on the goose in front of the woman. The goose is made from a similar, possibly identical, die as the Golden Goose.

The correct name of the toy is unknown. It could have been manufactured either by Marx or Strauss. The Mother Goose toy is fairly common at toy shows. Add $50 to the price of the toy with box.

                                                                                      55   100

MERRYMAKERS: c. 1931. 6-1/2" long x 8-3/4" high (with mouse). One of Marx's best toys, the Merrymakers toy is a mouse band. One mouse rocks back and forth as he plays the upright piano. To the left, another mouse beats a drum. Reminiscent of the Marx jigger toys, a third mouse dances at the pianist's right. A fourth mouse, which came in two variations, sits on top of the piano. In one variation the mouse waves a baton as his arms move out and down, while in a second variation, the mouse plays the fiddle. The piano has a start/stop lever.

The Merrymakers toy is decorated completely in red, white, and black. While the red sometimes has faded to orange, the toy still has an elegant appearance. The mice are nattily attired in black coats, black and white high-button shoes, white shirts and gloves, and red waistcoats. All have wire-thin arms and legs.

The piano is decorated with lithographed, full-figure mice, and the two chairs are decorated with the heads of cats. One of the cats' heads decorates the top of the drum, and the mouse beats on top of him. The Merrymakers came with or without an illustrated, moon-shaped backdrop which fits into the piano back. The backdrop is illustrated with two mice dancing while a cat plays the tuba. Lettering above the dancing mice reads "Merry Makers", but the back of the piano has lettering that reads "Merrymakers" as one word. A large Marx logo also appears on the back of the piano with lettering that reads "Louis Marx & Co., 200 5th Ave., N.Y., U.S.A." Five patents are listed below the lettering as well as the words "Other Patents Pending".

There are four variations of the Merrymakers toy. The most available version is that with the bandleader minus the backdrop, while the most desirable version is the violinist with the backdrop.

The toy appeared in 1931 catalogs for 98 cents. Strangely, the only version of the Merrymakers pictured in catalogs is the one with the bandleader minus the backdrop. The other variations were probably manufactured later. The Marx Merrymakers was also made in England.

Patents on the Merrymakers Piano: As with other patents used by Marx, Samuel Berger of Unique Art submitted all of the patents for the Merrymakers Piano. Berger designed patents for both Marx and Strauss. Oddly enough a similar toy made by Unique Art, L'l Abner Dogpatch Band, was not made until the mid-1940s while the Strauss toy, Ham and Sam Piano, was made in the early 1920s. The Ham and Sam toy was also marketed by Unique Art under the name Hott and Tott.

The first patent listed on the back of the Merrymakers piano is for a motor mechanism. It is number 1,393,936 and was filed June 1, 1921. The second patent is for a toy motor brake. It is number 1,595,702 and was filed August 16, 1924. The third patent, number 1,742,844, was filed March 21, 1925 and is for the Ham and Sam toy by Strauss. The patent illustration shows two white minstrels at a piano. The piano is like that of the Merrymakers toy; the figures are like those of the Charleston Trio (see Black Toys chapter). The seated figure plays the piano while the figure to his right plays the banjo. The design patent, number 69,559, shows a similar illustration with black minstrels (see Patents appendix). The design patent also has cut-out sections in the base of the piano and chair. Although the Strauss patent resembles the actual Merrymakers toy more closely than the design patent, the former shows the piano with a cloth over the top of it, which the actual toy does not have.

The fifth patent listed on the toy is design patent number 73,223 which was filed May 14, 1925. The simplified drawing of the patent shows a violinist standing right on the piano keys.

Licensing by Disney: It is generally believed that in the early years, Marx failed to get a license from Walt Disney to use the Mickey Mouse character. Yet the mice of the Merrymakers toy resemble Disney's early Mickey Mouse without the use of the Disney name. There are other toys that are rumored to represent well-known figures but are unlicensed to use the popular names. One is the Funny Face large walker, which resembles Harold Lloyd, and the other is the Roadside Rest,

A variation of the popular Marx Merrymakers. The toy was manufactured c. 1931 and measures 6-1/2" long x 8-3/4" high. This variation also came with the addition of a backdrop. C. Weber Collection. T. Parrish photograph.

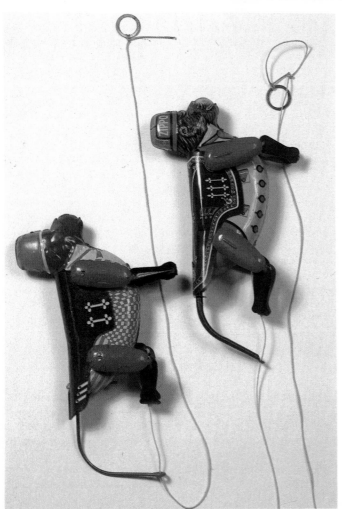

which resembles Laurel and Hardy. (For Funny Face toy, see Large Walkers chapter. For Roadside Rest, see Automobiles chapter in Volume II.)

The proof that Marx finally received a license from Disney is shown by such 1950s toys as the Mickey Mouse Dipsy Car and Mickey the Driver, as well as earlier Marx toys such as Donald Duck Duet, Pinocchio, and Dumbo (see Walt Disney Toys chapter).

The box for the toy is difficult to find and is illustrated with a dancing mouse and mouse musicians seated in tiers on either side of the dancer. If any Marx toy deserves to be called outstanding, it is the Marx Merrymakers. It is a strikingly handsome toy and quite desirable. Add $125 to the price of the toy with box and $80 to the price of the toy with backdrop.

350   900

MONKEYS

ACROBATIC MARVEL: 7-1/2" long x 13-1/2" high (fully extended). The Acrobatic Marvel is a monkey on a pole. The pole is a flexible tin strip attached to a rocking base. The monkey has fixed metal arms and jointed fiberboard legs which move as the animal swings back and forth and somersaults. A wooden wheel is between each of the monkey's arms and its body. The Acrobatic Marvel is brown with a flesh-colored face and smiling red mouth. He is dressed in a red coat with a yellow vest and bow tie.

The lithography on the base of the toy is very colorful. Yellow lettering reads "Acrobatic Marvel" on one side of the

Two variations of the Climbing Monkey shown unstrung. Sold in the early 1920s, Jumbo (left) was one of the first Marx toys. Zippo (right) was sold in the late 1930s. W. Maeder Collection. R. Grubb photograph.

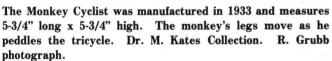

The Monkey Cyclist was manufactured in 1933 and measures 5-3/4" long x 5-3/4" high. The monkey's legs move as he peddles the tricycle. Dr. M. Kates Collection. R. Grubb photograph.

The Acrobatic Marvel is a monkey which swings back and forth on a flexible metal pole. The monkey has metal arms and fiberboard legs. The toy measures 7-1/2" long and, with the metal strip extended, 13-1/4" high. W. Maeder Collection. R. Grubb photograph.

red background. The Marx logo appears between the words of the title. An elephant, ringmaster, monkey, and clown appear under the title. A hippo, lion, zebra, and tiger are on the other side of the base. The top of the base pictures the Acrobatic Marvel in action, a young boy also on a trapeze, and a clown watching the performance.

An acrobatic figure on a tin strip with a rocking base was also manufactured as Pinocchio the Acrobat. Like the Acrobatic Marvel, Pinocchio has jointed fiberboard legs but they are shaped differently. The Pinocchio the Acrobat toy is much sturdier than the Acrobatic Marvel. The metal pieces which are part of Pinocchio's arms are larger, and the tin strip which supports Pinocchio is stronger than those of the other toy. The base of the Acrobatic Marvel has rounder sides than that of the Pinocchio toy. (For Pinocchio the Acrobat listing, see Walt Disney chapter.)

The Acrobatic Marvel is similar in several ways to other Marx toys. The Acrobatic Marvel and Ranger Rider have the same metal piece under differently-shaped bases, which facilitates the rocking motion. The Monkey Cyclist, which has jointed fiberboard legs, and the Tumbling Monkey with Trapeze are both similar to the Acrobatic Marvel.

The hands of all three of the monkey toys differ. The Acrobatic Marvel's hands are bent at the corners and formed as part of the piece attached to the flexible strip. In contrast, the Monkey Cyclist has holes through its hands for the handlebars, while the Tumbling Monkey has hands like hooks to fit on the rings of his trapeze.

The original box is almost as colorful as the toy. Bright illustrations are on all four sides. A boy and the monkey on a trapeze are colorfully illustrated on two sides. On the other two sides, the lettering "Acrobatic Marvel" is spotlighted in a circus ring with a spectator pointing up. Add $30 to the price of the toy with box.   **30 100**

CLIMBING MONKEYS

THE CARTER CLIMBING MONKEY: 1921. 8-1/2" long. The first monkey advertised under the Marx name was actually manufactured by C. E. (Nick) Carter. Possibly the first ad for the Marx company appeared in the April 1921 issue of **Playthings** magazine. The ad refers to the popular toy as "Carter's Climbing Monkey" and the illustration shows a little girl holding a string on which the monkey climbs. The Marx name and Fifth Avenue address in New York is listed at the bottom. The ad urges the buyer: "To be assured of delivery, order now. It is getting very late."

Two months later, in June 1921, the Climbing Monkey ad in **Playthings** appeared under steel toys, rather than tin. The following information was added: "Send for Catalog and Free Samples."

A 1922 ad shows the same illustration as previous ads, but no longer identifies the monkey as Carter's. But Carter's name is credited to the Dapper Dan toy in the ad (see Black Toys chapter). According to the January 1922 ad in **Playthings** magazine, the 8-1/2" long monkey has a body lithographed in two colors and a coat lithographed in bright blue. The ad shows the monkey with striped pants. The Carter Monkey also came with a green coat, yellow waistcoat, solid red pants, and a tasseled red hat with the addition of a chin strap. It is possible that the Carter monkey came in other variations. The toy came in a box with the names of both the C. E. Carter Company and the Louis Marx & Company.

In the late 1930s, the Carter Company was still producing a Climbing Monkey which was possibly made from the original dies of the first Climbing Monkey toy. While the original production was made from lithographed steel stampings, the late 1930s monkey was manufactured from steel stampings with sprayed flock, a fuzzy material that adhered to the metal.[7] (For more information on the C. E. Carter Company, see Chapter II.).

Add $20 to the price of the toy with box.   **35   70**

JOCKO: 1950s. Marx's 1930s Zippo monkey was renamed Jocko in the 1950s. The new name appears in some ads earlier than 1950. Add $10 to the price of the toy with box.   **25   40**

JUMBO: 1923. 9-3/4". Jumbo the Climbing Monkey has a brown head with tiny white eyes. His arms and legs are black, but later models have brown limbs to match the head. The monkey is dressed in a blue coat with two white frog closings, a red- and white-checkered vest, and short red- and yellow-striped pants. The monkey's short coat sleeves and pants legs are red and unpatterned. In the ads, Jumbo is shown with the striped pattern on its pants legs, and the toy was probably made with both striped and plain-colored pants legs. The actual Jumbo toy wears a red hat with a yellow stripe. In the ads, the hat is shown with a tassel. Whether or not a variation exists with the tassel is unknown.

The 38" long string that the monkey climbs passes through five circular holes in the monkey's body. One hole is at the end of the tail, and another hole joins his feet together. A third hole is in his stomach, a fourth joins his hands together, and a fifth is in his chest. When the string is held taut under a child's foot, the monkey climbs up the string. When the string is slackened, the monkey descends.

Although Carter had been manufacturing one climbing monkey for him, Marx had bought another die for the monkey from his former employer, Ferdinand Strauss, when Strauss had financial problems. Jumbo is believed to be the climbing monkey made from the Strauss dies, but the toy lacks manufacturer's information and logo.

An ad in the 1923 **Sears** catalog mentions two different Marx monkeys. One is probably that manufactured by the Carter Company, and is described as "Smaller, not as good quality, 7-3/4" high." The toy sold for 17 cents. The new monkey is believed to have been from the Stauss die, which Marx was known to have improved, making it larger and more colorful. This monkey has a checkered vest and is described as follows: "Extra quality. The one we recommend. 9-3/4" x 3". Finished in attractive colors which please the child's eye." The toy sold for 23 cents. This larger monkey continued to appear in Marx ads. It is possible that Carter continued to produce his own or both monkeys for Marx until Marx had his own manufacturing facilities.

In February 1923, **Playthings** magazine advertised Marx's new large climbing monkey, Jumbo. In the ad, Jumbo has a checkered vest and two frog closings on his jacket, but lacks the chin strap. The ad also features Strauss and Unique Art toys, although the names of the manufacturers are not credited.

The 1925 Fall/Winter **Sears** catalog advertised only the larger, 9-1/2" Jumbo monkey. Interestingly, the ad copy boasted: "There are cheaper monkeys on the market, but they are not as satisfactory as this one." Other manufacturers, Lindstrom and Lehmann, made similar climbing monkeys.

With a few exceptions, Jumbo continued to appear in ads unchanged for many years. The toy came in an illustrated box on which a little boy was shown playing with the toy. Add $25 to the price of the toy with box.   **40   50**

ZIPPO: 1938. 9-1/2". Due to the changes in the 1923 Jumbo, the climbing monkey was renamed Zippo about 1938. The more elaborately lithographed Zippo monkey has fur on his face and larger eyes. His arms and legs match his brown face. The tail is thicker and sturdier though not quite as curved. The monkey wears a blue coat with a fancy white border and three frog closings. His vest is yellow with red buttons and bow tie, and his sleeves and pants are red.

The Marx logo is at the base of the monkey's coat. Lettering on his hat reads "Zippo". In ads, his red hat does not have a tassel. Zippo sold for 25 cents in 1938. The 1949 Zippo was advertised as measuring 8-3/4" and sold for 74 cents. Add $10 to the price of the toy with box.

1938   **30   50**

MONKEY CYCLIST: 1933. 5-3/4" long x 5-3/4" high. There are two variations of the Monkey Cyclist toy. The figure of the first variation is completely tin and resembles the bear cyclist figure. The monkey's head is brown and flesh-colored, and his arms are flesh-colored with red arm bands. The figure wears a red vest and red bow tie, and his legs are green with yellow boots. The monkey is connected to the orange tricycle so that his legs move with the wheels.

The figure of the second variation, believed to be the later of the two toys, has jointed fiberboard arms and legs and more clearly resembles a monkey.

Both monkey figures drive tricycles with one large front wheel and two small back wheels. The wheels, with white trim and red centers similar to some eccentric car wheels, are lithographed with different designs. The tricycle's mechanism is activated by a lever. The second variation of the Monkey Cyclist has a tricycle with a wider frame and a large piece on the back of the cycle.

The first variation of the Monkey Cyclist has a face and body similar to the Marx Tumbling Monkey and Trapeze, described later in this section. The two toys have different lithography and hands. The Monkey Cyclist has flat hands with holes to fit the handlebars of the cycle, while the Tumbling Monkey has hands like hooks to fit on the rungs of the trapeze. The Monkey Cyclist has jointed knees, but the Tumbling Monkey has legs jointed only at the hip.

The illustrated box for the Monkey Cyclist toy has lettering that reads "Monkey Cyclist" and "Louis Marx & Co., New York, U.S.A." on one side. The monkey is shown on his tricycle. The end of the box has lettering that reads "Monkey Cyclist". Illustrated instructions for fastening the monkey on the tricycle and the operation of the toy appear on the other side of the box.[8] Add $10 to the price of the toy with box.

    40   85

TUMBLING MONKEY: c. 1942. 4-1/2". The monkey wears a red outfit with black and white stripes and six white buttons. He has a small cap on his head. The Marx logo is printed near the monkey's waist. The monkey holds two chairs with its arms while somersaulting between them. The chairs are yellow, red, and black. Mr. and Mrs. C. Weber Collection.

A firm named Shuco made a balancing monkey with chairs, but, unlike the Marx monkey, the Shuco monkey is made of cloth as well as tin. Toys of this type were also made in Japan.

The Tumbling Monkey sold for 39 cents in 1942. The toy came in an illustrated box. Add $20 to the price of the toy with box.   **45   90**

The Tumbling Monkey was manufactured c. 1942 and measures 4-1/2". The monkey somersaults between the two chairs. Mr. and Mrs. C. Weber Collection. T. Parrish photograph.

TUMBLING MONKEY AND TRAPEZE: 1932. 2-1/2" long x 4" wide x 5-3/4" high. The monkey is brown with a partially flesh-colored face. His arms and green legs are jointed. He wears a red jacket with small polka dots. The monkey's hook-shaped hands can be detached from the rings of the trapeze. The base of the toy is green and yellow. There are no identifying marks on the toy.

In the 1932 Fall/Winter **Sears** catalog, the Tumbling Monkey and Trapeze was sold with four other Marx toys at five for one dollar. The toy was described as follows: "Monkey on trapeze who can show you some real acrobatic stunts, and when set on the floor can turn somersaults." According to an ad in the 1934 Fall/Winter **Sears** catalog, the monkey also does stunts from the side bar of the trapeze.

The Tumbling Monkey is similar to one of the Monkey Cyclist variations except for the lithography and the monkey's hands and legs. The Monkey Cyclist has openings in his hands for the handlebars of the cycle, and its legs are jointed at both the hip and knees. The Tumbling Monkey's legs are jointed only at the hips.

The Tumbling Monkey came in a box with lettering that reads "Tumbling Monkey and Trapeze. Made by Louis Marx & Co., New York" on one side. On the other side, the monkey is shown in various positions on the trapeze.

Marx also made a number of trapeze toys with human figures in celluloid (See Miscellaneous Toys chapter, Volume II). Linemar, Marx's Japanese subsidiary, made trapeze toys with the figures of Mickey Mouse, Donald Duck, and Pluto. Unique Art's tin monkey, "Bombo", somersaults from a tree.

Add $10 to the price of toy with box.   **25   50**

MULES: See Horses, Donkeys, and Mules section, this chapter.

POOR FISH: See Fish, this chapter.

RING-A-LING CIRCUS: 1925. 7-1/2" diameter base. The Ring-A-Ling Circus is one of Marx's most delightful and colorful toys. A ringmaster stands in the center of a circus ring. A clown and various animals surround him. As the ringmaster revolves to face each performer, one of his jointed arms raises the whip and the performer does a stunt. The clown turns around on his bar, the monkey climbs up and down on a pole, and the elephant and lion rise up on their hind legs.

The ringmaster wears a red coat, yellow pants, black top hat, and black boots. The chubby little clown is dressed in a blue outfit with a white ruffled collar. The brown monkey wears a red cap and pants, plus a jacket with a fancy border. The elephant has a turbaned rider seated on his head. Across his back, the elephant has a red blanket with tassels and the same fancy border as the monkey. The lion holds a hoop in its mouth and is the same figure as the dog on the Charleston Trio toy with different lithography. (For Charleston Trio, see Black Toys chapter.)

The base, which acts as the floor of the ring, came in either a soft green or, less frequently, in a rose color. Lettering on the base of the toy reads "Louis Marx & Co., N.Y., U.S.A." On the other side, near the start/stop lever, lettering reads

The outstanding Ring-A-Ling Circus was manufactured in 1925 and measures 7-1/2" in diameter. As the ringmaster revolves and raises his whip, the clown turns around on his bar, the monkey climbs up and down the pole, and the elephant and lion rise up on their hind legs. W. Maeder Collection. R. Grubb photograph.

"Ring-A-Ling Circus". Although early catalog ads do not show illustrations around the base, the actual toy has never been seen without base illustrations. It appears that later ads, which show the toy with base illustrations, were corrected. A circus parade is shown on the base. A performer rides on horseback, hippos pull a lion cage, a clown sits on a pig, and a man rides on a camel. An elephant with a canopied seat, or howdah, on its back leads the circus preceded only by clowns that hold a sign which reads "Ring-A-Ling Circus". All of the parade participants head toward a circus tent.

Instead of a lion, early catalog illustrations show a clown figure holding a hoop. Perhaps the clown was meant to appear as if waiting for the lion to jump through the hoop. In addition, the elephant figure is shown without a rider. The ads quickly corrected the clown and lion, but the elephant continued to be

The Tumbling Monkey and Trapeze was manufactured in 1932 and measures 2-1/2" long x 4" wide x 5-3/4" high. The monkey performs tricks on the trapeze. Dr. M. Kates Collection. R. Grubb photograph.

shown riderless suggesting that the toy was possibly made in a variation with a riderless elephant.

There are three patents connected with the Ring-A-Ling Circus toy. The design patent, number 70,798 was filed May

15, 1925. This design patent, of the three, most resembles the toy except the elephant does not have a rider, nor is the base illustrated. The patent shows the ringmaster with a longer coat, shoes instead of boots, and no stripe in his hat.

The second patent, number 1,600,237, was filed on December 31, 1924. This patent looks less like the toy, but the ringmaster's clothing is closer to that of the actual toy. In the patent, the lion appears to be on stilts, the elephant still has no rider, and the clown seems to have a different bar. Except for two triangular pieces on each side of the ring, the toy in the patent illustration has no base.

The third patent, number 1,681,304, was filed on December 1, 1926. The toy in the drawing does not resemble the toy much but both have the same round base. It is possible that Marx had planned to make another circus toy from this patent. The patent drawing has a lady walking a tightrope, a circus tent, and a giraffe. Among several other figures, one man appears to be hitting another with a bat.

"New" in 1925, the toy sold for 89 cents. The toy came in an attractive green and yellow, illustrated box. The Ring-A-Ling Circus toy can still be found, but it is expensive. Add $200 to the price of the toy with box.   **170   300**

1 **Marx Toy Collector Newsletter**, Vol. 1, No. 5, p. 5.

2 **Kovels' Antiques and Collectibles Price List, 17th edition** (New York: Crown Publishers, 1984), p. 758.

3 Don Cranmer, **Cast Iron & Tin Toys of Yesterday** (Gas City, Ind: L-W Promotions, 1976), p. 27.

4 Information from T. Riley, a Marx Toy collector.

5 Information from Dr. M. Kates, a Marx Toy collector and 1987 President of the Antique Toy Collectors of America.

6 Eric Matzke, **Greenberg's Guide to Marx Trains** (Sykesville, MD: Greenberg Publishing Co., 1985), p. 86.

7 Correspondence from E. Carter, March 21, 1984 and May 16, 1986.

8 Information from Dr. M. Kates.

INTRODUCTION

While some of Marx's finest toys appear in this chapter, by today's standards the names of the toys are disturbing and derogatory. But at the time the toys were made, Marx was not the only manufacturer to use them.

The Alabama Coon Jigger was one of the first dies Marx obtained. As explained in previous chapters, Marx acquired the dies for this toy from his former employer, Ferdinand Strauss, when Strauss went out of business. The patent Strauss used for the toy was number 959,009 by Walter S. Hendren, May 24, 1910 (see Patents appendix). This date appears on the underside of the jigger's base. The Hendren patent, which expired at the time Marx bought the dies from Strauss, was later used for the Dapper Dan toys.[1] While Marx did not start production until 1921, the 1910 date of the patent appears on several black toys.

The black toys are similar to the "Oh-My" toy, produced by the German toy manufacturer, Lehmann. According to the outstanding book **Lehmann Toys** by Jurgen and Marianne Cieslik, the Hendren patent was confirmed for Germany in February 1911. But Lehmann modified the American invention so that it no longer resembled the Hendren patent and registered a patent of his own. It is a possibility that Lehmann, in turn, licensed his patents to the United States and that some U.S. toys are based on his designs.[2]

The Marx toys listed below are tin lithographed windups unless otherwise noted.

AMOS 'N' ANDY FRESH AIR TAXICAB: See Film, Radio, and Television Toys chapter.

AMOS 'N' ANDY WALKERS: See Large Walkers chapter.

BUSY DELIVERY: 1939. 9" long x 3-1/4" wide x 7-3/4" high. A figure drives an open, three-wheeled cart. The figure is black and dressed in a pointed red hat with a yellow band and feather, a white T-shirt with red circles, and a yellow neckerchief and belt. The three wheels of the vehicle are red and very sturdy. A rectangular design is indented on the sides of the bin, and the motor is on the bottom of the bin. The frame of the rear single wheel is yellow. When wound, the figure's legs pedal and the vehicle goes forward. The rear single wheel is attached so that it can pivot.

The Busy Delivery is similar to the Pinocchio Delivery toy except for the differently lithographed clothes and skin color. The Busy Delivery, of course, does not have Pinocchio's long nose. There are two variations of the Pinocchio Delivery, and the Busy Delivery toy has characteristics of both. One variation of the Pinocchio toy has the same wood-grained bin entitled "Busy Delivery" on the sides. The Marx logo and a sign "Phone 00-000" also appear on the sides. On the front and back of the bin are the words "We Deliver In All Directions" and "Snappy Service". However, the Pinocchio figure has metal arms. A second Pinocchio variation has both fiberboard arms and legs, like that of the Busy Delivery, but the lithography on the bin varies.[3]

Another variation of the Busy Delivery toy is shown in the 1941 **Shure Winner No. 136 Wholesale Catalog**, though the toy actually came out in 1939. In the 1941 ad, the driver retains his dark skin color, but resembles Pinocchio in dress and has the long nose. Other ads show the figure with a normal-sized nose. The bin shown in the **Shure Winner** ad has the wood-grained design, but the lettering reads "Mrs. Jones—Wet Wash—Incropolated (sic)". The word "Incropolated (sic)" also appears on the Amos 'n' Andy Taxi. The toy in the ad measures 9-1/2" long x 4-1/2" wide x 7" high and sold for $3.92 per dozen.

The Busy Delivery is not commonly seen.   **150 300**

CHARLESTON TRIO: 1926. 3-1/2" long x 5" wide x 9" high. The Charleston Trio is a colorful toy with fine lithography and clever action. Three figures perform on top of a red cabin roof. A large, black figure dances as he turns around in a circle, a black child figure plays a violin, and a dog with a cane in his mouth moves up and down. With a change in lithography, the dog was also used as a lion in the Ring-A-Ling Circus toy, which came out at about the same time. (For Ring-A-Ling Circus, see Animal Toys chapter). One scene on the cabin shows the three figures performing on a stage in front of an audience. Another scene on the cabin side shows three different black figures dancing in front of an audience.

Of the performers on the cabin roof, the dancer figure is dashingly dressed in a red coat with green lapels; a spotted red and white bow tie; navy- and white-checked pants; high-button shoes; and a red, green, and white cap. The child violinist wears an orange shirt, blue pants with an orange stripe, plain shoes, and a cap with a strap under the chin.

Besides the Marx logo and name, lettering on the base of the toy reads "Patented October 1921". According to the 1926 Fall/Winter **Sears** catalog, the Charleston Trio is a new toy for that year and sold for 45 cents. The Charleston Trio in the Sears ad features an outdoor scene quite different from the stage scene described above. In addition, the large figure does not have a cap. In an ad from the December 1927 **American Wholesale Corporation** catalog, the audience sits around a cabin rather than a stage. The first ad for the Trio in the **Montgomery Ward** catalog appeared in 1928 and shows the toy as listed above. By 1930, the ad in the Fall/Winter **Sears** catalog also resembles the toy described above. Whether the different ads are a result of artistic license or show actual variations of the toy is unknown. Reader confirmation is requested.

A rarer variation of the Charleston Trio features a large dancing figure that resembles the Marx Somstepa figure, described later in this section. This rare version of the Trio is pictured in the interesting book by Ward Kimball, **Toys—Delights from the Past.**

The history of Marx toys includes the work of Samuel Berger of Unique Art and Ferdinand Strauss. Nowhere is the Marx-Strauss-Berger interrelationship more evident than in the attractive Charleston Trio. In **Greenberg's Guide to Marx**

Trains, Eric Matzke provides the following interesting information: "Louis Marx and Sammy Berger had been close friends for many years. Sammy directed Unique Art, a New Jersey Toy manufacturing company. Marx both sold toys for him and purchased Unique toys to re-sell, and it was not uncommon for tools and dies for toy parts to be exchanged between the New Jersey and Girard plants."[4]

In the Charleston Trio, it is difficult to tell where the manufacturers of Strauss and Unique Art left off and Marx began. Both Strauss and Unique Art produced the Jazzbo Jim toy with either one large dancer or with both the dancer and violinist. Strauss, Unique Art, and Marx made similar Jazzbo Jim figures which resemble the dancer of the Marx Charleston Trio. Strauss and Unique Art made additional variations of the dancer with differently lithographed clothes and a banjo. The scenes on the Marx Jazzbo Jim differ from those of the Charleston Trio. (See Jazzbo Jim below.)

Both Unique Art and Strauss manufactured a single, white clown figure called Dandy Jim which is similar to Marx's dancer figure but with different lithography. Like the Charleston Trio, Dandy Jim came with a violinist. The figures of the Ham and Sam toy by Strauss, also known as Hott and Tott by Unique Art, resemble the Charleston Trio dancer. Marx's Japanese subsidiary Linemar produced a version of the Hott and Tott toy as well. A piano similar to that used in the Ham and Sam toy was designed by Samuel Berger and used by Marx in his Merrymakers toy.

The figure that completes the trio, the dog, is a Marx addition.   **225   300**

DAPPER DAN JIGGERS

Marx manufactured more than one Dapper Dan Jigger toy and there is confusion concerning which of these toys are actually to be attributed to Marx. One reason is that Marx sold other manufacturers' toys as well as his own and did not always identify the manufacturer in the advertisements. An ad in the February 1923 **Playthings** magazine is a case in point. Some of the pages featuring Marx toys in mail order catalogs included a few toys from other manufacturers that were not identified in the ad.   **175   350**

CARTER'S DAPPER DAN COON JIGGER: 1922. 4-1/2" wide x 10" high. The dancing figure is strikingly dressed in a red- and white-checked jacket, blue- and white-striped pants, blue and white tie, white shirt, yellow vest, and gray derby.

The mechanical workings of the toy are in a yellow base decorated with three figures elegantly lithographed in black with dashes of red and white. Red lettering reads "Dapper Dan Coon Jigger". Another Dapper Dan figure has a spotted coat.

An ad placed by Louis Marx in the January 1922 issue of **Playthings** magazine identifies the manufacturer of the Dapper Dan Coon Jigger as C. E. Carter. On the base of the toy, the names of both the Carter and Marx companies appear. The Hendren patent, number 959,009, dated May 24, 1910, is also referred to on the bottom of the toy. (For additional information about the Hendren patent, see the introduction to this section and the Patents appendix.)

Another ad for the Dapper Dan Coon Jigger appears in the December 1925 issue of the **American Wholesale Corporation Catalog**. The toy sells for $3.68 a dozen. The ad states that the toy measures 3-1/4" long x 4-3/8" wide x 11-1/2" high, but the toy actual toy is only 10" high. According to the ad, the toy is lithographed in eight bright colors and has a jointed figure with striped trousers, a red and yellow coat, and wide blue hat. A regulator on the side controls the action.   **300   400**

DAPPER DAN BANK: 1923. 10" high. Marx manufactured the Dapper Dan figure as a bank. The ad for this toy appeared as early as 1923 in the February issue of **Playthings** magazine. Dapper Dan's coat is unpatterned in the ad, but the figure also actually came in a patterned coat. Reader confirmation is requested. As in the Dapper Dan toy, the figure wears striped pants and a spotted bow tie. The ad shows a hand inserting a penny into the slot on the top of the platform. When the penny is inserted, Dapper Dan dances. Lettering on the front of the box reads "See Dapper Dan the Famous Coon Jigger". A crowd is shown in front of a theater where admission to see Dapper Dan ranges from 1 to 25 cents.

A similar bank, Thrifty Tom's Jigger Bank, was produced at about the same time by Strauss. The figure resembles that of the Dapper Dan Bank but wears a spotted coat and differently-shaped hat.   **NRS**

DAPPER DAN THE JIGGER PORTER: 1924. 9-1/2" high. Another Dapper Dan toy was made as a porter dancing on the top of a trunk. The porter wears a red coat with yellow lapels and cuffs. His pants are blue- and white-striped. He wears a flat cap with a peak similar to that of the Lehmann porter. The porter dances on a trunk decorated with travel labels. Lettering on the base of the toy reads "Dapper Dan Coon Jigger the Jigger Porter".

The **Dictionary of Toys Sold in America** by Earnest Long, states that the toy was manufactured in 1924. The dictionary describes the toy as follows: "...finished in seven colors, with hotel and baggage labels. It has a speed regulator and dances with perfect mechanical action."

Dapper Dan the Jigger Porter also bears the patent date May 24, 1910 on the base, referring to the Hendren patent number 959,009. (See introduction to this section and Patents appendix for further details.)   **250   350**

HEY HEY THE CHICKEN SNATCHER: 1926. 8-1/2" high. The Chicken Snatcher figure holds a chicken in his right hand and shouts in surprise as a dog bites the seat of his pants. He wears blue overalls, a white shirt, a red and yellow vest with yellow lapels, and large black shoes. He has a black string tie around his neck and, like some of the Crazy Car drivers, a yellow hat with a red band. In fact, the head of the Chicken Snatcher is the same as that of the Funny Flivver and a few other drivers. When not in motion, the figure appears to lean forward and to one side because the upper half of his body can pivot from side to side.

A hook in the dog's mouth attaches to a loop in the Chicken Snatcher's pants. The dog is white with brown and black markings. The chicken is also attached with a hook to a loop made by two of the figure's fingers. The chicken is lithographed in great detail and is the same one found on the Travelchiks toy by Ferdinand Strauss.

On the soles of the figure's oversized shoes is the following information: "Hey Hey The Chicken Snatcher/Trade Mark Louis Marx & Co., New York, U.S.A."; the Marx logo; the design patent 69,900; and the publication date of the patent, April 13, 1926 (see Patents appendix). This patent describes the toy just as it was produced. Another patent was submitted by Samuel Berger, who designed patents for both Marx and

The 1926 Hey Hey the Chicken Snatcher measures 8-1/2" high. The toy walks on big feet, the soles of which bear the toy's name, patent number, and Marx logo. W. Maeder Collection. T. Parrish photograph.

The Busy Delivery toy is similar to the Pinocchio Delivery toys. It was manufactured in 1939 and measures 9" long x 3-1/4" wide x 7-3/4" high. W. Maeder Collection. R. Grubb photograph.

The 1926 Charleston Trio has three moving figures. The large figure dances, the child plays the violin, and the dog jumps up and down. The toy measures 3-1/2" long x 5" wide x 9" high. W. Maeder Collection. R. Grubb photograph.

Strauss. While Berger's patent, number 1,674,943, was published about two years after the Marx patent, it was submitted almost one year earlier. The illustration of Berger's patent is of a similar figure, except that he is white, wears a helmet, and lacks the chicken and dog.

Hey Hey The Chicken Snatcher appeared in the 1926 Fall/Winter **Sears** catalog where it sold for 45 cents. It was advertised as "one of the new, most novel toys of the year." The toy continued to appear in the catalog for a few years.

Later Marx published a patent with a figure resembling Harold Lloyd, known as "Funny Face". The patent number is 1,764,330. The illustration shows the figure holding a chicken and being attacked by the dog, as is the Chicken Snatcher, but this time the figure is smiling.

Three other figures that resemble the Chicken Snatcher are Boob McNutt, the Iceman, and Tom Twist. Boob McNutt and Tom Twist are Strauss toys. The Iceman is credited to Marx in Lloyd Ralston's April 7, 1984 **Antique Toy Auction Catalog.** (Iceman is listed in Volume II, Miscellaneous Toys chapter.)

Other toy manufacturers produced a toy with a dog biting the seat of a figure's pants. In the October 20, 1984 Lloyd Ralston **Antique Toy Auction Catalog**, a black celluloid boy dressed in an outfit made of cloth is shown with a dog biting his pants. Instead of holding a chicken, the child eats watermelon. There is also a German toy with a black figure made of tin and the same dog-biting-pants action.   **175 250**

JAZZBO JIM: 1920s. 3-1/2" long x 5" wide x 9" high. Identical to the dancer of the Charleston Trio, the single figure of Jazzbo Jim dances on a cabin roof. The cabin roof is a solid dark red, lacking the yellow slashes of the Charleston Trio's roof. The lithography on the cabin sides also differs from that of the Charleston Trio. One side shows a man playing a banjo while, to the left, three children listen as they sit on the ground. A sign tacked to the cabin wall above the group reads "Jazzbo Jim" and "Trade Mark" in red letters. To the right of the banjo player, a man peeks out of an open doorway. A donkey also listens appreciatively with his head sticking out of a window.

A scene on the other side of the toy shows three children seated on a bench to the right. Above them the sign reads "Jazzbo Jim". The banjo player sits in a doorway while to the left, a little girl dances. Two figures look out through an open window near the start/stop lever.

Two sides of the toy have the same scene. A little boy clutches a woman's hand amidst some chickens. Above them, a child sits in a window.

Lettering reads "Jazzbo Jim The Dancer On The Roof" on the base, which also has a lithographed clown. Other lettering reads "Copyrighted" and "Patented October 1921". Notably, the Marx logo is missing.

The toy's red box has the Marx logo and lettering that reads "Jazzbo Jim The Dancer On The Roof". The smiling dancer figure illustrated on the box, very similar to the toy itself, is shown dancing in front of an audience.[5]   **NRS**

JIGGER: c. 1920s. 8" high. The Jigger wears a patterned suit with a cap and is attached to a rod on a circular base. He resembles the dancer from the Charleston Trio. Both have a large spotted bow tie, high-button shoes, and a design under the bow tie that might be a sparkling stickpin.

Although it is uncertain who manufactured the Jigger, the toy does have a resemblance to a Marx patent, number

1,538,541, "Mechanically Operated Dancing Toy" by T. Raymond Arden. While the patent shows a striped suit, instead of the patterned one on the toy, the illustration accurately depicts the figure's cap and the toy's attachment to a rod on a circular base. Gerritt Beverwyk, former Editor of the **Marx Toy Collector Newsletter**, spotted the likeness between this Marx patent and the Jigger.[6] Mr. Beverwyk also located an ad for a similar toy produced by the American toy manufacturer, Linstrom, called "Shufflin' Sam Dancing Coon", which sold for 25 cents. The ad for the Linstrom toy shows that the toy resembles the Jigger except for its suit pattern.[7] **NRS**

MAMMY'S BOY: See Large Walkers chapter.

SOMSTEPA: 1926. 8" high. The dark-skinned figure of the Somstepa toy has small, sloping shoulders. The figure wears a red coat with a fancy front, yellow-striped trousers, a dotted bow tie, and a red cap.

The base on which Somstepa dances is illustrated with black children on the banks of a river. Lettering on the front of the base reads "Somstepa". One side of the base reads "Coon Jigger". The other side reads "Louis Marx & Co., 200 5th Ave., N.Y.C." and has a large Marx logo.

The 1926 Fall/Winter **Montgomery Ward** catalog advertises that the figure is 8" high and dances by means of a Marx spring, which was guaranteed against overwinding. Interestingly, the Somstepa is advertised with the Climbing Monkey. Fifty-seven cents bought two toys.   **NRS**

SPIC AND SPAN: 1924. 6-1/4" long x 10" high. One of this toy's two figures sits on a bass drum which is turned sideways, plays a snare drum, and bangs the cymbals with his right foot. One drumstick automatically beats the drum. The other figure manages to dance a jig and play the violin. Both figures are dressed in red coats with yellow trim, red hats and bow ties, and blue-striped trousers.

Lettering on the base of the toy reads "Spic and Span The Hams What Am". These words also appear on a yellow banner held at each end by two men in front of a red backdrop. "Spic and Span" is in red letters; "The Hams What Am" is in black letters. The bass drum is red and pictures a man and woman.

The Spic and Span toy appears to have come from a combination of two patents, both filed in March 1923, but published at different times. The first patent, number 1,519,410, published December 16, 1924, shows three figures, only one of which resembles the actual Spic and Span toy's dancing violinist. The second patent, number 1,570,268, published January 19, 1926, clearly illustrates the figure seated on the drum as in the actual toy (see Patents appendix).

The Spic and Span toy is mentioned as early as 1924 in the February issue of **Playthings** magazine. According to the ad: "The toy embodies a remarkable amount of syncopated action." The same ad refers to a Marx toy Polar Bear, which is not known to exist.

The **Dictionary of Toys Sold in America** shows a 1924 ad for the Spic and Span toy which describes it as follows: "red, blue, black and yellow uniforms, red drums with gold trim. With speed regulator..." The pair is shown in the ad with top hats, but the figures of the actual toy wear derbys.

The Spic and Span toy does not appear in the **Sears** catalog until 1926, when the toy sold for 69 cents. According to the ad, the toy measures 6-1/4" long x 10" high. The toy is shown with top hats in this ad as well, but it is not known if a variation was ever actually made with hats.

The 1922 Fall/Winter **Sears** catalog lists a toy with two figures, one of which resembles the seated figure of the Spic and Span toy. This figure bangs the cymbals with his right foot. He does not play the drum, but "pats" out the beat with his hands. The other figure, unlike the Spic and Span toy, is also seated and plays the accordion. The toy has a platform similar to the Spic and Span toy.　　　　**200　400**

SPIC COON DRUMMER: 1924. 3-1/4" long x 4-3/4" wide x 8-1/2" high. This toy is actually made from the drummer figure of the Spic and Span toy. As with that toy, the figure is seated on the bass drum, plays the snare drum with his hands, and bangs the cymbals with his foot. The automatic drumstick is now on the right side of the toy instead of on the left as in the Spic and Span toy. The patent for the Spic Coon Drummer, number 1,570,268, was filed March 1923 and published January 19, 1926 (see Patents appendix).

Apart from not having the dancing figure who plays the violin, the other major difference between the Spic Coon Drummer and the Spic and Span toy is the illustrations on the base. The Spic Coon Drummer features the same three elegant figures as on the Dapper Dan Coon Jigger. A large Marx logo appears on the side of the base.

The **Dictionary of Toys Sold in America** shows a 1924 ad for the Spic Coon Drummer, the same year that the Spic and Span toy is advertised. Interestingly, the ad for the Spic Coon Drummer shows the figure in a derby, instead of the top hats shown in the ads for the other toy.

Both toys also appeared in the December 1925 **American Wholesale Corporation Catalog.** Reportedly, the measurements for the Spic Coon Drummer are 3-1/4" long x 4-3/4" wide x 8-1/2" high. The toy sold for $4.35 a dozen. No ad was found in the **Sears** catalog for the Spic Coon Drummer.　　**500　700**

WALKING PORTER: 1930s. 8" high. The porter is dressed in a red jacket with blue and white lapels, pockets, and belt. He wears red- and white-striped trousers and shoes. A badge on the upper left of the coat reads "Red Cap Porter". He does, in fact, wear a red cap edged in black and white. His exaggerated mouth is smiling.

The Walking Porter is not as old or rare as the toys previously described in this section. It is different from the earlier toys because it is much less realistic. For instance, the arm pieces, inserted halfway down the trunk, are lithographed up to where the shoulders should be. Since the figure's trunk is straight with a circular, indented ridge at the top, the toy actually does not have shoulders at all. Above the trunk of the body, the head is attached so that it can pivot up and down as the toy walks. The design of the figure's legs are the same as in the Walking Popeye With The Parrot Cages. In fact, the trunks of both figures are the same, as are the arm pieces, although the heads are different in shape and the Popeye head does not move.

The Porter carries two suitcases covered with travel labels. On the Popeye toy, the suitcases are lithographed as parrot cages. Each suitcase/parrot cage has wooden wheels at the edges to facilitate movement of the toy. (See Comic Strip Character Toys chapter for Popeye listing.)

A similar toy was made by the Unique Art Manufacturing Company. The legs of Unique Art's "G.I. Joe And The K-9 Pups" appear to be the same as the Porter and Popeye, with different lithography. Other characteristics of the toys are

The 1930s Walking Porter, measuring 8" high, is similar to the Walking Popeye, but the Porter's head moves. **W. Maeder Collection. T. Parrish photograph.**

similar but not identical. The head and body of the G.I. Joe figure are of one piece, his shoulders are designed differently, and he is taller than the other two toys.

The Walking Porter has not been found in any catalog, but the Walking Popeye appears in catalogs from 1932 to 1936, so it is likely that the Porter was made at about the same time.　　**100　150**

1 "Louis Marx: Toy King ," **Fortune,** January, 1946, p. 127.

2 Jurgen and Marianne Cieslik, **Lehmann Toys** (New Cavendish Books, 1982), pp. 142-143.

The 1920s Jazzbo Jim figure is the same as the dancing figure of the Charleston Trio. The toy measures 3-1/2" long x 5" wide x 9" high. Ferdinand Strauss and Unique Art also manufactured a version of this toy. Dr. M. Kates Collection. R. Grubb photograph.

3 Information for Pinocchio Delivery toys supplied by Dr. M. Kates.

4 Eric Matzke, **Greenberg's Guide to Marx Trains** (Sykesville, MD: Greenberg Publishers, 1985), p. 86.

5 Information from Dr. M. Kates.

6 Gerritt Beverwyk, "Coon Jiggers," **Marx Toy Collector Newsletter,** Vol. 1, No. 6, pp. 8-9.

7 Gerritt Beverwyk, **Marx Toy Collector Newsletter,** Vol. 2, No. 2, p. 7.

CHAPTER VII: COMIC STRIP CHARACTER TOYS

INTRODUCTION

Although some of the toys listed below may seem to be equally appropriate for other listing chapters, these toys are more easily associated with the comic character from whom they were modeled. All of the toys are lithographed tin windups unless otherwise indicated. Catalog numbers listed are from the June 1977 **PB 84** (Parke Bernet) catalog.

B. O. PLENTY: See Dick Tracy, this chapter.

Blondie's Jalopy was manufactured in 1941. It measures 16" in length and is the same car as the Charlie McCarthy and Mortimer Snerd Private Car. Dr. M. Kates Collection. R. Grubb photograph.

The spark-shooting Buck Rogers 25th Century Rocket Ship measures 12" long and was manufactured in 1934. Dr. M. Kates Collection. R. Grubb photograph.

BLONDIE

The popular "Blondie" comic strip was created by Chic Young in 1930. "Blondie" was made into a series of movies which began in 1938 starring Penny Singleton and Arthur Lake. Often, the 1930s dates that appear on the Blondie toys refer to the copyright of the comic strip.[1] If the Cookie character appears on the toy, then the toy was manufactured about 1941 since Cookie was not in the comic strip until that date.

BLONDIE'S JALOPY: 1941. 16" long. This attractively decorated red and yellow car with black trim is actually a version of the Charlie McCarthy and Mortimer Snerd Private Car with different lithography. Similar heads of two figures are in the car. One head represents Dagwood, and the other represents Baby Dumpling, later known as Alexander. Except for the substitution of a yellow hat for a red one in some variations, the Dagwood head is like that of Dagwood the Driver, which is an eccentric car. When the front or rear bumper of the jalopy hits an obstacle, the direction of the car is reversed while the characters' heads turn.

Lettering on the front fenders reads "Blondie's Jalopy", although Blondie does not drive the car. Blondie is pictured on the left side door of the car, Cookie on the right side door. Daisy the Dog is pictured on the rear fenders.

Blondie's Jalopy is not commonly available. Add $300 to price of the toy with box.   **200 600**

DAGWOOD THE DRIVER: See Eccentric Cars section, Automobiles chapter, Volume II.

DAGWOOD'S SOLO FLIGHT: 1941.   8-1/2" long with 11-1/2" wingspan. The metal airplane with celluloid propeller is predominantly yellow and red with some white and blue. With only his movable head and yellow bow tie showing, the Dagwood figure pilots the plane. The head is the same one used on the Dagwood the Driver car and Blondie's Jalopy, but for this toy, Dagwood does not wear a wooden hat. The plane has two large landing wheels and a smaller tail wheel. It moves in an eccentric manner, and even tips over on its nose.

On the left side of the plane, Daisy the Dog is pictured on the body, Baby Dumpling on the wing. A picture of Cookie appears on the right side of the plane with Blondie on the wing. As with other Blondie toys, the Cookie character dates the toy circa 1941. Catalog advertisements describe the toy as being new in 1941.

Dagwood's Solo Flight is similar to both the Popeye the Pilot plane (see Popeye, this chapter) and the Rookie Pilot (see Airplanes chapter, Volume II). But Dagwood's plane has a larger wingspan and the wings are tapered at a sharper angle.

Add $125 to the price of the toy with box.   **125 375**

BUCK ROGERS

The "Buck Rogers" comic strip by Phil Nowlan began in 1929. John F. Dille, whose name appears on the Buck Rogers Rocket Roller Skates, was then president of the National Newspaper Syndicate of America. It was Mr. Dille who suggested that the name "Buck" be used instead of the hero's original name, Anthony. After agreeing with Phil Nowlan to make Rogers into a comic strip hero, Dille assigned his best staff cartoonist, Dick Calkins, to draw the illustrations.[2]

BUCK ROGERS 25TH CENTURY ROCKET SHIP: 1934. 12" long. The rocket ship is multicolored in red, yellow, blue-green, white, and black. The nose, tail, and wings are striped. Sparks shoot from the rocket exhaust in the rear. The

piece that holds the spark-producing flint, just beneath the removable tail, is often missing.[3] There are wheels under the wings. A wing, cockpit dome, and four bubbles are on top of the ship. On the left side of the ship, Buck Rogers and Dr. Huer appear in the windows, but on the right side, Buck is shown with his girlfriend, Wilma Deering. All wear space helmets.

Near the wings, red and white lettering on a black background reads "Buck Rogers". A stripe and dot design is next to the lettering. The Buck Rogers rocket ship was marketed in 1934 for 94 cents. The patent date, March 15, 1927, appears on the ship, but the patent, number 1,621,266, was actually filed on June 14, 1924. Not surprisingly, the patent drawing, which preceded the comic strip by several years, does not resemble the actual toy. The patent does show the gearing and sparking mechanisms, as well as two cars with the sparking mechanisms—one of them a racer, possibly the Sparks racer (see Automobiles chapter). Rocket Racer, a car with a rocket ship body, was also produced but did not spark.

In his excellent book, **A Celebration of Comic Art and Memorabilia,** Robert Lesser reveals that John Dille, publisher of "Buck Rogers in the 25th Century" wanted toys produced by the Daisy Manufacturing Company to appear in the comic strip for the subtle advertisement of those toys. Without realizing it, Marx showed his 1934 Buck Rogers Rocket Ship with Buck and Wilma wearing headgear produced by Daisy, providing free advertising for his competitor.[4] Another toy manufacturer called Tootsietoy produced smaller Buck Rogers rocket ships in die-cast metal at about the same time.

The Buck Rogers Rocket Ship was marketed in a nicely illustrated box that shows a helmeted man and woman figure waving at the rocket ship in the sky. It is a very desirable toy and considered one of Marx's best. Add $200 to price of toy with box.   **100 400**

BUCK ROGERS 25TH CENTURY POLICE PATROL: 1935. 12" long. The rocket ship is predominantly red and blue-green. A particularly appealing feature of this toy is a porthole lithographed to look like an eye, which gives the toy an animated appearance. The wings of the Police Patrol are lithographed to resemble a group of rocket exhausts, similar in shape to those on the rocket ship described above.

The Police Patrol was advertised in 1935 and sold for 94 cents. Similar in appearance, both the Police Patrol and Flash Gordon ships have open cockpits with single figures firing guns. However, similarities between the earlier Buck Rogers rocket ship and the Police Patrol have been pointed out by Dick Martin, an illustrator and contributor to the **Marx Toy Collector Newsletter.** According to Mr. Martin, both Buck Rogers ships have rocket bodies printed in five colors, gray-blue tail fins with black stripes, gray front wheels, and support for the rear wheels. On both ships, the front wheels have an inner rim stamped in the metal and the rear wheel has two metal hubcaps. The Flash Gordon ship has none of these features. In addition, though the cockpits of the Police Patrol and Flash Gordon ships are similar, the cockpits are made of different materials with the rim of the former being made of aluminum and the latter of steel. The above facts led Dick Martin to conclude correctly that the Buck Rogers Police Patrol was issued closer to 1934 than to 1939.[5]

The Buck Rogers Police Patrol came in a plain box with the description: "a flashing, roaring, speeding model of Buck Rogers Famous Inter-Planetary Police Patrol." Add $250 to the price of the toy with box.   **150 450**

The Buck Rogers Rocket Roller Skates were manufactured in the 1930s with the picture and name of Buck engraved on the sole. Skates are pictured with original art for the box of a different pair of skates. Note the misspelling of the words "featuring" and "gauge". W. Maeder Collection. R. Grubb photograph.

BUCK ROGERS ROCKET ROLLER SKATES: c. 1934. Standard-size, unique roller skates made of heavy-gauge steel. Designed to look like rocket ships, the skates have a raised-dot design on the steel and reflectors on the tails. The front wheels have the scalloped edges of wings.

Fancy lettering engraved in the soles of the skates reads "Buck Rogers". A head and shoulders portrait of Buck appears above his name. Below the name, standard lettering reads "Licensed under Copyright 1930-1935 John F. Dille" and "Louis Marx & Co., U.S.A." (see introductory paragraph to Buck Rogers section).

The patent for the skates is probably number 2,058,164, submitted on September 13, 1934. Although the patent drawing is slightly different than the actual skates, the patent has more similarities to the skates than any of Marx's other patents for roller skates.   **NRS**

DICK TRACY

The "Dick Tracy" comic strip was created by Chester Gould in 1931. Marx made many Dick Tracy toys—cars, guns, and games. The Dick Tracy cars came in many different variations and were frequently colored green or blue.

B. O. PLENTY: Late 1930s or early 1940s. 8-1/2" high. The walking toy "B. O. Plenty" was modeled after the character from the Dick Tracy comic strip. He has brown hair and a beard and is dressed in a yellow shirt and hat, orange tie, blue vest, and brown pants with white stripes. His daughter Sparkle, with blonde hair and long white dress, is lithographed on his right arm. A red-ribboned package with the lettering "For Baby Sparkle" is in his left arm.

B. O. Plenty is made from the same die as Mortimer Snerd. Not only do both figures hold a package, but they have the same walking action while their hats, also alike, tip up and down. The action of the hat results from a rod in the figure's head which moves up and down.

The Marx logo appears on the back of the figure with lettering that reads "B. O. Plenty". The June 1977 **PB 84** auction catalog lists number 194 for this toy. B. O. Plenty was marketed in a plain, unillustrated box. Add $65 to the price of the toy with box.   **50   135**

DICK TRACY POLICE STATION AND RIOT CAR: Late 1940s or early 1950s. The tin Police Station is 9" wide and nicely illustrated with several characters from the Dick Tracy comic strip. Winding the station's crank opens the plastic

The 1935 Buck Rogers Police Patrol measures 12" in length and has an animated appearance. Dr. M. Kates Collection. R. Grubb photograph.

Manufactured in the late 1930s or early 1940s, B. O. Plenty walks and his hat tips up and down. W. Maeder Collection. T. Parrish photograph.

This 6-1/2", friction drive Dick Tracy Squad Car was manufactured c. 1949. W. Maeder Collection. T. Parrish photograph.

The 6-1/2" Dick Tracy Squad Car with gun pointing out of windshield. E. Owens Collection. G. Stern photograph.

The 1939 Flash Gordon Rocket Fighter measures 12" in length. The ship was re-issued in 1951 without Flash Gordon. Dr. M. Kates Collection. R. Grubb photograph.

doors and ejects a 7-1/2" Riot Car. The Riot Car has a friction motor. Sparks shoot from a machine gun sticking out of the right windshield. Lettering reads "Riot Car" on the side and "Dick Tracy" on the hood. The June 1977 **PB 84** auction catalog lists 3236 as the catalog number for this toy. The Dick Tracy Police Station and Riot Car set was marketed in an illustrated box. Add $100 to the price of the toy with box.

75   100

The automatic firehouse and fire chief car is the same toy with different lithography (see Automobiles chapter, Volume II).   **NRS**

A similar Riot Car, also 7-1/2" long, has the Captain, one of the other characters from the Dick Tracy comic strip, holding a gun in his hand. This variation is dark green with the license plate "#LM53", rubber tires, and a copyright symbol on the rear fender. A badge with Dick Tracy is pictured on the trunk of the car. The Marx logo is on the roof.[6]

A third Riot Car of the same size came with a siren, friction motor, and sparking mechanism.   **NRS**

DICK TRACY SIREN POLICE WHISTLE: Made of tin.[7] Add $20 to the price of the toy with box.   **10   50**

DICK TRACY SQUAD CAR: c. 1949. 11-1/4" long. The popular Dick Tracy Squad Car has a siren and flashing red spotlight. The light housing holding the bulb is either red or white. Some variations have a gun sticking through the windshield. Tracy drives the car and other characters from the comic strip are pictured in the windows. In order to show both a front and side view of the characters in the car, there are sometimes two drawings of each. A full-face drawing appears in the windshield, a profile in the side window.

Lettering reads "Dick Tracy" on the hood, "Police Dept." and "Squad Car No. 1" on the side. The back of the car has dummy lights, the license number "LM52", and the word "Police" above the license plate. Dick Tracy and his badge are pictured on the door.

The squad car was advertised in the 1950 **Sears** Christmas catalog but was available at least one year earlier. The ad describes the lithographed steel toy as having dummy headlights, bumpers, grille, and adjustable front wheels. The use of a flashlight battery and a motor wound by key are also mentioned. The toy sold for $1.87.

At least two variations of the car are known to exist. Gerritt Beverwyk, former editor of the **Marx Toy Collector Newsletter**, describes a deep green variation with an added grille, bumper, and lights which were made of pressed tin, chrome-coated, and fastened over the printed grille of the car. This car, which is the more popular variation, has a key-wound motor and two rubber and two wooden wheels. Mr. Beverwyk describes a second variation which is metallic blue in color with a friction-style motor and four rubber wheels. These two variations are somewhat different. Both have a battery space of the same size, but in different positions. The lever to turn on the light is also in different places.[8]

The smaller variations measure 6-1/2" and came in two different versions, one green and the other blue. The blue car has a sparking machine gun. Both cars have dummy lights and grille. No further information is known about the smaller blue car.

The green car has the usual lettering which reads "Dick Tracy" on the hood, "Squad Car No. 1", and "Police Car" on the side. The badge with Tracy's picture appears on the door. The words "Police Dept." and "Squad Car No. 1" are on the

side of the green car, but in opposite positions in comparison to the 11-inch car. The car has additional lettering that reads "Friction Drive" on both the hood and the side. The copyright symbol and "F.A. Synd." appears under the badge. The license plate reads "#305" with the Marx logo above it. A dummy light, the word "Police", and a paper label with instructions for the car are on the roof.

Linemar, Marx's Japanese subsidiary, also made variations of Dick Tracy cars. It is believed that Marx produced many other versions of these cars.

Add $100 to the price of the 11-1/4" car with box.

140   300

Add $25 to the price of the 6-1/2" car with box.   **40   75**

DICK TRACY TARGET GAME: See Games chapter.

FLASH GORDON

The "Flash Gordon" comic strip was created by Alex Raymond in 1934. Three movie serials known for their elaborate sets were produced in the 1930s and 1940s. Buster Crabbe starred as Flash and also played Buck Rogers in a similar serial.

FLASH GORDON RADIO REPEATER CLICK PISTOL: See Guns chapter.

FLASH GORDON ROCKET FIGHTER: 1939. 12" long. An attractive and colorful toy, the Flash Gordon Rocket Fighter is predominantly red and yellow with some black and white. The Flash Gordon figure aims a gun from an open cockpit. A mask covers the lower part of his face.

Along with the copyright symbol, lettering on the nose of the ship reads "Flash Gordon" and "King Features Syndicate". A lightning design and portholes decorate the front of the ship as well. Behind the figure are bubbles and rocket exhausts. On the side of the ship, the Marx logo appears above lettering that reads "Rocket Fighter". On the wing, lettering reads "Flash Gordon". A large number "5" appears on the wing as well. The Flash Gordon Rocket Fighter resembles the Buck Rogers Police Patrol toy. For a detailed comparison see Buck Rogers 25th Century Police Patrol listed previously in this chapter.

The Flash Gordon Rocket Ship was produced in 1939. In 1951, Marx re-issued the Rocket Fighter but the Flash Gordon name disappeared. One version still retained the number "5" on the wings, but in a second version this too disappeared. The June 1977 **PB 84** catalog lists number 1925 as the catalog number for the Rocket Fighter version without the number "5" on the wings.

In the 1951 **Montgomery Ward** Christmas catalog the variation with the number "5" on the wings is listed. The description reads as follows: "Rocket Ship shoots harmless sparks, runs ahead or in circles, 'rat-a-tats.' Lithographed steel, spring motor." The toy sold for $1.79. (Another rocket, Moon Rider Space Ship, is listed under the Rockets section of the Airplanes chapter, Volume II.)

Add $100 to the price of the toy with box.   **125   300**

FLASH GORDON SIGNAL PISTOL: See Guns chapter.

FLASH GORDON TWO-WAY TELEPHONE: The two-way telephone consists of two circular holders which are red or yellow with black centers and metal handles. The string that connects the telephone runs through a hole in the center of the holders. A fine illustration of Flash and Dale on a card came

Flash Gordon Two-Way Telephone with original card. Mr. and Mrs. C. Weber Collection. T. Parrish photograph.

with the toy. It is thought that the toy was sold from the 1940s to the 1950s. Add $50 to the price of the toy with box.

50   100

FLASH GORDON WATER PISTOL: See Guns chapter.

LITTLE ORPHAN ANNIE

Introduced on August 5, 1924, the "Little Orphan Annie" comic strip was created by Harold Gray. The comic strip character became popular on radio and was known as Radio Orphan Annie. In the 1970s, Little Orphan Annie inspired a Broadway show and movie.

LITTLE ORPHAN ANNIE SKIPPING ROPE: 1931. 5" high. Little Orphan Annie is brightly colored with orange-red hair, red dress with white collar, white socks, and black shoes. Lettering reads "Little Orphan Annie" on the figure's belt, and "Harold Gray" on the figure's shoes.

This ingenious toy is described in the 1931 Fall/Winter **Sears** catalog as follows: "New, unique and clever. When mechanism is wound, Orphan Annie skips rope. If she falls, she gets up herself to an upright position, never stopping her rope jumping regardless of whether she falls on her back or on her face." The toy sold for 25 cents.

The clever design of the toy was pointed out by David Longest in his beautiful book **Character Toys and Collectibles.** "Actually the Little Orphan Annie tin windup toy never leaves the ground as a unique mechanism simply allows the rope to pass under the figure's feet as a jump is simulated and balance is maintained." [9] There are four gears in Annie's feet which permit her wire jump rope to pass under her feet.

Add $100 to the price of the toy with box.

100   200

LITTLE ORPHAN ANNIE STOVE: c. 1938. 5/1-2" long x 10" wide x 8-1/4" high. This handsome electric stove is pale green and cream. There are four gold-colored metal plates on the stove lithographed with two different illustrations. One shows Little Orphan Annie serving cake to her dog Sandy; the other shows Annie holding a piece of cake with red lettering that reads "Little Orphan Annie". On the upper right side of the stove is an oven compartment and on the left, two burners. All

The Girard Toys stove, though similar to the Little Orphan Annie stove, is a paler green with cream-colored panels instead of lithographed plates. It measures 5-1/2" long x 9-1/2" wide x 9" high. Mr. and Mrs. C. Weber Collection. T. Parrish photograph.

the oven doors can be opened. Four lines of lettering are embossed underneath the stove and read "Louis Marx & Co.", "New York, N.Y. U.S.A.", "Catalog K44", "Rating 115v - 250W".

A similar stove measuring 9-1/2" wide x 8-1/2" high, but not identified as a Marx toy is advertised in the 1938 **Sears** Christmas catalog for 98 cents. This is believed to have been the approximate date for the Orphan Annie stove described above. While the advertised stove has the same illustrated plates, three burners take the place of the upper oven compartment. The Sears stove also came with six utensils: frying pan, sauce pan, stew pan, pie tin, and two mixing spoons. But both the Sears stove and the one described above

The 1930s electric Little Orphan Annie Stove has metal lithographed plates and measures 5-1/2" long x 10" wide x 8-1/4" high. Mr. and Mrs. C. Weber Collection. T. Parrish photograph.

The Moon Mullins and Kayo Handcar features the Mullins character on a box of dynamite and the Kayo character opposite. The toy measures 6" long. Erie archives, 1977.

have hooks on the burner backboard for hanging utensils. The Sears stove has two hinged, handled oven doors and a cord and plug for 110V A.C.

Other Orphan Annie Stoves that are not identified as Marx toys also exist. These are similar in design and have the same gold plates as the Marx stove. Some of these stoves, red in color or, more commonly, green and cream, as the one described above, are not electric.[10]

In addition, an electric "Girard Toys" stove is similar to the Marx stove described above. (See Chapter II: The Rise of the Factories for information about the Girard factory.) Measuring 5-1/2" long x 9-1/2" wide x 9" high, this stove is a paler green and cream, but identical in shape to the Marx stove except for a small ledge on the upper left side above the burner backboard.[11] The Girard Toys stove has cream-colored panels in place of the gold plates. Lettering in the oval temperature gauge reads "Girard Toys". The box for this toy is numbered "47".

Add $45 to the price of the Orphan Annie Stove with box.

	50	80
Add $25 to the price of the Girard stove with box.	40	75

MYSTERY SANDY DOG: 1938. 8-1/2" long. Orphan Annie's dog Sandy is made of colored metal and was marketed in a carton used for his dog house. An ad in the 1938 **Sears** Christmas catalog describes the Mystery Sandy Dog as follows: "Two-way motor. Any little tot can work it. Press down tail or push back—away he goes rolling his wood ball

This prototype of the Popeye Express has a movable head. The wheelbarrow, to which Popeye's body is attached, reads "Erie 12/2?/38" on its base. (The question mark represents a number that is illegible.) Mr. and Mrs. P. Sadagursky Collection. P. Summers photograph.

Brutus Horse and Cart was manufactured in 1938 and was sold with the Brutus figure as shown, the Popeye figure as described below, or no figure at all. W. Maeder Collection. R. Grubb photograph.

between his paws." The toy sold for 39 cents. Annie was not sold with Sandy, but she is shown on the box saying, "Oh! I know he's in there."

The Sandy Dog resembles the earlier Mystery Cat toy in appearance and size, and both toys have the same wooden ball. (See Mystery Cat, Animal Toys chapter.) A later toy similar to Mystery Sandy is Walt Disney's Mystery Pluto produced later. Pluto does not have the wooden ball, his head is lower to the ground, and his legs are lithographed. (See Mystery Pluto, Walt Disney Toys chapter.)

Add $50 to the price of the toy with box.   **50   150**

WALKING SANDY: 1931. 5" long x 4-1/4" high. Walking Sandy is orange-brown with black spots, and white snout and tail tip. Lettering reads "Sandy" on his collar. The dog was sold in either a standard box or a cardboard box that was also his kennel. The latter was illustrated with both Sandy and Annie. The toy was sold at the same time as Little Orphan Annie Skipping Rope. In 1931, Walking Sandy sold for 48 cents.

Although several ads mention that Sandy carries a basket in his mouth, the actual toy has a satchel or valise with Orphan Annie's name on it. Today, collectors often find that the satchel is missing from the toy. Add $100 to the price of toy with box.   **50   150**

MOON MULLINS

In 1923, Frank Willard created the "Moon Mullins" comic strip. Although there are many characters in the strip, Marx focused on two for toy manufacture, Moon (short for Moonshine) Mullins and the precocious young Kayo.

MOON MULLINS AND KAYO ON A HANDCAR: Mid-1930s. 6" long. The Moon Mullins figure, 4-3/4" high, and Kayo, 2-3/4" high, are on a railroad handcar that comes in a deluxe and regular version.

Both handcars have two-dimensional figures at opposite ends of the car that pump the handles with the aid of their jointed arms and legs. The figures wear derbies and checked pants in both versions, but the color of the clothing differs. Both versions could run on tracks.

The deluxe version came with 118" of track in a figure-eight design. The toy has a clockwork motor and is equipped with a bell and wheels that could also run on the floor. New in 1934, it sold for 79 cents in the 1934 **Sears** Christmas catalog. In the 1935 Fall/Winter **Sears** catalog, the regular version of the toy sold for only 25 cents. This less expensive model had a spring motor with flanged wheels to run on two-rail track.

The regular version of the toy is the most popular and features Kayo standing on a box of dynamite mounted to a black tin base. Lettering on the sides of the dynamite box reads "Dynamite Danger" and "Dynamite, 48 Sticks, Do Not Jar". On the deluxe toy, Kayo stands on a red platform which almost reaches from one side of the handcar to the other. The platform is mounted to a yellow, heavy-gauge steel base. The figure's names are printed on the side of the red platform.

The deluxe version was marketed in a red box with white lettering. An illustration shows Moon Mullins and Kayo speeding toward an angry bull.

According to Eric Matzke, a third version of the handcar was manufactured in the mid-1930s. As in the regular version, Kayo stands on the box of dynamite. But the car has a higher

quality windup motor, heavy underframe, and flanged O Gauge wheels. [12]

Add $150 to the price of the toy with box.

Regular	**175**	**400**
Deluxe	**200**	**450**

POPEYE

The "Popeye" character was created by E. C. Segar in 1929. Before Popeye, Segar's comic strip was known as "Thimble Theatre" with Olive Oyl and another character as her boyfriend.

Marx made a large number of fine Popeye toys, probably more than of any other comic strip character. Popeye is always dressed in his sailor suit, and although the toy came with a small pipe in the side of his mouth, today the pipe is often missing. From toy to toy, the color of Popeye's cap and pants may vary. On some toys, such as Popeye the Champ, Popeye Dippy Dumper, and Popeye the Pilot, the figure wears a white sailor cap. On other toys, such as Popeye Express, Popeye Jigger, and the Walking Popeye, his cap is navy blue. Likewise, on toys such as the Popeye Express and the Walking Popeye, the figure's pants are usually striped, but some of the walkers have been seen with navy pants. The Popeye Jigger and celluloid Popeye also have navy pants. Other variations in the color of caps and pants probably exist as well.

Marx's closest competitor for the Popeye toy market was Chein, a company that also made many excellent Popeye toys similar to those of Marx.

BRUTUS DIPPY DUMPER: See Eccentric Cars chapter.

BRUTUS HORSE AND CART: See Popeye Horse and Cart, this chapter.

POPEYE THE CHAMP: 1936. 7" long x 7" wide. Celluloid figures of Popeye and Brutus, mounted on metal pieces, fight in a boxing ring. The toy has a square boxing ring with four corner posts joined by four pieces of rope. When the bell rings, the mechanism randomly selects which figure is knocked out. Attractive lithographed scenes with characters from the Popeye comic strip decorate the base of the toy. On one side, there is a scene of clench-fisted characters with a sign that reads "Big Fight: Popeye the Champ".

The same celluloid figures were used for the Popeye Horse and Cart toy as well as for the Dippy Dumper and Funny Fire Fighters eccentric cars. Since celluloid is not a durable material, it is often difficult to find the figures of this toy in good condition.

The Popeye the Champ toy was marketed in 1936 for under one dollar. Marx produced a similar toy called "Knockout Champs" at the same time. This toy's two celluloid boxing figures are of young boys. The base of the boxing ring has different lithography. (See Knockout Champs, Miscellaneous chapter, Volume II.) The Strauss toy company manufactured a similar boxing toy called Knock-Out Prize Fighters.

The red and blue box for the Popeye the Champ toy is very well illustrated. It shows Popeye delivering a walloping punch to Brutus. The members of the audience, including an excited Olive Oyl, are depicted in detail. This toy is one of the most desirable of the Popeye toys. Add $800 to the price of the toy with box.   **400   700**

POPEYE EXPRESS: 1932. 8-1/2" long x 3-1/4" wide x 8-1/4" high. The Popeye Express, lithographed in bright colors, shows Popeye walking with a trunk on top of a wheelbarrow. As he walks, a parrot pops his head in and out of the trunk. The toy was produced with a small flap at the side of the trunk that covered the parrot's head. Unfortunately, today the flap is frequently missing. Popeye wears striped trousers, a sailor's shirt with pocket and buttons, and a cap. The trunk's luggage strap and padlock are lithographed as is a "New York" label on the trunk. Lettering on the side of the wheelbarrow reads "Popeye Express".

The Popeye Express was marketed in 1932 and sold for 59 cents. One variation of the toy exists in which the parrot is stationary. A second variation is believed to exist without a parrot, as illustrated in the 1937 **Paramount Salesman** wholesale catalog. The toys are similar except for some lithographed differences. On the variation, Popeye's trousers are not striped, his shirt has no pocket or buttons, and he does not wear a cap.

A prototype of the Popeye Express has a movable head. The figure's body is attached to the side of an unlithographed, empty wheelbarrow. Printing on the bottom of the wheelbarrow reads "Erie 12/2?/38". The question mark represents a number following the "2" that is illegible.

Another toy called the Popeye Express is similar to the Honeymoon Express toys (see Honeymoon Express chapter).

200   350

POPEYE FLYER: See Flyers in Airplanes chapter, Volume II.

POPEYE HANDCAR: 1935. 6-1/2" handcar; 4-5/8" figures. The rare Popeye Handcar is metal with rubber Popeye and Olive Oyl figures, which are known to deteriorate with age. Olive Oyl, in a red dress, stands on the handcar and pumps energetically with both hands while Popeye sits on a box of spinach, unwillingly pumping with one hand. Like the deluxe Moon Mullins and Kayo Handcar, the Popeye Handcar has a long red platform mounted to a green base. Swee' Pea crawls along the side of the base. The Handcar came with eight sections of curved track. It is believed that a variation of this car came with floor toy wheels.

Marketed in 1935, an ad described the Popeye Express as follows: "These rubber bodies sway and are flexible when toy is in motion. Handcar travels around...(the) circle of track approximately 12 times to one winding." A dozen sold for $17.50 in this ad, but other ads offer the toy at a cheaper price.[13]

The blue and orange box for the toy shows Popeye fuming and spluttering while Swee' Pea stands near Olive Oyl. The box from the D. McLain Collection has 49 cents written in pencil as the price of the toy. Add $150 to the price of the toy with box.   **180   400**

POPEYE HORSE AND CART: 1938. 7" long x 5-1/2" high. This metal windup toy has a celluloid Popeye figure in a cart pulled by a very small horse. Red on the outside and yellow inside, the cart has black disc-shaped wheels. A white horse with black markings pulls the cart with the aid of a small wheel on one of its hind legs. In 1938, the toy sold for 25 cents.

The Horse and Cart toy was made with the Brutus figure, known also as Bluto. Both celluloid figures were used for the eccentric cars and the Popeye the Champ toy. Because celluloid figures are fragile, it may be hard for collectors to find them in good condition today. The Horse and Cart toy was also advertised without a figure.

The Popeye Horse and Cart toy came in a plain unillustrated box which reads "Mechanical Horse Cart with Driver". Add $100 to the price of the toy with box.

Popeye Horse and Cart	200	300
Brutus Horse and Cart	50	200

POPEYE JIGGER and **POPEYE AND OLIVE OYL JIGGER:** 4-5/8" long x 3-1/8" wide x 10" high. The jiggers, made of tin, came in either a single Popeye figure or with Popeye and Olive Oyl on the roof of a cabin. The latter is the most popular version and one of the few tin toys that Marx made with the Olive Oyl figure. Others are the Popeye Flyer and a Linemar Olive Oyl Ballet Dancer. Unlike the Popeye Handcar, this time Olive sits on a box of spinach. Swaying, she plays the accordion while Popeye dances. Olive is dressed in a red blouse and black skirt. Her high-buttoned shoes are yellow. Popeye's name is printed at the waist of his sailor outfit. The Marx logo is on the bottom of the cabin's base.

The box for this toy shows Popeye wearing a top hat. However, the actual figure of the toy wears a sailor's cap. Similarly, while the box shows Olive Oyl singing, the actual figure has a closed mouth. The details of illustrations found on Marx toy boxes occasionally differ from the toy inside.

The lithography on the base of the toy is very fine. One scene is of an angry Olive, apparently after she fell into the water. Wimpy is also in the water holding onto a plank. Beside them in a green boat marked "Spinach" is a character which is probably supposed to be Brutus. Another scene on the side of the base shows Wimpy serenading a cow with a guitar. A third scene shows a creature hitting someone on the chin while holding Swee' Pea. On the back of the base, Wimpy suffers from the noise of a band of musicians. The toy sold for $4.15 a dozen in 1936.

The cabin beneath the figures was possibly meant to have been a boat deck because the roof is lithographed to look like wooden planks, and a coil of rope lies in the corner at Olive's feet.

While one 1937 ad shows the exact same scenes for both the single- and double-figure jiggers, another 1937 ad for the single-jigger figure has illustrations different from those on the double-jigger base. On the front of the base, Olive Oyl and Wimpy are standing on a boat. An illustration of Wimpy and the cow is on the side of the base, but the guitar is missing. The toy sold for 50 cents.[14]

Add $125 to the price of the single jigger toy with box.

175   375

Add $300 to the price of the double jigger toy with box.

200   400

POPEYE THE PILOT: 1936. 8-3/4" long with 8-1/2" wingspan. This attractive red, white, and blue airplane has the head of the Popeye figure in an open cockpit of a single-propeller plane. The plane may also have come in red, yellow, and blue. Multicolored lettering on the wings of the plane reads "Popeye the Pilot". In a 1936 ad the toy sold for $8.00 per dozen and is described as follows:

...modern streamline airplane with Popeye at the controls. Plane runs backward, forward, in a circle and also tips over on its nose. Popeye's head also moves up and down, very amusing action, equipped with a clock spring motor. Constructed of heavy sheet metal and brightly lithographed.[15]

The Popeye the Pilot plane came in at least two variations. One has a grille design on the nose of the plane. The Popeye figure's collar can be seen. The number "47" appears on the side of the plane. The second variation lacks the above features, but has a decorative design on the side. Sometimes the Popeye the Pilot plane has a flag mounted on the wing. In addition, Linemar produced a version of the toy. The Marx Rookie Pilot is similar to Popeye the Pilot. (For Marx Rookie Pilot, see the Airplanes chapter in Volume II.)

Add $75 to the price of the toy with box.

Early version	150	325
Later version	75	150

POPEYE PIRATE PISTOL: See Guns chapter.

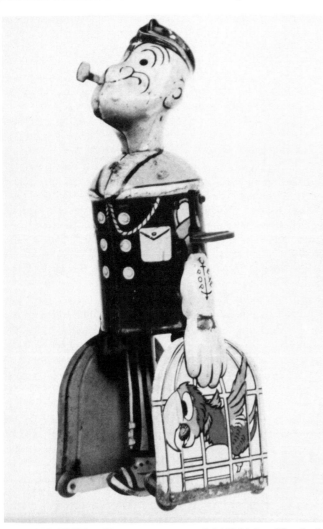

The 1932 Walking Popeye measures 8-1/4" high. The body was used as a model for several different toys. W. Maeder Collection. T. Parrish photograph.

WALKING POPEYE: 1932. 8-1/4" high. Popeye walks rapidly while carrying a caged green parrot in each hand. The Popeye toys were usually produced with either navy or white caps, but for several years, some ads show the Walking Popeye with no cap at all. Marketed in a September 1932 **Butler Brothers** catalog, the toy came in an illustrated box and sold for $2.25 a dozen.

Marx used the body of the Walking Popeye for several different toys. For example, the Walking Porter is the same toy with a different head and lithography. Popeye's parrot cages become the Porter's pieces of luggage. Other Marx toys with the Popeye body are Tidy Tim and the Drummer Boy.

The G.I. Joe and the K-9 Pups by Unique Art has a body similar to the Popeye toy. Though the soldier's cages are wider than Popeye's, the cages of both toys are equipped with a wheel at each end joined by a yellow metal strip. Both the soldier and Popeye have the same legs and rapid walking action.

The Walking Popeye is the most commonly available of the Popeye toys. Add $125 to the price of the toy with box.

175   375

This interesting prototype is entitled "Wimpy's Hamburger Stand". The piano was also used in the Merrymakers toy. Mr. and Mrs. P. Sadagursky Collection. P. Summers photograph.

WIMPY'S HAMBURGER STAND PROTOTYPE: A very interesting Popeye comic strip prototype was made from the piano of the Merrymakers toy. The prototype is the property of Stephanie and Paul Sadagursky, well-known dealers and collectors. The front of the tan piano, illustrated with dishes and utensils, resembles a food counter. An illustrated Wimpy wearing a chef's hat stands behind the counter. Salt and pepper shakers, a napkin stand, and a cash register are at his side. In front of the counter is an unpainted, metal, three-dimensional figure resembling Wimpy in shape. The figure of Swee' Pea is dressed in blue and playing the saxophone on top of the piano. Lettering on the left side of the piano reads "Wimpy's Hamburger Stand". Exemplifying Marx's sense of humor, the back of the piano shows a wood-grained design with two doors, one is marked "Ladies" and the other is marked "Gents".

SMITTY SCOOTER: 1932. 5" long x 8" high. In this rare toy, a two-dimensional figure of the young office boy Smitty is on a scooter. The figure is from the "Smitty" comic strip created by Walter Berndt in 1922. Smitty is brightly dressed in an orange sweater with black stripes, short black pants, cap, bow tie, long socks, and ankle-high shoes. He has a tiny nose, freckles, and orange-red hair. His round eyes are similar to those of Little Orphan Annie

The Superman Turnover Tank measures 4" in length and bears the date 1940. The flat superman figure under the tank appears to lift the tank and turn it over. W. Maeder Collection. R. Grubb photograph.

Smitty's foot fits into a slot on the scooter so that the figure can be removed from it. The scooter is orange with black stripes, a red handle, and red wheels. Black lettering reads "Smitty Scooter" on the side.

The 1932 Fall/Winter **Sears** catalog advertises the Smitty toy with four other toys; the entire group sold for one dollar. According to the ad, the toy has a spring motor and scoots in a zig-zag fashion.

Add $700 to the price of the toy with box.   **500   1300**

SUPERMAN

The "Superman" character, created by Jerry Siegel and Joe Shuster, was introduced to the public in **Action Comics** in 1938.

SUPERMAN AND THE AIRPLANE: 1940. 6" long with 6" wingspan. A three-dimensional Superman figure kneels on one knee at the rear of a single propeller plane. He is attached by a wire and appears to be rolling the plane over. Superman wears his traditional blue and red outfit. A villain with goggles and a brown helmet pilots the red plane. A circled star appears on each of its yellow wings. The plane is usually red, but also came in blue or aluminum. Its fin and side are numbered "12". The plane was used for the Marx Rollover Plane.

The Superman and the Airplane toy is not commonly available. Add $500 to the price of the toy with box.   **300   800**

SUPERMAN TURNOVER TANK: c. 1940. 4" long. A two-dimensional Superman figure underneath a tank appears to lift up and turn over the tank. The copyright symbol, "1940", and "Superman, Inc." are on the back of Superman's red cloak. The Marx logo reads "Made in the United States of America" and is on both the tank's turret and the back of the Superman figure. Superman's feet are slightly cut off, the amount varying somewhat from toy to toy. The tank is unlithographed gold with a predominantly blue turret and lithographed white hatch cover. Two large and two small wooden wheels are underneath the tank.

The Superman Turnover Tank is similar to other Marx Turnover Tanks. In fact, a Turnover Tank made in 1952 is almost identical, even to the same colored turret and hatch cover with the addition of some colorful lithography. In place of the Superman figure, a metal lever turns over the tank.

The Superman Turnover Tank was also made by the Marx Linemar division of Japan. The United States and Japanese versions are similar in appearance and size, but the Linemar tank is army green with lithographed details. Superman's suit is not blue but yellow. The Marx Linemar division also made several other Turnover Tanks with characters such as Popeye, Casper the Ghost, The Flintstones, and The Jetsons. In the 1950s, Linemar produced a large, three-dimensional Superman figure with a tank.

Add $100 to the price of the toy with box.   **75   200**

1 Gerritt Beverwyk, "Blondie and Dagwood," **Marx Toy Collector Newsletter,** Vol. 2, No. 3, p. 4.

2 Robert Lesser, **A Celebration of Comic Art and Memorabilia,** (New York: Hawthorne Books, Inc., 1971), p. 170.

3 Gerritt Beverwyk, "Spaceships," **Marx Toy Collector Newsletter,** Vol. 1, No. 3, p. 1.

4 Robert Lesser, p. 70.

5 Dick Martin, **Marx Toy Collector Newsletter,** Vol. 1, No. 3, p. 4.

6 Gerritt Beverwyk, "Dick Tracy," **Marx Toy Collector Newsletter,** Vol. 1, No. 4, p. 6.

7 Richard O'Brien, **Collecting Toys,** (Alabama: Books Americana, 1982), p. 393.

8 Gerritt Beverwyk, "Dick Tracy," **Marx Toy Collector Newsletter,** Vol. 1, No. 4, p. 4.

9 David Longest, **Character Toys and Collectibles,** (Kentucky: Collector Books, 1984), p. 67

10 David Longest, pp. 70 and 72.

11 Information from Marx Toy collector, Dr. C. Weber.

12 Eric Matzke, **Greenberg's Guide to Marx Trains,** (Sykesville, MD: Greenberg Publishing Company, 1985), p. 42.

13 **Blackwell Wielandy Company Catalog,** St. Louis, 1936.

14 **Decatur & Hopkins Catalog,** Boston, 1937.

15 **Blackwell Wielandy Company Catalog,** St. Louis, 1936.

CHAPTER VIII: WALT DISNEY TOYS

INTRODUCTION

Louis Marx & Company modeled attractive toys from the characters of the wonderful Walt Disney cartoons. Many of these toys are still available today, but are somewhat expensive perhaps because they appeal to both toy and Disney collectors.

Marx's Japanese subsidiary, Linemar, made practically every Disney figure, even the lesser characters like the Mad Hatter of Alice in Wonderland. This listing, however, will present only Marx Disney toys made in the United States. Unless specified otherwise, all of the following toys are lithographed tin windups.

DISNEY CABIN PROTOTYPE: 4-5/8" long x 2" high. A fine, hand-painted prototype was made from the cabin of the Popeye Jigger (see Comic Strip Character Toys chapter). The wood-grained roof and the coil of rope from the Popeye toy is retained. The cabin is illustrated on all sides. One side, probably the front, pictures Mickey Mouse, Donald Duck, and the Cold-Blooded Penguin from the 1945 Disney cartoon "The Three Caballeros." Horace Horsecollar and Clarabelle Cow appear on the back. The left side shows one of the Three Little Pigs; the right, a running Pluto. The Marx logo is on the bottom of the base in red with "X-708".

DONALD DUCK BANK: c. 1940. Various markings on different versions of the appealing Donald Duck Bank show that the toy was manufactured by Marx in the United States and by Linemar in Japan.

Lithography on the front of the tin bank shows Donald Duck wielding a mallet while Mickey Mouse points with a cane to the lever. When the lever is pulled, the bank tallies the amount of money or "score," as lettering reads on the bank. Donald Duck's nephews look at an elephant on the side of the bank.

The illustrated box pictures a happy Donald regarding the coins that pour out of the open bank door. The June 1977 **PB 84** catalog lists 728 as the catalog number for this toy. Add $25 to the price of the toy with box.   **30   75**

DONALD DUCK DIPSY CAR: See Eccentric Car section, Automobiles chapter, Volume II.

DONALD DUCK DUET: 1946. 10-1/2" high. This colorful toy features Donald Duck with jointed arms and Goofy standing on drums fastened together. Somewhat reminiscent of the earlier Marx jigger toys in movement, Donald beats the smaller drum while Goofy dances on the larger one. The copyright date "1946" appears on the toy's base. The Donald Duck Duet sold for $1.49 in 1946.

The squat Donald Duck figure is dressed in his sailor outfit with red bow tie. Despite the title, "Donald Duck Duet", the Donald figure is considerably smaller than that of Goofy. The smaller drum, on which Donald beats, has a circular pattern on the top and a triangular pattern around the outside.

Goofy has rubber ears and wears a red shirt, blue pants, open vest, and cap. A similar figure of Goofy was used for the toy, "Goofy the Gardener". Goofy dances on a white drum lithographed with musical notes and pictures of Donald Duck and Goofy. Lettering reads "Walt Disney's Donald Duck Duet".

The toy's illustrated box shows both Donald and Goofy dancing. The June 1977 **PB 84** catalog lists 362 as the catalog number for this toy. Well worth owning today, the Donald Duck Duet is not hard to obtain. Add $200 to the price of the toy with box.   **200   300**

DONALD THE DRIVER: See Mickey the Driver later in this section.

DONALD THE DRUMMER: 1940s. 10" high. A moving plastic figure of Donald beats a tin drum. Linemar made a smaller tin version of Donald the Drummer. Add $50 to the price of the toy with box.   **50   100**

DONALD THE SKIER: 1940s. 10-1/2" high. The plastic Donald the Skier figure is similar to Donald the Drummer, but he wears metal skis. Small wheels inserted in the skis facilitate movement.

Today, Donald the Skier is more common than Donald the Drummer. Add $15 to the price of the toy with box.   **40   85**

DOPEY WALKER: 1938. 8" high. Dopey walks by rocking from side to side as his blue eyes move up and down. He has large feet and some of the same movement as other Marx Walkers such as B. O. Plenty, (Comic Strip Character Toys chapter); Charlie McCarthy and Mortimer Snerd, (Film, Radio, and Television Toys chapter); and Pinocchio, (Walt Disney Toys chapter). He has pink cheeks and wears a tan cap and long yellow coat with two pink buttons that resemble his round pink nose.

Lettering on the top of his cap reads "Dopey". The Marx logo, copyright symbol, date "1938", and "W. D. Ent" (Walt Disney Enterprises) appear on his back. The toy sold for 25 cents in 1938.

Strangely, Dopey was the only tin character made from the film "Snow White and the Seven Dwarfs." Marx did not even manufacture Snow White. Perhaps Dopey was not a good seller or interest in the Snow White characters may have dwindled. In the 1950s, however, Marx manufactured Snow White and the Seven Dwarfs as miniature plastic figures.

Add $50 to the price of the toy with box.   **70   150**

DUMBO: 1941. 4" high. The charming Dumbo toy, an excellent likeness of its film counterpart, was modeled from the 1941 Walt Disney film about the baby elephant. The toy begins in a sitting position, somersaults, and returns to a sitting position when the key is wound.

Dumbo is gray and wears a lithographed red and yellow blanket and hat. The two front legs are lithographed, but the back legs are separate from his body.

Lettering on his big ears reads "Walt Disney's 'Dumbo'". The Marx logo is under the blanket and lettering that reads "Louis Marx & Co., Inc., Made in U.S.A., New York, N.Y." is on the blanket. The copyright symbol and lettering that reads

This prototype, made from the cabin of the Popeye Jigger toy, measures 4-5/8" long x 2" high. The front view pictures Mickey Mouse, Donald Duck, and the Cold-Blooded Penguin. The right side of the prototype shows Pluto running. The back view shows the Disney characters, Horace Horse Collar and Clarabelle Cow. The left view illustrates one of the three Little Pigs. Mr. and Mrs. P. Sadagursky Collection. P. Summers photograph.

"Walt Disney Productions" is near one ear. Near the other ear is the date "1941". The toy sold for approximately 45 cents in 1941.

Dumbo resembles the Marx Flippo Dog in build and action except that Flippo has separated, jointed front legs and is one-half inch smaller than Dumbo. The toys were manufactured at about the same time. (For Flippo listing, see Animal Toys chapter.)

Possibly the small size of the toy—only 4" in height—makes Dumbo a somewhat less impressive toy to some than if it were higher. But after all, Dumbo is a baby elephant. Though not a common toy, Dumbo is not very highly priced. Add $45 to the price of the toy with box.   **150   230**

FERDINAND THE BULL: 1938.   5-1/2" long x 4" high. Marx made an engaging toy from Disney's Ferdinand, the peace-loving bull. Ferdinand's metal tail spins rapidly around as the bull turns in a circle, in an attempt to escape a movable

The 1938 Dopey Walker measures 8" high and walks with a rocking motion as his eyes move up and down. Dopey is the only tin version of the Seven Dwarfs that Marx manufactured. W. Maeder Collection. T. Parrish photograph.

The 4" high Dumbo, manufactured in 1941, somersaults and returns to a sitting position. W. Maeder Collection. R. Grubb photograph.

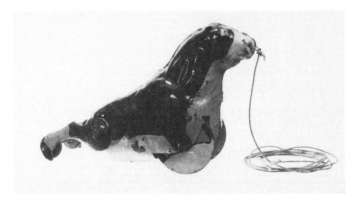

This prototype for a Ferdinand the Bull pull toy has wheels for the front legs and jointed back legs. Two smaller wheels are also positioned between the back legs. Lettering on the base reads "5/20/38 Erie 1652". Mr. and Mrs. P. Sadagursky Collection. P. Summers photograph.

metal bee attached to a small hole in his body. The turning action of the toy is similar to other turning Marx toys such as the Lone Ranger (see Film, Radio, and Television Toys chapter).

Ferdinand the Bull is reddish-brown with a yellow chest and stomach. He has soulful eyes and hard, fiber-like horns curved around his face. In his mouth, Ferdinand holds a yellow cloth flower. The color of the flower may vary. The horns and flower are frequently missing from the toy today.

The Marx logo, copyright symbol, date "1938", and lettering that reads "W. D. Ent" are printed on the bull's stomach. Yellow lettering reads "Ferdinand" on the bull's right side just above the windup key.

An ad in the 1938 **Sears** Christmas catalog shows Ferdinand in a steel wagon pulled by the same horse which pulls a cart with Popeye or Bluto. A farmer figure similar to those found on Marx tractors drives the wagon. Ferdinand in the steel wagon, plus the horse and farmer, sold for 59 cents. According to the

Sears ad, the cart measured 11" x 5-1/4" x 3/4". Two years later, in 1940, Ferdinand was sold without these accessories for 25 cents.

An interesting prototype, owned by Stephanie and Paul Sadagursky, shows Ferdinand with wheels instead of front legs and jointed back legs. Two small wheels are on an axle between the back legs. String to pull the toy is attached to the animal's nose. The base of the toy reads "5/20/38 Erie 1652".

The production toy has a blue and green box which pictures two calves gamboling at Ferdinand's left side. The top and bottom of the box show Ferdinand's head and shadow in green. Add $50 to the price of the toy with box.   **60   250**

FERDINAND THE BULL AND THE MATADOR: c. 1938. 8" long x 5-1/2" high. Facing one another, Ferdinand and the matador each stand on a lithographed, wheeled stand joined by a metal strip. The lithography on the stand is almost identical to the lithography on some variations of the Honeymoon Express toys. The bull and matador move back and forth.

The Ferdinand figure, unlike the one with the bee, stands hunched over, ready to attack the matador. Instead of the metal tail of the previous toy, his tail is believed to be made of cloth. But like Ferdinand with the bee, the Ferdinand with the matador is reddish-brown with a yellow chest and stomach. Lettering reads "Ferdinand" on his side. Additional lettering that reads "Walt Disney Ent" and "1938" as well as the copyright date appear on his stomach. The tin matador is colorfully dressed in a red, yellow, and blue costume. Holding his red cape, the matador has a rather evil smile.

In the 1930s, a similar toy of approximately the same size was made. The manufacturer was possibly Gebr. Einfalt. Both the matador and bull are on wheels joined by a tin strip to allow back-and-forth action. The matador wields a long knife or sword. It is unknown which toy was produced first, but one toy was probably influenced by the other. Another toy with the steel strip on wheels and back-and-forth action is the Maggie and Jiggs toy manufactured by the German firm, Nifty.

Ferdinand and the Matador is more difficult to find than the single Ferdinand the Bull figure. When the former is located, it frequently has missing parts.

Add $75 to the price of the toy with box.   **150   300**

FIGARO: 1940. 5" long. The cat character, Figaro, is from the 1940 Disney film "Pinocchio." Marx's Figaro toy is not quite as successful in capturing the essence of the delightful film character as, for example, the Dumbo toy. Figaro the cat has brownish-black fur; rubber ears; white paws, tail tip, and snout; and flesh-colored face. Lettering reads "Figaro" and "From Walt Disney's Pinocchio" on the back of the figure.

Figaro's roll-over action was described in two patents. The first, designed by Willis Rexford, is number 2,182,642, application date April 1939. The patent drawing resembles the roll-over Pluto toy described later in this chapter. The second patent, number 2,189,759, application date June 3, 1939, was designed by Raymond Lohr and Richard Carver (see Patents appendix). While both patents describe the roll-over action, only the later patent shows the reversing roll-over action.

A possible variation of the Figaro toy has the same markings on its back as that described above, but the figure holds a ball in its front paws. Figaro with a ball has legs separate from its body, rather than lithographed to it like the toy described above. Whether this toy was a prototype or a less common variation of the Figaro toy is unknown. Reader confirmation is requested.

The Figaro toy is commonly available and inexpensive to obtain. Add $25 to the price of the toy with box.   **30   75**

GOOFY THE GARDENER: c. 1940s. Goofy the Gardener is almost identical to the Goofy figure on the Donald Duck Duet toy described previously. It is estimated that both toys were marketed at about the same time. The Goofy figure holds a wheelbarrow with lettering that reads "Goofy The Gardener".

According to the April 1983 Lloyd Ralston **Antique Toy Auction Catalog,** Goofy the Gardener was manufactured in Great Britain. It is unknown whether an American version of the toy exists, but Goofy the Gardener is not a common toy. Add $75 to the price of the toy with box.   **75   125**

MICKEY MOUSE DIPSY CAR: See Eccentric Car section, Automobile chapter, Volume II.

MICKEY MOUSE EXPRESS: See Honeymoon Express chapter.

MICKEY THE DRIVER: 1950s. 6-1/2" long x 4-1/2" high. A plastic Mickey drives a small, flat car decorated with the names and pictures of various Disney characters. The figure has a spring in his neck which allows his head to shake. The Mickey Mouse figure is the same as that of the Mickey Mouse Disney Dipsy Car, but the cars differ in shape and lithography, though both feature Disney characters. Unfortunately the Mickey figure often has broken arms because they protrude from both the Driver and Dipsy cars.

The red, blue, pink, white, and black tin car has a plastic steering wheel and lithographed headlights. An intriguing feature of the toy is the "works" lithographed to the underside of the car. Various Disney characters are lithographed on the car. Mickey and Minnie figures appear on the hood, and Pluto and Goofy are on the doors. Donald Duck is shown on the trunk. The Marx logo, copyright, and lettering that reads "W. D. P." are on the right side of the car near the picture of Goofy. The same car, with different lithography, came in two versions with a boy or girl driver believed to be Dan and Dottie.

Like the Marx Mystic Motorcycle and the Tricky Taxi, the car was designed to turn before it falls off of a table's edge. Occasionally, the car does fail to swerve in time.

It is believed that a Donald the Driver toy also exists. The plastic Donald figure of the Donald Duck Disney Dipsy is similar to the Mickey figure and could have also been used in a Donald the Driver toy. In addition, Linemar, Marx's Japanese subsidiary, produced a similar version of the Mickey the Driver as well as Donald the Driver car, but both were made of tin.

Add $100 to the price of the toy with box.

Mickey	**100**	**300**
Donald	**150**	**300**

PARADE ROADSTER: 1950. 11" long. A strikingly attractive toy, the tin Parade Roadster is a large, flat convertible. Disney figures, garlands, and blue ribbon are lithographed on the red, white, and blue car. A plastic figure of Donald is in the driver's seat with plastic Mickey, Minnie, and Pluto figures as passengers.

In the 1950 **Montgomery Ward** Christmas catalog the toy sold for 98 cents. The ad describes the toy as follows: "Made of metal, lithographed in pastel colors, bottom completely enclosed, rubber wheels, transparent windshield, spring motor..." In compliance with safety regulations, Marx was

The 1938 Ferdinand the Bull measures 5-1/2" long x 4" high. In an attempt to escape the movable metal bee, Ferdinand turns in a circle and spins his tail. S. Stoughton Collection. R. Grubb photograph.

Manufactured in the 1950s, Mickey the Driver car has the same figure as the Mickey Mouse Disney Dipsy eccentric car and measures 6-1/2" long. The car was made to turn before falling off of a table's edge. W. Maeder Collection. T. Parrish photograph.

beginning to produce toy cars with a completely enclosed bottom as described above.

The toy is not hard to find, but occasionally some of the figures are missing. Add $50 to the price of the toy with box.

125   350

PINOCCHIO

The Pinocchio character originated in the tale "Pinocchio: The Story of a Puppet" created by a 19th century writer, Carlo Collodi. In 1940, Walt Disney presented his full-length, animated movie version of Pinocchio.

PINOCCHIO THE ACROBAT: 1939. 16" high x 11" wide. Pinocchio the Acrobat is a striking toy with lithographed metal arms attached to metal strips.[1] The strips are connected to a metal rod projecting upward from a rocking base. When wound, Pinocchio somersaults as he swings back and forth. Like the figure of the Pinocchio Busy Delivery, Pinocchio the Acrobat has jointed legs made of composition cardboard. The figures of the two toys also have a similar face and body.

The base of the toy has the same shape as the Marx Range Rider base and is attractively lithographed with characters from the film, such as Pinocchio, Figaro, Jiminy Cricket, and the imposing Monstro the Whale. Letters in various colors read "Pinocchio the Acrobat" on one side of the base. Red lettering reads "Watch Him Go!" on the other side of the base. The Marx logo, copyright symbol, copyright date "1939", and lettering that reads "Walt Disney Prod." also appear on the base.

The 1939 Walking Pinocchio is similar to other Marx walkers and measures 8-1/2" tall. As Pinocchio walks, his eyes move. W. Maeder Collection. T. Parrish photograph.

The 1939 Pinocchio the Acrobat measures 16" high x 11" wide. The figure somersaults as it swings back and forth. Dr. M. Kates Collection. R. Grubb photograph.

The idea for Pinocchio the Acrobat was used in a similar toy called "Acrobatic Marvel" in which a monkey does tricks while suspended on a less sturdy metal strip (see Animal Toys chapter).

Pinocchio the Acrobat came in an illustrated box entitled "Acrobatic Pinocchio". The toy itself is entitled "Pinocchio the Acrobat". Pinocchio the Acrobat is fairly common in the toy market. Add $50 to the price of the toy with box.   **80 250**

PINOCCHIO BUSY DELIVERY: c. 1939 to 1940. 9" long x 3-1/4" wide x 7-3/4" high. The Pinocchio figure sits on a unicycle facing the attached, open two-wheeled cart. After the cart rolls forward, the unicycle pivots in a different direction. Pinocchio holds the handlebars and pedals the cart with his legs when the toy is wound.

All of the long-nosed Pinocchio figures are dressed as Disney's movie character. The outfit consists of a white shirt;

The Pinocchio Busy Delivery toy with lithographed wood pattern was manufactured c. 1939 to 1940 and measures 9" long x 3-1/4" wide x 7-3/4" high. The figure has metal arms and jointed cardboard legs. Dr. M. Kates Collection. R. Grubb photograph.

red, short-legged overalls; pointed yellow hat with a red feather; and a large blue bow tie.

The Pinocchio figure has lithographed metal arms and composition cardboard jointed legs. The handlebars of his cycle are merely extended pieces of his metal arms, bent into the shape of a handlebar.

Black lettering reads "Busy Delivery" on the wood-grain lithography of the cart's sides. The Marx logo is in the left lower corner. A small notice reads "Phone 00-000" in the right lower corner. The back of the cart has one notice which reads "We Deliver In All Directions" and another notice which reads "Snappy Service". The base of the cart is black.

In a variation of the toy, Pinocchio has composition cardboard arms in addition to the composition cardboard jointed legs. The handlebar is now a separate metal piece. Instead of the lithographed wood pattern, the cart is yellow and lithographed with several characters from the Pinocchio film, such as Geppetto, Figaro, and Jiminy Cricket. Red lettering reads "Pinocchio Delivery". The Marx logo, copyright date

"1940", and lettering which reads "W. D. Prod." appears on the lower part of the cart. The base of the cart is blue.

Marx's Busy Delivery toy is similar to the Pinocchio Delivery toys with elements of both Pinocchio variations. The black figure is from the same die but lithographed differently and without Pinocchio's long nose. (See Busy Delivery in Black Toys chapter.)

The two variations of the Pinocchio Delivery toy are the rarest of the Pinocchio toys. Add $50 to the price of the toy with box.   **90   200**

WALKING PINOCCHIO: 1939.   8-1/2" high.   Walking Pinocchio is similar to a number of other Marx walkers with large feet such as B. O. Plenty, Charlie McCarthy, Dopey, and Mortimer Snerd.   Like the Dopey Walker, the Walking Pinocchio has eyes that move up and down.   The copyright symbol, Marx logo, and lettering that reads "1939 Walt Disney Ent." appear on the back of his collar.

The 1940 variation of the Pinocchio Busy Delivery toy has both cardboard arms and legs. The cart is lithographed with characters from the "Pinocchio" movie. Dr. M. Kates Collection. R. Grubb photograph.

The toy came in an illustrated box and is the most common of all the Pinocchio toys. Add $50 to the price of the toy with box.   **100 250**

PLUTO

MYSTERY PLUTO: 1948. 8" long. The yellow-tan Pluto crouches to sniff the ground. His legs are not separate appendages, but are lithographed. Two red wheels on each side of the toy obscure a view of the dog's hind legs. Mystery Pluto has a red metal tail, which is rather long and flat at the sides. Pluto has the same rubber ears as the Goofy figure of the Donald Duck Duet. Except for its tail and wheels and the lack of a red sweater, Mystery Pluto is identical to Roll-over Pluto.

The mystery in the toy's title probably refers to the way in which the toy's mechanism is activated. Pushing down on Pluto's tail starts the toy forward; the tail rises as the spring unwinds.

Though the copyright date printed on the toy is "1939", the earliest advertisement found for Mystery Pluto appeared in 1948 when the toy sold for 98 cents. As mentioned in previous descriptions, the copyright date does not necessarily coincide with the manufacture date.

The patent number 2,001,625 is printed on Mystery Pluto. The patent was submitted February 23, 1935, and pictures a car, but the patent states the toy could be an animal, too. This patent was not designed by Marx employees but by Heinrich Müller of Nuremberg, Germany.

Marx manufactured toys similar to Mystery Pluto, such as Mystery Sandy, the dog from the Little Orphan Annie comic strip, and Mystery Cat (see Comic Strip Character Toys and Animal Toys chapters). Unlike these other toys, Mystery Pluto

The 1948 Mystery Pluto measures 8" long. Pushing down on Pluto's tail activates the toy's mechanism. W. Maeder Collection. T. Parrish photograph.

does not have the wooden ball between his paws and his head is lower to the ground.

Mystery Pluto came in an illustrated box. It is commonly available today. Add $50 to the price of the toy with box.

50   100

ROLL-OVER PLUTO: 1939. Roll-over Pluto's yellow-tan body has a lithographed red coat with lettering that reads "Watch Me Roll Over—Pluto". Additional lettering reads "1939 Walt Disney Prod." beneath the coat. A whimsical touch, typical of Marx, is the lithographed paws on the base of the toy. On one side of the toy, a windup key activates the toy's mechanism. Roll-over Pluto has a thin, curved metal tail with a small metal ball on its end. The tail turns around as the dog rolls over.

An ad in the 1941 **Shure Winner No. 136 Wholesale Catalog** shows Roll-over Pluto without the coat or lettering described above. It is unknown whether this variation of the toy actually exists. According to the ad, Pluto "runs along the ground and at intervals rolls completely over sideways, lands on his feet and continues in his forward action." The toy sold at $4.25 for one dozen.

Unlike the Mystery Pluto, Roll-over Pluto does not have a patent number printed on the toy. Because the Pluto toys have different mechanisms, the patent for each toy probably differs. The patent for Roll-over Pluto is possibly 2,182,642, submitted April 1, 1939, which is for a roll-over toy. The patent illustration shows a dog similar to Pluto. Marx used the roll-over action for other toys, too, such as the roll-over cats, listed in the Animal Toys chapter.

Roll-over Pluto, the most popular Pluto toy, came in an illustrated box and is commonly available today. Add $50 to the price of the toy with box.

100   200

WISE PLUTO: 1939. Wise Pluto is yellow-tan with a rubber tail. He is similar to the Roll-over Pluto, but does not have a red coat.

In the 1942 **Montgomery Ward** Christmas catalog the toy sold for 54 cents. The advertisement describes the toy as follows: "Inquisitive Pluto sniffs along your table right to edge but never quite falls." This action is not infallible and occasionally the toy does fall off of the edge.

Wise Pluto, the least common of the Pluto toys today, also came in an illustrated box. Add $50 to the price of the toy with box.

100   200

THE THREE CABALLEROS

"The Three Caballeros" is a 1945 Walt Disney cartoon starring Donald Duck, a parrot named Jose Carioca, and a rooster named Panchito.

THE THREE CABALLEROS PROTOTYPE: c. 1945. 7-1/4" long x 5-3/4" high. The Three Caballeros prototype is a yellow piano with a Latin-American flavor. The piano is illustrated on all sides with various characters from the cartoon. Sheets of music which appear above the keys read "The Three Caballeros". South American village scenes decorate the piano on either side of the music. A rousing scene on the back of the piano shows the Three Caballeros, all in white sombreros, singing on a stage. The Cold-Blooded Penguin, also from the cartoon, is pictured on the right side of the piano wearing a cap, scarf, and mittens. The winged donkey character, known as the Flying Gauchito, appears on the left side of the piano flying above the clouds.

"The Three Caballeros" prototype inspired by the 1945 Disney cartoon. The sides and back feature characters from the film. The left view of the prototype shows the Flying Gauchito. The back view features Jose Carioca the Parrot, Panchito the Rooster, and Donald Duck. The right view of the prototype pictures the Cold-Blooded Penguin. Mr. and Mrs. P. Sadagursky Collection. P. Summers photograph.

The Caballero piano is of a different shape than the Merrymakers Piano and, unlike that toy, does not have attached figures.

TRAIN-RELATED TOYS: Described after Walt Disney's Television Car.

WALT DISNEY'S TELEVISION CAR: Late 1940s or early 1950s. 7-1/2" long. The Television Car is a colorful yellow friction car. The word "Television" in the toy's name refers to a lighted, transparent screen made of plastic in the car's roof. As the car moves, the heads of Mickey Mouse and Donald Duck appear on the screen.

The lights, grille, and various Disney figures are lithographed on the car. Donald Duck is lithographed in the driver's seat, and Mickey Mouse sits beside him. The figures are lithographed twice in order to show front and side views as on the Dick Tracy Car. In the back seat are Goofy with one of Donald Duck's nephews. Bambi is shown on the left door, and Thumper is on the right one. Lettering on the hood reads "Walt Disney's Television Car".

Walt Disney's Television Car is not as common as other cars with Disney figures such as the Parade Roadster. The toy was marketed in a yellow and red illustrated box. Add $100 to the price of the toy with box. **100   200**

TRAIN-RELATED TOYS

Marx made many attractive toy trains, some with more realistic detail than others. Model railroad enthusiasts will find the realistic trains in Eric Matzke's excellent book **Greenberg's Guide to Marx Trains**. This section lists only Disney toy trains.

DISNEYLAND EXPRESS: c. late 1940s or early 1950s. This set came with an articulated toy passenger train consisting of a locomotive and three tin cars. Articulated train cars came in a number of varieties over many years but commonly have only one set of wheels and are partially supported by the car ahead of it.   The Disneyland Express train is lithographed with various Disney characters.

The set has a 21-1/2" long sheet metal base with a channel track. This colorful base has one tunnel in the right corner and is illustrated with many Disney characters such as Snow White and the Seven Dwarfs, and Mickey and Minnie Mouse. The same lithographed base with two tunnels in different locations was used for the Walt Disney Train Set (described later in this chapter).

Add $100 to the price of the toy with box.   **100 200**

DISNEYLAND TRAIN: c. 1950. Goofy drives the locomotive of this small, articulated train with three tin cars. Similar in appearance to the Casey, Jr. Disneyland Express, the Disneyland Train is lithographed with several Disney characters. The locomotive is believed to be a combination of tin and plastic (reader confirmation is requested). Add $25 to the price of the toy with box.   **75 100**

MICKEY MOUSE EXPRESS: See Honeymoon Express Toys chapter.

WALT DISNEY TRAIN SET: c. 1950. The Ranger-sized train set includes a blue, 3-3/4" long, 376 Locomotive with Donald Duck as the engineer and Goofy reclining on the running boards. The red, 2" long, 3462 Tender has lettering that reads

"Donald Duck R.R." and pictures both Mickey's and Donald's nephews.   The blue, 3" long gondola is not numbered but pictures the Three Little Pigs and Pluto. A yellow, 3" long, 049 Boxcar has lettering that reads "Mickey Mouse Express" and pictures Mickey and Minnie Mouse, a parrot, and three of the Seven Dwarfs. A red, 2-1/2" long caboose, also not numbered, pictures Pinocchio and Jiminy Cricket.

The set includes a red, sheet metal base which is 21-1/2" long and has a channel track.   The multicolored base is lithographed with Walt Disney characters such as Snow White and the Seven Dwarfs, Bambi, Thumper, Pluto, Dumbo, Mickey and Minnie Mouse with nephews, and Donald Duck with nephews.   The base has lithography similar to that of the Disneyland Express, but the two tunnels are located on the outer middle sides.   The set was also sold without the base.[2]

The set came in a blue box with a yellow train.   A large, plain, 376 Locomotive is pictured.   Lettering reads "Walt Disney Train Set" on the cover.

The train from the Walt Disney Train Set is similar to the Ranger manufacturer's 390 Freight Set and 395 Passenger Set. The trains of both manufacturers are quite similar in construction, style, lithography, size, and scale.   All are lithographed tin windup toys.[3]   **150 400**

---

[1] Information for Pinocchio the Acrobat and the Pinocchio Delivery Toys provided by the well-known Marx toy collector, Dr. M. Kates.

[2] Information for the Walt Disney Train Set provided from the Allan Collection.

[3] Edward B. Pinsky, "Look-A-Likes," **Atlantic Division Express,** Summer 1978, p. 7.

CHAPTER IX: ELONGATED TRAFFIC TOYS, HOME TOWN BUILDINGS, AND NEWLYWED'S ROOMS

The Main St. (foreground) and Big Parade (rear) were manufactured in the late 1920s and measure 24" long x 3-1/2" wide x 7-3/4" high. Figures and traffic move through slots in the street. W. Maeder Collection. R. Grubb photograph.

INTRODUCTION

The elongated traffic toys are especially appealing and exemplify Marx toys at their best. As the category implies, the toys are quite long and measure 24" long x 3-1/2" wide x 3" high. But the Busy Bridge, considerably higher, measures 7-3/4" high. Slots are utilized along the length of each toy in this group through which figures and traffic can move continuously when activated.

The patent for the traffic toys, number 1,674,293, was published June 19, 1928 and entitled "Traffic-Simulating Toy". The patent drawing resembles the "Main St." toy with a policeman in the center of it. (Note the abbreviation of the word "Street" in the name of the toy.) But all of the elongated traffic toys have the same long, narrow shape with two sets of arches, as shown in the patent drawing. Airplanes and zeppelins are also shown attached to a loop at the top of the toy, but this feature is not on any of the actual toys. However, the Big Parade was produced with a single airplane.

The patent was subsequently revised as number 1,704,012, published March 5, 1929, and entitled "Parade-Simulating Toy". The revised patent is similar to the patent described above, except for the airplanes and zeppelins, and resembles the Big Parade toy.

A separate patent for the Busy Bridge, somewhat different from the Main St., Big Parade, and West Point Parade toys, has not been located.

BUSY BRIDGE: 1937. A tin windup lithographed in white, black, and red. Six cars and buses drive over the Busy Bridge lined with lamp posts. In the center of the toy is a flat lithographed piece that reads "Police" and has pictures of two officers, one in a booth, the other standing near "Stop" and "Go" signs.

The buildings at each end of the bridge are amusingly lithographed. In one, the dry goods store, a party is going on in the upper part of the building with one man seated in the window. Lettering on the end of the building reads "Main St." and there are clocks on two sides of the building that read 3 p.m. The same lettering and clock appear on the Main St. toy.

The "Main St. Terminal" building is at the other end of the Busy Bridge. It has the same clock as the dry goods store and some amusing scenes as well. In one scene, a man having his shoes shined appreciatively eyes a lady in a short coat. In the background, a barber attends to a customer. Upstairs, a crowd similar to the one in the dry goods store makes merry. A scene at the end of the building shows a policeman arresting someone, a peddler selling his wares, and a man buying cigars.

With the addition of four metal pieces lithographed to look like bridge piers, the Busy Bridge is basically the same toy as the Big Parade. The bridge piers raise the toy high enough so that other toys can travel beneath it. Metal cables are also attached to the arches and reach to the buildings at each end of the toy so that it more closely resembles a bridge.   **125 200**

MAIN ST.: 1927. As explained previously, the name of the Main St. toy contains the abbreviation for the word "Street." The Main St. buildings are predominantly red and the street is black. The street came in other colors too, though less commonly. For example, one toy has a street with a red brick design and yellow-tan block pavement. It is believed that the street also came in tan. Six vehicles on Main St. measure 1-1/2" long x 3/4" high and are lithographed in great detail considering their size.

Main St., a lithographed tin windup, is similar to the other elongated traffic toys but has figures that do not appear on those toys. A large three-dimensional policeman with his raised right hand dominates the center of the toy. He is slightly taller than the toy's flat metal statue of a man mounted on a horse. Unlike the policeman, the two other figures are flat, two-dimensional, and much smaller, reaching only to the policeman's chest. One of these is a man with a sly expression who sells fruit from a cart. The other figure, a woman, is the same piece as the man with different lithography. Both of these figures were used on a toy called "Pinched" which was also marketed in the late 1920s.

The Main St. buildings are lithographed with the same scenes as those of the Busy Bridge except for the side of one building where a couple is shown kissing. Other people in the scene are engaged in various activities. A large clock stands in the middle of the street near the policeman. This clock, like the two lithographed on the buildings at each end, reads 3 p.m.

The Main St. toy appears in the 1927 Fall/Winter **Sears** catalog, and, depending in which city the catalog was issued, the toy sold for either $1.00 or $1.15. Page numbers also vary between catalogs as do some of the toys shown. The **Sears** catalog advertisement describes the toy as "The Newest Sensation — A Whole Town In Itself" and further states that it would normally sell for $1.50.

Marx was not the only manufacturer of elongated traffic toys. Gotz of Germany produced a similar toy in the 1930s. The Gotz toy is pictured in the informative book by Martyn L. Schorr entitled **The Guide to Mechanical Toy Collecting**.[1] Another toy, the Lincoln Tunnel produced by Unique Art, is so similar to Marx's Main St. that it is possible the same dies were used. Occasionally, Marx was known to exchange tools and dies with his friend Samuel Berger of Unique Art.[2]

A demonstrator model of the Main St. toy was also sold. One such toy, owned by Toney Florey, was pictured in the **Marx Toy Collector Newsletter**. The dimensions of the demonstrator are 29-1/2" long x 8-3/4" wide x 6-1/2" high, measurements slightly different from the actual production toy. An instruction sheet for motor care, found inside the door of the demonstrator, states that with the proper care, the motor would run indefinitely. According to Toney Florey, the motor of his demonstrator Main St. toy still runs smoothly.[3]   **225 400**

THE BIG PARADE: 1928. The Big Parade, a tin windup, is colorfully lithographed in red, white, blue, and yellow.

Two-dimensional soldiers parade in pairs, some marching, some on horseback. A two-dimensional bandstand with a lithographed audience is in the center of the toy. Somewhat reminiscent of the toy New York, flat metal pieces on both sides of the toy's arches are lithographed as skyscrapers. Four buildings are lithographed on each metal piece and a crowd of people is lithographed in front of the skyscrapers. At each end of the street, where the parade turns around, three-dimensional buildings are decorated with soldiers.

An ambulance and airplane are the only vehicles on the Big Parade. The airplane is on the right side of the toy, near its key, but is frequently missing on the toy today. Lettering reads "insert aero here". A start and stop lever is below the key.

The toy appears in the 1928 Fall/Winter **Sears** catalog and is described as "new" and "fascinating." It sold for one dollar. An ad for the Big Parade also appears in the September, 1928 **Butler Brothers** catalog but the toy is shown without an airplane. Whether Marx actually produced the toy without the airplane is unknown (reader confirmation requested). In addition, according to the same ad, the Big Parade has the statue figure mounted on a horse like the Main St. toy. But neither the toy itself nor other advertisements show the Big Parade with the Main St. statue. Interestingly, the ad in the **Butler Brothers** catalog shows the Main St. toy without the statue. Marx sometimes made different models for each catalog house. K. Wills observation.

A modern version of the Marx Big Parade was displayed at a recent toy show. This newer toy, with the Marx name, had large separate figures of the soldiers and was battery-powered.   **150 250**

WEST POINT PARADE: 1929. 14-1/2" long x 5-1/4" high. The West Point Parade is similar to the Big Parade but, instead of a street with arches, the cadets march on an incline. The side of the incline is lithographed with cadets. According to the ad in the 1929 Fall/Winter **Montgomery Ward** catalog:

Wind the guaranteed unbreakable Marx spring in the guard house beneath to see them in action. At a distance it is quite impossible to tell what causes this perpetual procession. Made entirely of metal lithographed in realistic colors showing cadets, trees and shrubbery.

The toy sold for 59 cents. Although West Point Parade appears in ads, as the one described above, the actual toy has not been seen. Reader confirmation of the existence of this toy is requested.

A toy similar to the West Point Parade called Soldier's Parade was manufactured by Henry Katz. It is obvious from the similarities that one toy was influenced by the other, but which came first is unknown. The Katz toy is slightly different in size, measuring 16" long x 4" high, and the soldiers do not march up an incline.   **NRS**

BUILDINGS

HOME TOWN BUILDINGS: 1930. 5" long x 2-3/4" wide x 3-1/4" high. The buildings are tin with three walls and attached floors. There is no wall at the front of the building, so that the lithographed interior of the walls and patterned floors can be seen. Not all of the floors are patterned. The backs of the buildings are not lithographed but are colored blue. The buildings came with loose two-dimensional metal figures that

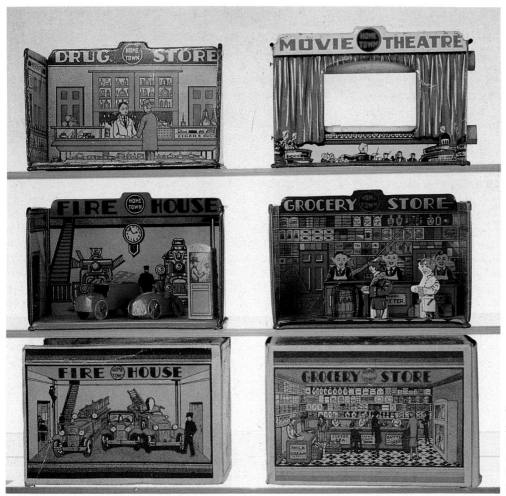

The 1930 Home Town Buildings measure 5" long x 2-3/4" wide x 3-1/4" high. The stores were intended to be used with the Main Street toy. T. Riley Collection. C. Myers photograph.

were used for other toys as well. Furniture was also supplied with the toy in loose pieces which are frequently missing today.

An interesting advertisement in the 1930 **Butler Brothers** catalog shows the Main St. toy flanked by four buildings: a firehouse, drug store, movie theatre, and meat market. The ad refers to the buildings as Main St. Stores, although the buildings actually have the words "Home Town" printed at the top of the center wall with the words enclosed in a circle. In the December 1930 **Butler Brothers** catalog, the Main St. toy and the four buildings sold for $8.50 per dozen.

Home Town buildings not mentioned in the ad are the Grocery Store, Savings Bank, Police Station, and Your Favorite Store, which could be marked as either a Woolworth or Kresge store. A Post Office and School House are believed to exist as well.

While some stores were marketed with the Main St. toy, others were sold in a boxed set of four or in individual boxes.[4] Of those sold individually, the Fire House is numbered 186, the Meat Market, 181. Your Favorite Store was numbered 182 and since neither the Woolworth nor Kresge name appears on the box, the same catalog number was probably used for both versions of the store. The boxes are nicely illustrated with the interior of each building as well as the figures and furniture included. Since the toys are frequently found with mixed up figures and furniture, the box illustrations give some clues as to the correct contents for each store. The stores also came in a

complete set of eight in a single box which pictures the Home Town buildings on the top and sides. The set number "840" and "Home Town Stores" is printed on the ends of the box.[5]

HOME TOWN DRUG STORE: The Drug Store is lithographed in light blue, dark blue, orange, and black. The back panel pictures a pharmacist with a patron dressed in an overcoat and hat. The end wall shows a luncheon counter with a seated female patron. The Drug Store came with separate metal pieces including a counter and clerks, a table, stools, and possibly other pieces. The base is orange and black.   **20   30**

HOME TOWN FIRE HOUSE: The Fire House has blue and red walls with a dark pink floor. Lithographed details on the walls show a pumper and a ladder truck with firemen standing by. A clock reads "2:55", the same time as that in the Police Station. On the left side, a fireman slides down a pole while on the right side, two firemen are shown near a window.

The Fire House came with three separate small metal stampings, namely, a red ladder truck, a chief's car, and a telephone booth. At least two metal firemen were also included.   **20   45**

HOME TOWN GROCERY STORE: The Grocery Store has delightful details including a separate metal counter with three obliging clerks and two stamped metal patrons. On the counter, lithographed signs read "Fresh Butter", "Spice", and "Tea". A barrel reads "Sugar", while a sign to the left reads "Fresh Eggs 65 cents". On the back panel, a lithographed clerk with a long pole is shown reaching for a bottle on the top shelf. The store illustrated on the box is more elaborate than the actual toy.   **20   35**

HOME TOWN MEAT MARKET: The Meat Market is blue-gray, red, white, and yellow. The toy has a separate metal piece with three clerks behind a counter. Various cuts of meat are lithographed on the counter's shelves. On the walls behind the counter, a lithographed butcher attends to a woman customer with a child. The Market is lithographed in detail with a scale, different cuts of meat suspended from racks, and apples shown in the windows. The floor has a red and white diamond pattern. A separate metal refrigerator, stools, and metal figures also came with the toy. (See Newlywed's Rooms section below for photograph.)   **25   30**

HOME TOWN MOVIE THEATRE: The Movie Theatre is lithographed in red, yellow, and dark green. Lithographed red curtains and an orchestra pit surround the cutout section of the screen. Two wooden spools can be turned to roll the "film", a comic-illustrated paper outlined in black and entitled "Bobby's and Betty's Trip To Jungleland". Lettering on both sides of the theatre reads "Turn knobs to wind and unwind reels. Do not overwind." Interestingly, although the instructions on both sides are identical, they are not in the same locations, perhaps so that each scene could be shown to best advantage.

The scene on the left side shows a man at the ticket office and lettering reads "Louis Marx & Co. N.Y." In the scene on the right, a man and woman dressed in evening clothes wait in a lounge decorated with palm trees.

The Movie Theatre is somewhat different from the other buildings. It is the only building that does not come with figures or furniture. Whereas the other buildings have open ends that face front so that the interiors can be seen, the Movie Theater has its open end facing the rear. In the 1931 **Sears** catalog, in one ad the Movie Theatre was marketed with nine other toys, some of which were produced by Marx, that sold at ten for $1.00.

A variation of the Movie Theatre is believed to exist which features a different movie. It is believed that the movie is called "Bobby's and Betty's Trip to China".   **60   125**

HOME TOWN POLICE STATION: The Police Station has a tin lithographed piece which shows a policeman at a desk and a man seated at a table. The center wall is dark pink with two lithographed cell doors that are closed. A lithographed clock reads "2:55", and two pictures hang on the wall. The clock reads the same time as that in the Fire House. The two side walls have lithographed prisoners which can be seen through open cell doors. The floor is light blue and unpatterned. The toy came with at least two standing metal figures and a policeman on a motorcycle. The box illustration differs slightly from the actual toy.   **30   55**

HOME TOWN SAVINGS BANK: A separate metal piece shows two tellers seated at their windows in the Bank. The sign above the left window reads "Paying Teller" while the one on the right reads "Receiving Teller". Additional windows with other tellers who wait on bank patrons are lithographed on the back wall, behind the two tellers. Three lithographed light fixtures hang from the ceiling. The floor is patterned. This toy probably came with at least two standing metal figures and counters.   **20   30**

HOME TOWN YOUR FAVORITE STORE: As mentioned previously, Your Favorite Store could be entitled as either a Woolworth or Kresge store. The store has lithographed counters, clerks, and pillars. A separate metal counter has signs that read "Toys" and "Candy". A female clerk behind the counter serves separate metal male and female customers standing nearby.   **20   35**

ROOMS

NEWLYWED'S ROOMS (COTTAGES): Late 1920s or early 1930s. 5" long x 2-3/4" wide x 3-1/4" high. The Newlywed's Rooms or Cottages are a series of rooms that include a Kitchen, Bathroom, Bedroom, Dining Room, Parlor, and Library. The Cottages are the same size as the Home Town Buildings, but the latter have a small protrusion on the center wall where "Home Town" is printed. The cottages have no lettering on them at all. The backs of the Newlywed's Rooms are painted gray.

Newlywed's Rooms measure 5" long x 2-3/4" wide x 3-1/4" high and were manufactured circa the late 1920s or early 1930s. Shown from left to right are the Library, Bedroom, and for comparison the Home Town Meat Market, and the Dining Room. W. Maeder Collection. R. Grubb photograph.

Additional Newlywed's Rooms are the Parlor, Bathroom, and Kitchen. Unlike the Home Town series, the Newlywed's Rooms do not appear to have people in them. W. Maeder Collection. R. Grubb photograph.

The cottages came with furniture but no figures, neither the two-dimensional ones of the traffic toys nor the two-dimensional, lithographed ones of the Home Town Buildings. The lithography on some of the pieces of furniture was changed in order that it could be used in different rooms. For example, a kitchen cabinet, china closet, highboy, and bookcase are the same piece with different color and lithography.

Like the Home Town Buildings, the Newlywed's Rooms were sold individually and probably also came in boxed sets of four or eight. The boxes for the rooms that were sold individually have illustrations of the room's interior and furniture. Notably, none of the rooms have figures in them. On each side of the room, the boxes show the faces of what appear to be five little girls—each of them different. Presuming the illustrations are of little girls, the Newlywed's Rooms would be a rare example of an early Marx toy for girls. The catalog number listed on the box is 193 for the Parlor and 195 for the Library. In addition to the Marx company name and address, the box's end flap reads "Continental Folding Paper Box Co. Ridgefield, N.J."

No catalog illustrations of the Newlywed's Rooms are known to exist, but it is believed that they were manufactured at about the same time as the Home Town Buildings.

Although the Home Town Buildings are in more demand than the Newlywed's Rooms, both buildings are more popular than the Main St. and the other traffic toys.

NEWLYWED'S BATHROOM: The bathroom is lithographed in red, white, and yellow. The walls are colored with a rectangular green and white pattern and a few red tiles. Lithographed red curtains, picture, and light fixtures decorate the walls. The floor is patterned with green and yellow diamonds. The toilet, sink, and bathtub are separate white metal pieces. The box illustration also shows a stool.   **25   45**

NEWLYWED'S BEDROOM: The bedroom is lithographed in pink, blue, and white. The walls are primarily pink with

lithographed blue and white curtains that frame cutout windows. Room details such as light fixtures, picture, vases of flowers, and rounded door are also lithographed. The carpet has an ornate light and dark blue pattern. The separate pieces of furniture are dark pink and consist of a chest, vanity table, chair, and bed. Other chairs may have also been included.
                                                                              17   30

NEWLYWED'S DINING ROOM: The dining room is pink, pale gray, yellow, and red. Pink and gray walls have cutout windows with pink and gray curtains. A mantelpiece with a vase of flowers is lithographed in the center. A lithographed staircase and statues are on the left wall, and on the right, a lithographed window. The red and yellow carpet has an elaborate design different from that of the Bathroom and Bedroom. Separate multicolored metal pieces consist of a sideboard, grandfather's clock, chairs, a table, and a cabinet with lithographed dishes.   **17   30**

NEWLYWED'S KITCHEN: The kitchen is lithographed in red, white, pale gray, and blue. The center wall has two cutout windows with red-spotted, gray curtains. Lighting fixtures and a clock that reads "2:50" are on one wall. An open door is lithographed on the left wall and on the right, a telephone and list which reads "Today". The floor is lithographed with a red and white diamond pattern. A separate metal cabinet is lithographed with dishes at the top. Lettering on the bottom of the cabinet reads "Sugar", "Coffee", "Spice", "Tea", "Bread", and "Flour". Other separate pieces are a stove, sink, table lithographed with dishes and utensils, and a chair. These metal pieces are either gray or blue and gray.   **20   45**

NEWLYWED'S LIBRARY: This room is lithographed in red, yellow, and black. The patterned walls are yellow and red, with lithographed lighting fixtures, pictures, and a bird cage. The tables have books and vases of flowers. The red curtains surround cutout windows. The floor has the same richly patterned design as the bedroom but is red and black. The library has separate metal pieces which include a red bookcase, a red table, and a yellow chair which may be from a different room, although there was certainly one or more chairs.

17   30

NEWLYWED'S PARLOR: The parlor is dark red, white, and black. The center wall has two cutout windows surrounded by primarily red curtains. A fire glows in the fireplace. Two candlesticks and a vase with flowers are on the mantelpiece just below a picture of a sailing ship. Light fixtures, another picture, and a tapestry hang on the left wall. Double doors are on the right wall. The red and black rug has the same elaborate design as the dining room.

The multicolored separate metal pieces consist of a sofa, table, and sideboard. The box illustration also shows three armchairs.   **NRS**

[1] Martyn L. Schorr, **The Guide to Mechanical Toy Collecting,** (New Jersey: Performance Media, 1979), p. 48.

[2] Eric Matzke, **Greenberg's Guide to Marx Trains,** (Sykesville, MD: Greenberg Publishing Company, 1985), p. 86.

[3] Toney Flory, **Marx Toy Collector Newsletter,** Vol. 3, No. 2, pp. 4-5.

[4] Gerritt Beverwyk, "Stores," **Marx Toy Collector Newsletter,** Vol. 2, No. 4, p. 6.

[5] Introductory information is from Dr. Malcolm Kates, a Marx Toy collector. The Drug Store, Fire House, and Grocery Store have been described by Marx Toy collector, Trip Riley.

CHAPTER X: FILM, RADIO, AND TELEVISION TOYS

The 1930 Amos 'n' Andy Fresh Air Taxicab rolls forward, then shivers, shaking its occupants. W. Maeder Collection. T. Parrish photograph.

Note: The following toys are lithographed tin windups unless otherwise specified.

AMOS 'N' ANDY

Begun in the late 1920s, "Amos 'n' Andy" became a very popular radio show. Freeman Gosden played "Amos" with Charles Correll as "Andy." Both Gosden and Correll were personal friends of Louis Marx.

The Amos and Andy characters were later featured in the 1930 movie "Check and Double Check." In the 1950s, the show was produced on television but lasted only a short while.

AMOS 'N' ANDY FRESH AIR TAXICAB: 1930. 7-3/4" long x 3-1/2" wide x 5" high. The Taxicab toy, considered as one of the best Marx toys, has a unique mechanism that produces amusing action. The cab rolls forward for a short distance, then violently shakes its occupants, Amos and Andy. The cab resumes rolling forward for a few feet, only to repeat its shivering again. The cab was designed so that the motor housing and rear wheels can pivot. The separate front wheels have a single assembly on the axle which also enables them to

pivot. As a result, the entire chassis tilts or sways from left to right.

Amos sits in front, leaning over the steering wheel to which he is attached. He is dressed in a green shirt with rolled up sleeves, a light-colored vest, and checkered pants. Andy takes his ease in the back seat with crossed legs and a cigar. He is dressed in a blue coat, a hat with a green band, and light-colored pants. A white dog with black ears sits in the front seat next to Amos. Amos and Andy are attached to their seats with spring-action brackets which enable them to shake when the car is moving. The dog is attached loosely to the seat with tabs that allow some motion.

The cab is brightly colored in orange with black running boards. To appear worn, the tires are lithographed with patches. The following lettering appears in black: "Original and Genuine Authorized Fresh Air Taxicab, Amos 'n' Andy, Genuine Facsimile Signatures, Copyright Correll & Gosden" on the back of the car; "Made By Louis Marx & Co." on the lower left corner of the back; "New York, U.S.A." on the lower right corner of the back; "License Applied For Time After Time" on the trunk; "Fresh Air Taxicab Co. of America Incorpolated" (sic) on the hood;   "Rates Ask Amos", with the letter "s" printed backwards, appears on the left side of the car. Lettering reads "Amos 'n' Andy", with the letter "s" printed backward, on the back doors of the car. The style of lettering is erratic.   The title of the Amos and Andy film, "Check and Double Check", is printed on the sides of the car.   The words "Double Check" are in white lettering.   A meter with lettering that reads "Tariff" is attached to the right side of the windshield.

The toy is sometimes missing the crank under the left front bumper, the horseshoe-shaped radiator cap, or the white dog. Replacement reproduction horseshoes can be obtained at a reasonable price.   However, the white dog is much more difficult to replace.

The Amos 'n' Andy Taxicab has some of the same features as the eccentric cars. The wheels of the Taxicab are the same size as the front wheels of the earlier eccentric cars, such as the Coo Coo Car. Spokes are lithographed on the wheels. The hood is pointed, and the raised grille design and stamped Marx logo appear on the radiator.

A rare variation of the car has lettering on the front door that reads "Andy Brown Prez, Amos Jones Driver". This variation came both with and without headlights. Although some advertisements for the toy show the headlights near the fenders, the actual toy has the headlights on the hood, near the windshield.

Another, rarer variation of the taxi has a factory label on the door with the signatures of Amos and Andy. The label pictures a microphone and has a border. A photograph of this variation

Manufactured near the late 1930s, Mortimer Snerd Drummer walks rapidly as he beats his drum. The Charlie McCarthy Drummer is a similar toy. Dr. M. Kates Collection. R. Grubb photograph.

appears in the October 1979 Lloyd Ralston **Antique Toy Auction Catalog**.

Marx made two exceptions with the Amos 'n' Andy Taxicab. He introduced the toy in the spring, instead of at Christmas, and bought three full-page ads for this one toy. The first ad appears in the February 1930 **Playthings** magazine and focuses on an un-described sensational development, boasting that the toy: "will be just about the biggest thing that has ever been accomplished in the Toy Industry." In the March 1930 **Playthings** magazine a two-page spread reveals the name of the toy and boldly acclaims: "We feel confident that this is the hit of hits, and will be the biggest selling toy that we have ever offered to the trade." But a January 1946 **Fortune** magazine article was to report the unprofitable outcome of Marx's new plan:

The one time Marx defied the custom of introducing a major new mechanical toy only at Christmas, the results were unhappy. He crowded the counters one spring with the Amos 'n' Andy Fresh Air Taxicab. The toy sold so fast that he got set to make three million. Around a million and a half, sales began to fall; another half million and the toy was through. "When I make a mistake," Marx explained with grim frankness, "it is usually a whopper."[1]

Considering the price of the toy today, it might pain readers to know that in 1930, the toy sold for only 95 cents. But today's price has been known to fluctuate considerably.

The patent, number 82,440, was filed in March 1930 (see Patents appendix). Unlike other patents, the illustration closely resembles the toy except for some minor details. For instance, the illustration does not depict the lithographed "dents" on the actual toy. The black and white coloring of the lettering "Double Check" is slightly different in tone. The phrase "Rates Ask Amos" appears on the reverse side of the meter in the illustration.

The box for the Amos 'n' Andy Taxicab is attractively illustrated and a desirable addition to the toy. The 1930 Fall/Winter **Sears** catalog advertisement reveals that "the pictures on the four sides of the carton in which the taxicab is packed are provided with tabs to make attractive cutouts." One amusing picture shows a policeman being squirted from the back of the cab. Add $200 to the price of the toy with box.

200   550

AMOS 'N' ANDY WALKERS: See Large Walkers chapter.

AMOSANDRA DOLL: See Miscellaneous chapter, Volume II.

CHARLIE MCCARTHY AND MORTIMER SNERD TOYS

These two characters are the well-known dummies of the famous ventriloquist Edgar Bergen. He was popular on the radio for many years and also appeared in the movies and on television.

CHARLIE MCCARTHY DRUMMER and **MORTIMER SNERD DRUMMER:** Late 1930s. 9" long x 8" high. Charlie and Mortimer figures walk rapidly beating bass drums that they push along. Both toys have one long and one short arm, the long one beats the drum, the short one is under the winding key. The two toys are the same except for the heads and the lithography. Charlie wears a black top hat, red coat with frog closings, and blue- and white-striped pants and shoes. Mortimer does not wear a hat, but the rest of his costume is the same as Charlie's but reversed in coloring. He wears a blue coat and red- and white-striped pants and shoes.

Illustrations on the red, white, and blue drums show the characters' heads coming out of a burst drum. Lettering on the side of Charlie's drum reads "Strike Up The Band Here Comes Charlie", while lettering on Mortimer's drum reads "Mortimer Snerd's Home Town Band".

Another toy, the Drummer Boy, is the same as the Charlie and Mortimer Drummers except for its head. The Drummer Boy was made in 1938 and sold for 53 cents. Since no catalog information has been found on the Charlie and Mortimer Drummers, it is believed that all three of these toys sold at about the same time for approximately the same price. (The Drummer Boy is listed in the Miscellaneous chapter of Volume II.)

The bodies of the Charlie and Mortimer Drummers resemble the Marx Tidy Tim, the Walking Porter, and Walking Popeye with the exception of the heads and some of the arms of these toys.

The Charlie and Mortimer Drummers sell for a high price and are not as easily found as some of the other Charlie and Mortimer toys. Add $175 to the price of the toy with box.

Charlie Drummer   **200   375**
Mortimer Drummer   **200   450**

CHARLIE MCCARTHY AND MORTIMER SNERD ECCENTRIC CARS: See Volume II, Automobiles chapter, Eccentric Car section.

CHARLIE MCCARTHY AND MORTIMER SNERD PRIVATE CAR: 1939. 16" long. This toy has some of the most fantastic lithography of any Marx toy. Black and yellow stripes zig-zag on the fenders; red, white, and black stripes run on the yellow hood; and green and white squares checker the trunk. When the key is wound and the brake is released, the car speeds forward until one of its large bumpers encounters an obstacle. When the bumper is hit, the car reverses itself.

Charlie McCarthy, with black top hat, and Mortimer Snerd heads stick out of the car roof. The heads are the same as those used in the eccentric cars. As the car moves, the heads revolve. Through the Private Car windows, lithographed parts of the two puppet bodies can be seen. In the front windshield, there is an illustration of Charlie, which is not in proportion, with his hands gripping the steering wheel. Through each of the side windows part of the arms of each figure can be seen.

On the driver's side door, yellow lettering reads "We'll Mow You Down" and "1939, McCarthy, Inc." with the copyright symbol. On the passenger's side door, lettering reads "Charlie McCarthy Mortimer Snerd Private Car". The Marx logo is on the front of the car, near the windshield.

The box for the Private Car has lettering that reads "Charlie McCarthy Mortimer Snerd Coupe". Marx's box illustrations sometimes differed slightly from the actual toy. The illustration on the Private Car box shows an unpatterned car on a city street.

With different lithography, the Private Car is the same as Blondie's Jalopy (see Comic Strip Character Toys chapter) and the Reversible Coupe (see Automobiles chapter, Volume II).

Add $200 to the price of the toy with box.   **500 1000**

CHARLIE MCCARTHY and **MORTIMER SNERD WALKERS:** 1938. 8-1/2" high. The name on the box for the walking Charlie McCarthy is "The McCarthy Strut". Charlie is pictured on the box with lettering that reads "I'll Mow You Down". The toy waddles with a swaying motion as Charlie's

The 1939 Charlie and Mortimer Snerd Private Car reverses itself when it encounters an obstacle. The characters' heads revolve. W. Maeder Collection. R. Grubb photograph.

The 1938 Gang Busters Car is similar to the Marx "G" Man Pursuit Car. Dr. M. Kates Collection. R. Grubb photograph.

The Mortimer Snerd Walker was manufactured in the late 1930s from the same die as B. O. Plenty. As he walks, his hat moves up and down. W. Maeder Collection. T. Parrish photograph.

mouth moves up and down like Mr. Bergen's full-sized dummy. Charlie is in his usual costume, a black tuxedo and top hat, with a monocle over his right eye. In 1938, the toy sold for 25 cents.

The Mortimer Snerd Walker does not have a moving mouth, but his hat moves up and down. With different lithography, the Mortimer Snerd toy was made from the same die as the B. O. Plenty toy (see Comic Strip Character Toys chapter). Because of the die, the Mortimer Snerd Walker has a different head than that used for the eccentric car and private car. All of these toys, Mortimer, Charlie, and B. O. Plenty, stand on the same base made to look like feet.

Mortimer is dressed in a blue, windowpane-checked suit and blue hat. He holds a present in his left hand, a bouquet of flowers in his right. A lithographed note is pinned to his back with lettering that reads "Meet My Friend—Mortimer Snerd, Signed Charlie McCarthy". The Marx logo is below the note, then the copyright symbol and lettering that reads "1939 McCarthy, Inc." The toy came in an illustrated box that reads "Edgar Bergen's Mortimer Snerd".

An interesting prototype exists with Charlie McCarthy on roller skates. The prototype belongs to O. E. Gernand of

The 1938 Charlie McCarthy Walker waddles as his mouth moves up and down. Dr. M. Kates Collection. R. Grubb photograph.

Indiana and is shown in the **Marx Toy Collector Newsletter** with the following description: "The toy is made up of the regular walking Charlie, but underneath is a small windup spring motor with four small wheels. The body has a hinge to the feet, so as the wheels carry it forward, the body sways left to right as a skater would." [2]

Another interesting prototype for the Mortimer toy belongs to the well-known collector and author Robert Lesser, who wrote the fine book **A Celebration of Comic Art and Memorabilia**. The prototype, also seen in the **Marx Toy Collector Newsletter**, shows Mortimer in a tuxedo and top hat, with a flower in his right hand and a cane in his left. His three-dimensional arms are separate from his body in contrast to the lithographed arms of both the Mortimer and Charlie Walkers. The body of the prototype resembles the Popeye toy. The head is the same as that of the cars. The Mortimer Walker actually produced by Marx is much simpler than this prototype. [3]

Add $100 to the price of the toy with box.

Charlie McCarthy Walker	200	300
Mortimer Snerd Walker	150	250

FUNNY FACE (HAROLD LLOYD): See Large Walkers chapter.

THE GANG BUSTERS

Begun in the 1930s and continuing into the 1950s, the "Gang Busters" radio program dramatized real-life crime stories. A description of wanted criminals after each program actually aided law enforcement officials to capture some of them.

GANG BUSTERS CAR: 1938. 14-1/2" long x 5" wide x 5-1/2" high. According to the 1940 **Shure Winner No. 136 Wholesale Catalog**, the car speeds along in either a straight or circular path and is equipped with a brake. The Gang Busters Car has a cream-colored top, dark green sides, and black running boards and fenders. The wheels too are black with silver centers. The grille of the car is black with cream stripes. It has dummy taillights and front and back bumpers. A machine gun juts out of the front windshield of the car which sparks and sounds. The gun held by a G-Man is lithographed in cream, red, and black and has a black muzzle, a cream-striped barrel, and a reddish-colored handle.

The license number is "G-511". "Gang Busters" appears within a badge on the side of the car, one part of the name above, the other below, an eagle emblem. The cream trunk of the Gang Busters Car repeats the badge emblem within a black square. The black badge is outlined in dark green. Underneath the badge is the Marx logo and the markings "Patent No. 2,055,848 RE. No. 20,504". Black lettering above the side windows reads "Police". Cream-colored rectangles, six in all, appear on each side of the hood. "Gang Busters" in dark-green lettering is repeated on each half of the hood in reversed positions. Also on the hood, two circles on dark green backgrounds show saluting figures. [4]

The Gang Busters car sold for 98 cents in 1938. The June 1977 **PB 84** catalog lists number 7200 as the catalog number for this toy.

The Gang Busters Car is similar to the Marx G-Man Pursuit Car produced at about the same time. It is believed that the patent for both toys is number 2,055,848, entitled Toy Pursuit Car (see Patents appendix). Marx applied for the patent in October 1935; it was issued in September 1937.

Add $50 to the price of the toy with box.   **75   150**

GANG BUSTERS SUB-MACHINE GUN: See Guns chapter.

GANG BUSTERS TRAP DOOR TARGET GAME: See Games chapter.

HOP A' LONG CASSIDY

Books featuring the Hop A' Long Cassidy character date back to 1911. Hop A' Long Cassidy movies began to appear in the mid-1930s. In the 1940s and 1950s, the cowboy hero, played by William Boyd, became popular on the silver screen. In the 1950s, a Hop A' Long Cassidy show was aired on the radio. The cowboy also appeared on television in the 1950s.

HOP A' LONG CASSIDY: c. 1946. 11-1/4" long x 2-1/4" wide x 10-1/2" high. The cowboy figure is dressed in black with a red kerchief. He sits on a white horse that stands on a rocking base. The horse, Topper, has a blue blanket edged in red. Hoppy's left arm is jointed and in his left hand he holds a gun. In his stationary right hand he holds a wire lariat. When the toy is wound, the base rocks back and forth, Hoppy's lariat spins, and his jointed arm moves.

The base of the toy is multicolored with pictures of the heads of both Hoppy and Topper in a desert scene background. Red lettering reads "Hop A' Long Cassidy" in the illustration and on the top of the base.

The Marx Range Rider, which sold for 94 cents in 1946, is similar to the Hop A' Long Cassidy with different lithography. The Range Rider cowboy and horse came with a curved rocker that was close to the ground and in a variation with a raised base. (See Miscellaneous chapter, Volume II for more information on cowboy riders.)

The Acrobatic Marvel, which featured a monkey on top of a pole, has a rocking base similar to the Hop A' Long Cassidy toy. But the base for the Acrobatic Marvel is smaller and more rounded than the Hoppy base. (See Animal Toys chapter for the Acrobatic Marvel.) Pinocchio the Acrobat also has a rocking base similar to that of the Hop A' Long Cassidy toy. (See Walt Disney Toys chapter for Pinocchio the Acrobat.)

The horse of the Hop A' Long Cassidy toy is the same as the rearing horse of the Lone Ranger toy. The difference is that Hoppy's horse Topper has his left leg extended straight on top of a box, while the Ranger's horse Silver has his left leg bent under him. By changing the shape of a single leg, Marx was able to use the rearing horse in a different position. Incidentally, the box under Topper's leg is very close in pattern to some of the tunnels used in the Honeymoon Express toys.

The Hop A' Long Cassidy and Lone Ranger figures are the same; both have jointed, moving left arms and stationary right arms. But the Hop A' Long Cassidy lariat is thicker and lacks an extra piece of the Lone Ranger lariat. (See Lone Ranger later in this chapter).

Add $50 to the price of the toy with box.   **75   150**

JOE PENNER

Joe Penner was a comedian whose popular phrase was "Wanna buy a duck?" Penner started in burlesque stage shows and moved on to radio and films.

JOE PENNER AND HIS DUCK GOO GOO: 1934. 7-1/2" high. Joe is strikingly dressed in a black- and white-checked coat with blue lapels and a windowpane-patterned hat that moves up and down as the figure walks briskly forward. A big cigar rests in his mouth. He carries his rather large, multicolored duck Goo Goo in his right hand and a brown basket containing three white ducks in his left. A lithographed tag on the basket has facsimile handwritten lettering that reads "Wanna buy a duck? Sincerely Joe Penner".

In the September 1934 **Butler Brothers** catalog, the Joe Penner toy sold for $4.15 a dozen. The advertisement clearly says "Joe Penner" but oddly does not show his checked coat or the label on his basket. It is possible that the Joe Penner toy was confused with another Marx toy from the same die called the Butter & Egg Man. This figure has different lithography, and the label on his basket reads "Fresh Country Butter". (See Butter & Egg Man, Miscellaneous chapter, Volume II.)

The Joe Penner toy came in an illustrated box. Joe's cigar appears so large on the box that it covers the face of one of the ducks. The famous "Wanna buy a duck?" slogan is printed on the box. Add $100 to the price of the toy with box. **160 300**

JOE PENNER PROTOTYPE: The well-known New York toy dealers, Stephanie and Paul Sadagursky, own a fascinating prototype of a Joe Penner toy that was never produced. Joe Penner sits on a duck. The head, which is the same one used for the production of the Penner toy, can be tilted backwards while Joe's hat tips. Joe's body is much slimmer than that of the production version and his legs appear to be painted. Unlike some prototypes, this one had no information on the bottom of it.

THE LONE RANGER

The popular Lone Ranger radio program began in the early 1930s. Lone Ranger books started to appear in 1936 and continued at least until 1939. In the 1950s, the Lone Ranger appeared on television. But a 1981 movie entitled "Legend of the Lone Ranger" was poorly received.

LONE RANGER: 1938. 8" high. The Lone Ranger figure is seated on his rearing horse, Silver. The horse's tail rests on the ground to balance its two hind legs. As mentioned previously, the Lone Ranger and Hop A' Long Cassidy figures are the same. Both have a moving left arm holding a gun and a stationary right arm grasping a spinning lariat. When wound, the Lone Ranger toy turns in a circular vibrating motion, while the lariat spins. In 1938 the toy sold for 39 cents.

The masked Lone Ranger is colorfully dressed in a red shirt, gold/tan vest and hat, blue pants and kerchief, and brown boots. The blanket on his horse is red and edged with black and white. The Lone Ranger is nicely lithographed with such details as the fancy design on his boot and the draping of his shirt.

A yellow streamer across the Lone Ranger's knees has black lettering that reads "The Lone Ranger Hi-Yo Silver!" Lettering reads "Copyright 1938 The Lone Ranger" and the Marx logo appears on the right side of the horse blanket.

The Lone Ranger came in two variations. On the more common one, the horse is white like that of Hop A' Long Cassidy. On the other, the horse is silver. Otherwise, the colors of the two toys are the same except that the entire silver-horsed toy has a metallic finish. The box is red and green and shows a smiling Lone Ranger dressed in red and green on top of the rearing horse, Silver.

The Lone Ranger figure also came on a Hop A' Long Cassidy horse and Range Rider rocking base. The horse is in a standing position with one leg suspended on top of a box. The toy has a streamer with lettering that reads "The Lone Ranger Hi-Yo Silver!"

The Cowboy Rider, which is actually the same toy as the Lone Ranger, was made in 1942 and sold for 29 cents. The Cowboy Rider has different lithography, and lacks the Lone Ranger's mask and streamer. (See Cowboy Rider, Miscellaneous Toys chapter, Volume II.)

Add $100 to the price of the toy with box. **210 350**

LONE RANGER GAMES: See Games chapter.

LONE RANGER PISTOLS: See Guns chapter.

MILTON BERLE ECCENTRIC CAR: See Automobiles chapter, Volume II.

MORTIMER SNERD TOYS: See Charlie McCarthy and Mortimer Snerd, this chapter.

PORKY PIG

In the mid-1930s, the fussy Porky Pig made his debut in a Warner Brothers Looney Tune cartoon. Porky Pig was later put into comic books and still appears today on television in rerun cartoons.

PORKY PIG WITH UMBRELLA: c. 1939-42. 8" high. The most common variation of the toy has a figure that turns while his red- and white-striped umbrella twirls. Porky is dressed in a blue coat, white collar, and red bow tie. Behind Porky's head, his collar shows his name, the copyright symbol, the Marx logo, and the date, "1939". Lettering on the back of the collar reads "Leon Schlesinger", who was the producer of the cartoons. In various 1942 catalogs, the toy sold for 39 cents.

The least common variation of the Porky Pig with Umbrella has a top hat. It is built like the toy described above, but where the first Porky has a lithographed left arm, this Porky has a long, jointed left arm that raises and lowers a black top hat while he turns his umbrella. Both toys twirl the red- and white-striped umbrella in the right arm, which is shaped but not separate from the body. The Porky Pig with the top hat has a navy blue jacket instead of a lighter blue one. It sold for 39 cents in various 1939 catalogs.

Add $100 to the price of the toy with box.

Without Top Hat.	**100**	**200**
With Top Hat.	**70**	**180**

PORKY PIG THE COWBOY: 1949. 8" high. Porky Pig the Cowboy is elaborately lithographed in a western outfit. He wears a predominantly green shirt, yellow vest with design, and a red, western-style bow tie. His cowboy hat is rakishly perched over his left ear. The Porky Pig cowboy has a lithographed gun on each hip and western boots.

The cowboy Porky is different from the umbrella Porky in two ways. Instead of the umbrella, western Porky holds a spinning lariat, which is the same as that of the Lone Ranger. In addition, the umbrella Porky was made completely of lithographed steel, while the cowboy Porky has a plastic hat.

The copyright symbol, "1949", and "Leon Schlesinger" appears on the back of the figure's right arm. The Marx logo is on Porky's left wrist. On the umbrella Porky, the logo is on the back of the collar. Lettering reads "Cowpuncher Porky" on the back of cowboy Porky's collar. But the name on the box flap reads "Porky Pig the Cowboy".

On the front and back of the box for Porky the Cowboy, the umbrella Porky Pig with the top hat is shown and lettering reads "Porky Pig". The box could therefore have been used for at least two of the Porky Pig toys. An appealing illustration of Petunia, Porky's girl friend, also appears on the box. Add $70 to the price of the toy with box.   **60 180**

[1] "Louis Marx: Toy King," **Fortune Magazine** January 1946, p. 124.

[2] Gerritt Beverwyk, **Marx Toy Collector Newsletter,** Vol. 3, No. 1, p. 10.

[3] Gerritt Beverwyk, "Mort," **Marx Toy Collector Newsletter,** Vol. 2, No. 2, p. 8.

[4] John Fox, a well-known Marx Toy collector, provided detailed information and several drawings of the Gang Busters Car.

Prototype of a Joe Penner toy that was never produced. Note the use of the head from the original Joe Penner toy, which tilts backward as the hat tips. Stephanie and Paul Sadagursky Collection. P. Summers photograph.

Porky Pig with Top Hat has a long jointed left arm that raises and lowers his top hat while the umbrella twirls. Porky Pig with Umbrella turns, as his umbrella twirls. Porky Pig the Cowboy is equipped with a plastic hat and spinning lariat. W. Maeder Collection. T. Parrish photograph.

The 1936 "G" Man Tommy Gun measures 23" long, is made of wood and metal, and shoots sparks. Dr. M. Kates Collection. R. Grubb photograph.

One end of the Sheriff Signal Pistol is a flashlight, and the other end is a whistle. Shown are several color variations of the 5-1/2" long, plastic pistol. Mr. and Mrs. C. Weber Collection. T. Parrish photograph.

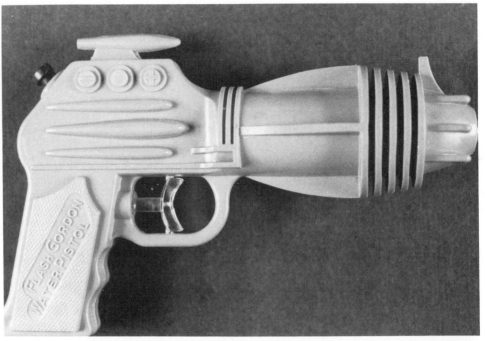

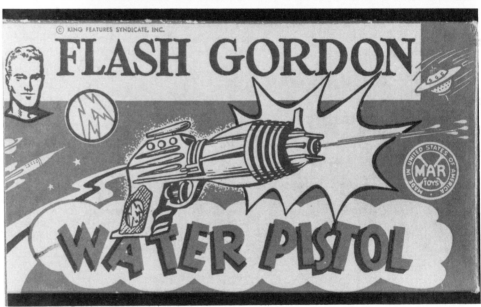

The 1940s Flash Gordon Water Pistol came in the illustrated box shown. Photographs are courtesy of Hake's Americana & Collectibles.

GANG BUSTERS "CRUSADE AGAINST CRIME" MACHINE GUN: c. 1938. 23" long. This lithographed metal gun has a wooden stock. It is similar in shape to the "G" Man Tommy Gun, but the magazine drum is on top of the gun instead of underneath it. A man and child are pictured near the trigger. The gun sparks and makes a noise.   **45   90**

HI-YO SILVER LONE RANGER PISTOL: The Lone Ranger is shown on the handle of this tin gun. The toy came in a box illustrated with the Lone Ranger and Silver. The **PB 84** catalog number is 96.   **35   75**

LONE RANGER CLICK PISTOL.[8]   **NRS**

LONE RANGER 45 FLASHER FLASHLIGHT PISTOL.[9] **NRS**

LONE RANGER SPARKLING POP PISTOL: The Sparkling Pop Pistol is made of lithographed tin. The **PB 84** catalog number is 096.   **35   75**

MAGNUM GUN: 7" long. The Magnum Gun is a gold, plastic click gun with a black handle. The trigger and hammer are metal and can shoot caps. Mr. and Mrs. C. Weber Collection.   **NRS**

MARXMAN TARGET PISTOL: 5-1/2" long. The black plastic Marxman Target Pistol is snub-nosed and shoots projectiles with trigger action. The Marx logo appears on the right side with lettering that reads "Target". Mr. and Mrs. C. Weber Collection.   **35   60**

NEVADAN PISTOL: 7" long. The plastic Nevadan Pistol has a clicking sound activated by the trigger. The pistol is predominantly black with embossed silver trimming. A cowboy is embossed on the handle and stars and feathers are embossed on the barrel and chamber. Mr. and Mrs. C. Weber Collection. **NRS**

OFFICIAL DETECTIVE-TYPE SUB-MACHINE GUN: The **PB 84** catalog number is 2146. **NRS**

OFFICIAL SPACE PISTOL: The **PB 84** catalog number is 105. **NRS**

PLAY BOY CANNON: 1929. 21" x 8" x 11". The steel Play Boy Cannon is black and battleship gray with 5-1/2" spoke wheels. The exceptionally strong plunger shoots wooden projectiles.[10] **NRS**

POP RIFLE: The **PB 84** catalog numbers are 217 and 218. **NRS**

POPEYE PIRATE CLICK PISTOL: Mid-1930s. 10" long. The handle of the tin pistol shows Popeye wearing a pirate hat. Lettering reads "Popeye Pirate Click Pistol" on the barrel. The Popeye pistol is the same as the Flash Gordon Radio Repeater Pistol and the later Tom Corbett Space Cadet Pistol. The **PB 84** catalog number is 68. **50   110**

REPEATING CAP PISTOL: The aluminum cap pistol has **PB 84** catalog number G375. **NRS**

REX MARS PLANET PATROL MACHINE GUN: 21-1/4" long. The gun is brightly colored with a red plastic muzzle end, and red plastic end-caps for the spring mechanism on the top. The plastic stock is blue and the plastic bottom panel is green.

The rear of the gun has a yellow tin body with red, silver, and black detailing. The front of the gun is blue with silver, yellow, and white detailing. The Planet Patrol gun has a tin body which is "riveted" with heat-flattened knobs to the gun's other plastic parts. The windup mechanism is tabbed into the fore-end of the gun which sparks and makes a machine gun noise when the metal trigger is pulled. The steel rod inside the spring mechanism is the only other metal piece on the gun. The popping sound is presumably made by something striking a fiber insert inside the winder.

On one side of the gun's fore-end, lettering reads "45 cal. Automatic", "Safe", "On", and "Off". On the other side of the fore-end, lettering reads "Full Auto". On one side of the tin body, lettering reads "X-92", "Official Rex Mars Planet Patrol", and "Density Gauge" enclosed in a black arrow. On the other side of the tin body, "Rocket-2" appears above the Marx logo.

The illustrated box for the toy pictures a gun which has different lithography and differences in the shape of the muzzle end and trigger. Illustrations on Marx boxes occasionally differed from the toys themselves. Lettering on the box reads "Official Rex Mars Planet Patrol", "Sparkling", "Space Gun", and "Realistic Plastic Stock and Fore-end". The Marx Company name, address, and logo appear on the box as well as the Marx slogan: "One of the Many Marx Toys—Have You All of Them?"[11] **50   100**

REX MARS PLANET PATROL SPARKLING PISTOL: 7" long. **NRS**

The rare Siren Sparkling Airplane Pistol measures 7" long and has a 9-1/2" wingspan. The wings detach for storage. W. Maeder Collection. R. Grubb photograph.

SHERIFF SIGNAL PISTOL: 1950. 5-1/2" long. The plastic Signal Pistol is a flashlight on one end and a whistle on the other. The light is at the end of the muzzle and is activated by pulling the trigger. An AA battery fits into the gun barrel. The hammer of the gun is the whistle. Lettering on the attached tag reads "Model #1652 same as sample in N.Y. 11/3/50". The toy comes in several colors: red, white, khaki, yellow with red baseplate, black with red baseplate, gray with green baseplate, and silver with green baseplate. Mr. and Mrs. C. Weber Collection.   **NRS**

SIREN SIGNAL SHOOTER: 6-1/2" long. The Siren Signal Shooter is a red plastic gun with a large round siren mounted on one side. The Marx logo appears on the gun. Mr. and Mrs. C. Weber Collection.   **NRS**

SIREN SPARKLING AIRPLANE PISTOL: 7" long. 9-1/2" wingspan. This pistol is made of heavy gauge, enameled steel and has a red body and blue wings. The wings detach for storage. The pistol has two celluloid propellers. Except for the addition of the wings, the shape of the Airplane Pistol is similar to the Flash Gordon Signal Pistol. The **PB 84** catalog number is 182.

The Siren Sparkling Airplane Pistol came in a red, white, and blue illustrated box. The box pictures a young boy holding the pistol. Although the Marx logo does not appear on the gun, it is on the box. It would appear that the box was printed about the time of World War II because lettering on one of the box flaps reads "For Defense, Save and Sell This Empty Carton."   **50   95**

SIREN SPARKLING PISTOL: The lithographed tin Siren Sparkling Pistol has **PB 84** catalog number 164.   **NRS**

SPARKLING ATOM BUSTER PISTOL: The **PB 84** catalog number of the aluminum Atom Buster Pistol is 46.   **NRS**

SPARKLING CELEBRATION PISTOL.   **NRS**

SPARKLING POP GUN: The **PB 84** catalog numbers are 98S and 198.   **NRS**

SPARKLING SIREN MACHINE GUN: 1949. 26" long. The machine gun is similar to the "G" Man Tommy Gun, except that it has a lower and thinner barrel tip and fewer ridges. The stock and muzzle are plastic, and the other parts are made of metal. The "new" machine gun appears in the 1949 **Sears** Christmas catalog.   **NRS**

SPARKLING SPACE GUN: Rifle.   **NRS**

STREAMLINE SIREN SPARKLING PISTOL: The **PB 84** catalog number for this lithographed tin pistol is 155.   **NRS**

TOMMY GUN: c. 1939. The Tommy Gun sparks and makes noise. It has a wooden stock and black barrel with a lithographed U.S. shield on the front handle. The ammunition drum, breech, and recoil mechanism box are lithographed.[12]   **NRS**

WATER PISTOL: 5-3/4" long. The plastic Water Pistol is red with black lettering or blue with white lettering. Script lettering reads "Water Pistol" on the top of the gun. The Marx logo is near the trigger. The Water Pistol is similar to the Sheriff Signal Pistol, but the former has a fixed hammer and a smaller barrel and no whistle. Mr. and Mrs. C. Weber Collection.   **NRS**

ZORRO FLINTLOCK PISTOL.[13]   **NRS**

ZORRO RIFLE.   **55   110**

GUNS ON MILITARY TRAIN

Several guns are also found on the Army Military Train which was manufactured in the late 1930s to early 1940s. Some of these guns were sold separately as well.

ANTI-AIRCRAFT GUN ON CAR: Gun measures 5-1/4" long x 2" high. The Anti-Aircraft Gun shoots projectiles by a spring-loaded mechanism and has adjustable elevation. The gun is similar to the Anti-Aircraft Cannon which came with the Soldiers of Fortune set. The gun on car and the cannon have the same intricate lithography, but the gun has a longer pedestal and two round holes on the left side of the pedestal, possibly to hold ammunition. Unlike the cannon, the gun does not have wheels. The car's **PB 84** catalog number is 572AA.   **45   95**

ARMY CANNON ON CAR 572G: See Military Cannon Truck and Army Cannon Trailer, Trucks chapter, Volume II.

FIELD GUN ON CAR: Gun measures 3-1/2" long x 2" high. The gun is mounted on a pedestal and has a protective shield. It rotates horizontally 360 degrees, is adjustable for elevation, and has a hand-operated clicker.   **NRS**

MACHINE GUN ON CAR: 3" long x 2-1/2" high. The Machine Gun is fixed with a simulated ammunition belt on the left side of the breech. A hand crank activates the rat-a-tat-tat noise and sparkler. There is a protective yellow shield for the gunner. The mount is khaki-colored. The same gun with longer legs on the mount came with a kneeling soldier (see Miscellaneous chapter, Volume II). The car's **PB 84** catalog number is 572MG.   **30   65**

1 Richard O'Brien, **Collecting Toys,** 3rd ed., (Alabama: Books Americana, 1982), p. 450.

2 O'Brien, p. 392.

3 Peter Fritz, **Marx Toy Collector Newsletter,** Vol. 4, No. 2, p. 7.

4 Peter Fritz, **Marx Toy Collector Newsletter,** Vol. 4, No. 2, p. 6.

5 Peter Fritz, **Marx Toy Collector Newsletter,** Vol. 4, No. 2, p. 7.

6 Gerritt Beverwyk, ed., **Marx Toy Collector Newsletter,** Vol. 3, No. 6, p. 9. The newsletter shows an advertisement that is a reprint from an unknown source.

7 O'Brien, p. 455.

8 O'Brien, p. 458.

9 O'Brien, p. 458.

10 Earnest A. Long, **Dictionary of Toys Sold in America,** Vol. 1, (published by the author, 1971), p. 52.

11 The listing for the Rex Mars Planet Patrol Machine Gun was provided by John Ritter, a Marx toy collector.

12 The listing for the Tommy Gun was provided by Eric Matzke, a Marx train and toy collector.

13 O'Brien, p. 441.

CHAPTER XIII: HONEYMOON EXPRESS
AND RELATED CIRCLE TOYS

INTRODUCTION

Honeymoon Express toys are lithographed tin windups with circular bases that measure 9-1/2" in diameter. Much descriptive information was graciously contributed by John Fox who has also estimated the dates of many of the toys. Mr. Fox, a knowlegeable collector who specializes in Honeymoon Express toys, believes that at least 40 variations of the toy exist. According to Richard Carver, former Design Foreman and Model Maker for Louis Marx & Company: "We made so many Honeymoon Expresses that it got to be a standing joke. Every year we would come out with a new Honeymoon Express model."

A double Honeymoon Express is believed to exist, at least as a prototype. William Kalsch, former head of the Lithography department and later Production Superintendent, believes the double express may have two trains on the same track, one following the other.

Marx was not the only manufacturer to make toys like the Honeymoon Express. The December 3, 1983 Lloyd Ralston **Antique Toy Auction Catalog** shows the "Roundabout Railroad" produced by the German manufacturer Gely. The 5" x 7" tin friction toy has a train speeding through a tunnel and bridge longer than those on the Marx toys. Another version of the toy, slightly larger than penny-toy size, is wound by hand.

A toy produced by Distler in 1926 closely resembles the Marx Honeymoon Express of the same year. The Distler toy is the same size and shape and has the same coloring as the Marx toy. Both toys even have a little red-roofed building and a key in the center. The Distler toy, however, has a small house next to the outer side of the track.

One die-cast toy like the Honeymoon Express has a base with three wheels that are geared to its express train. When the toy is pushed or pulled, the train circles the oval.·

A British toy, manufactured by Mettoy, and a Russian toy each have two connecting circles of cars. Some of the Japanese toys like the Honeymoon Express have two trains, and one has a train and bus.

Linemar, Marx's Japanese subsidiary, also made toys like the Honeymoon Express. Linemar's express is a few inches smaller than Marx's, and lettering on the house reads "Honeymoon Cottage". One version of Linemar's toy has a train that runs on circular track inside a square base; another, a train and an airplane which hovers over the toy.

An advertisement for Unique Art appears in the April 1945 **Playthings** magazine and pictures a Honeymoon Express among the manufacturer's other toys.

1926 HONEYMOON EXPRESS: A British steamer train runs on an open circular track with three tunnels. The train has blue and cream coaches. The tunnels are lithographed with brick and shrubbery. Some expresses have a red and blue flagman that signals the train with a red and white flag as it goes by. The predominantly green base has a pastoral scene with a grist mill, castle, and other buildings. Reminiscent of the illustrations found in early children's books, delicate scenes of

children playing with animals and being pulled in wagons by dogs and goats decorate the edge of the base. An intricately lithographed station with a red roof houses the winding key in the middle of the toy. The station has a brick design with lettering that reads "Richmond" at the lower left. A counter is shown with signs and items for sale.

The toy sold for 59 cents in a 1926 Fall/Winter **Montgomery Ward** catalog ad, the earliest one found for the Marx Honeymoon Express. The toy in the ad has the flagman and lettering that reads "Honeymoon Express" on the base. Actually, the earliest Honeymoon Express did not have the flagman or the "Honeymoon Express" lettering. Instead, lettering reads "Louis Marx & Co., N.Y., U.S.A." Since ads have not been found for Honeymoon Expresses earlier than 1926, it is a good estimate that the version without the flagman or name appeared in early 1926. By fall of 1926, the ads show the added flagman and the name, possibly an enhancement for the Christmas season.

Without flagman	**100**	**300**
With flagman	**150**	**350**

LATE 1920s: By the late 1920s, two variations of the Honeymoon Express were produced, both with the lettering "Honeymoon Express" lithographed on the base. One version has a flagman, the other does not. **85 200**

HONEYMOON SPECIAL: 1927. 6" diameter. Smaller than the other Honeymoon Expresses, the Honeymoon Special does not have a station and the key is underneath the base instead of in the center of the toy. A red, brick-patterned metal strip stretches from one side of the toy to the other. Each end of the strip is formed into a tunnel through which the red and yellow European steam locomotive runs. An arm under the center of the strip moves the train. The steam locomotive, without tender, has three coaches with red and yellow roofs and blue and white windows. Instead of the open grooves of the standard Honeymoon Express, the tracks of the Honeymoon Special are made of a slight indentation and lithographed red, pale blue, and black.

Additional lithography on the toy is quite charming. A group of children are shown swimming in a stream surrounded by bushes. A red train, more typical of American trains by having a tender, is lithographed around the base. A farmer waves to the train with a house, dog, and chickens completing the background. Also on the base, red lettering reads "Honeymoon Special, Trade Mark, Louis Marx & Co., N.Y., U.S.A." Black lettering reads "Pat's Pend'g". In the November 1927 **Butler Brothers** catalog the toy sold for $2.25 a dozen.

There is at least one variation of the Honeymoon Special which is similar to the toy described above, but has different lithography. While the wording on the base is the same, it is lithographed in a different style and placed differently. The lithographed tracks are white, red, and yellow. The bridge is yellow with black brick outline, but the toy also came in a variation with a red bridge. Foliage replaces the swimming

The 1926 Honeymoon Express with its name on the base. As the train goes by, the flagman signals. W. Maeder Collection. R. Grubb photograph.

children. The coaches of the European-style passenger train are yellow with red details; blue windows; and red, white, and blue roofs or red and yellow roofs. A red and yellow train is lithographed on the base with people, houses, and animals.

Patent number 1,644,933, filed April 10, 1925, resembles both the Honeymoon Express and the Honeymoon Special, but neither toy was made exactly as shown in the patent drawing. (See Patents appendix.)   75   150

1928 NEW YORK: A train, a plane, an entire city is at your fingertips! The New York Honeymoon Express has a flat, tin circular cutout strip elaborately lithographed with skyscrapers. A flat, blue and white airplane with a fixed propeller is attached by a rod to the red-roofed station marked "U.S. Post Office". The rod is detachable, and the plane is frequently missing from the toys today. The New York toy is the first of the Honeymoon Express type toys to have an airplane. The British steamer

coaches are red and cream. The three tunnels are square, like buildings, with horseshoe-shaped portals. Each tunnel building has a flat-roofed cupola, one of which has a clock.

Black and white lettering reads "New York" on the roof of the Post Office. Additional lettering reads "Insert Aero Here", "Trade Mark", and "Pat. Pending". "Louis Marx & Co., N.Y." is on the side. A detailed scene with skyscrapers and boats decorates the edge of the base.

The action of the toy is the same as that of the earlier Honeymoon Expresses. The train circles an open track with three tunnels. The airplane turns in the same direction as the train.

When the New York toy first appeared in 1928, it sold for 49 cents.

Without airplane	**200**	**700**
With airplane	**250**	**750**

The 1927 Honeymoon Special measures only 6" in diameter. Unlike the larger Honeymoon Express, there is no station, the key is underneath the base, and the tunnels are shaped differently. W. Maeder Collection. R. Grubb photograph.

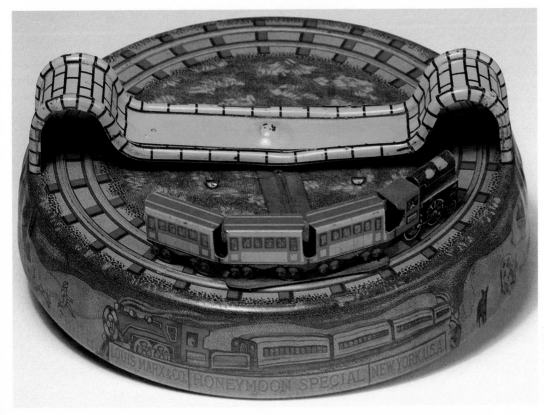

Honeymoon Special variation shown has different lithography. The bridge of this variation also came in red. Dr. M. Kates Collection. R. Grubb photograph.

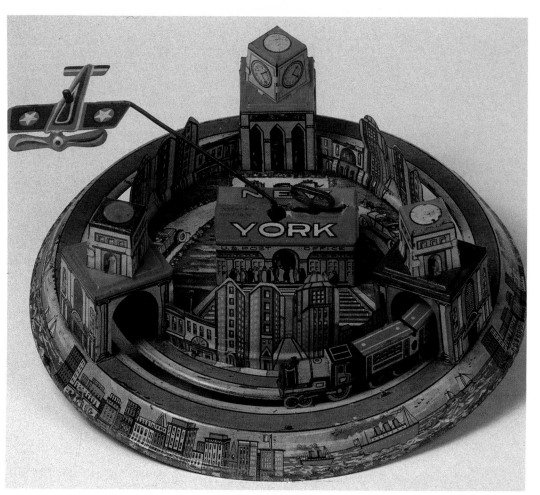

Skyscrapers make this 1928 New York Honeymoon Express unique. It also came with a train and airplane, though the latter is frequently missing today. W. Maeder Collection. R. Grubb photograph.

1930 HONEYMOON EXPRESS: The British steamer train of the early 1930s Honeymoon Express has red and cream coaches like the New York toy. One variation has a flagman, the other does not.

About 1930, the design of the Honeymoon Express base changed from that with the playing children to a train thought to be a steam passenger express.

The early Honeymoon Express box is red and green with an amusing scene of people running to catch the train. The scene includes animals, trees, a signal bridge, and figures watching the train from roof tops.

Without flagman	65	115
With flagman	115	165

EARLY TO MID-1930s HONEYMOON EXPRESS: The 1933 toy does not have the flagman. The 1934 ads still show the toy with the three brick design tunnels.   **75   125**

1935:   Circa 1935, the British steamer train was changed to an M-10000 streamline train with yellow sides, a red roof, and red windows. The toy now has only two tunnels; both are yellow, red, and green. The third tunnel was replaced with a bridge that has a pebble design.   **125   200**

POPEYE EXPRESS: 1936. The colorful Popeye Express is yet another spectacular variation of the Honeymoon Express. Like the New York toy, the Popeye Express has an airplane, but a Popeye figure's head and waving hand are in the plane. Popeye's blue plane with silver wings has a more defined shape

and is less flat than that of the New York toy. The Popeye head and plane were also used on a prototype in which the plane was attached to a train.[1]

Advertisements for this toy show an insert on the inner side of the track. The insert, made of paper on cardboard, is amusingly lithographed with Olive Oyl, Swee' Pea, Wimpy, and a barking dog chasing a motorcycle policeman with a ticket in his hand. Tabs on each end of the insert fit into the sides of the black, green, and orange pebble design or camouflage-colored bridge. Additional tabs on the bottom of the insert fit into the base.

The Popeye Express has a red base with pictures of Popeye's head, some with a cap and some without. A bridge and two tunnels also appear on the base. The two characters, Wimpy and Sappo, and lettering that reads "Hamburgers" are shown on the tunnels. The train is a red M-10000 Streamliner. Each coach roof has the name of one of the characters, Wimpy, Sappo, Olive Oyl, and Swee' Pea with a lithographed head of the figure jutting out of the window.

The same red-roofed building is in the middle of the toy with lettering that reads "Popeye's Blow Me Down Airport". A picture of Popeye's head and other sea-faring details such as an anchor, tiller, lifesaver, and rowboat are also shown. This version of the Popeye Express, which originally sold for about $4.00 a dozen, is considered the most desirable variation and is most often seen.

On a later version of the Popeye Express, the small building has the green, black, and orange pebble design like the bridge.

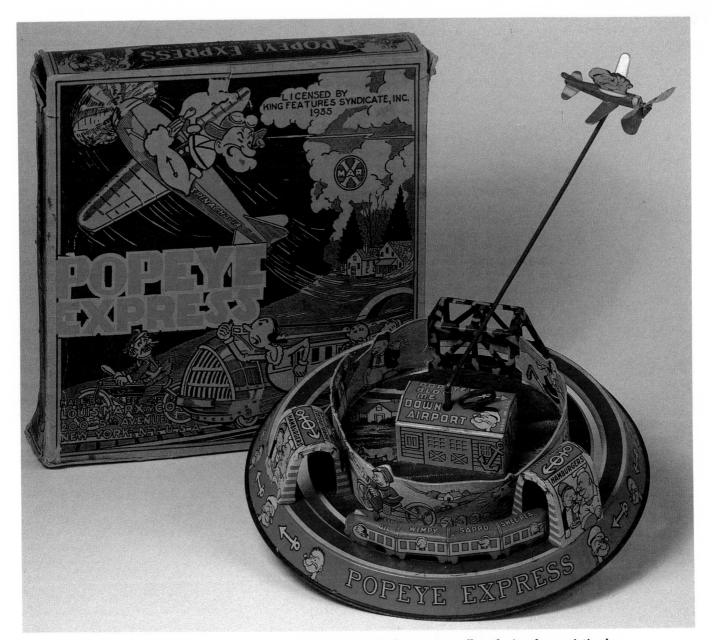

The 1936 Popeye Express has an insert made of lithographed paper on cardboard. Another variation has an airport with different lithography. W. Maeder Collection. R. Grubb photograph.

The lithography of the building described above disappeared. This less expensive variation also came with a cardboard insert.

It is possible that a variation of the Popeye Express was produced without the insert since it is often missing today.

The attractively illustrated box of the Popeye Express shows the Popeye figure to the waist and seated in the plane. Olive Oyl, a motorcyclist, and the other train occupants look up at Popeye from the ground. Lettering reads "Spinachovia" on Popeye's airplane. Additional lettering on the box reads "Licensed by King Features Syndicate, Inc. 1935".

The name "Popeye Express" was used for another toy of Popeye pushing a wheelbarrow. (See Comic Strip Character Toys chapter.)   **300   700**

1936 HONEYMOON EXPRESS: Begun on the New York and Popeye Express toys, Marx continued to use various planes on some, but not all, of the standard Honeymoon Express toys.

Since Marx used materials left over from other toys, the 1936 standard Honeymoon Express has the same tunnel as on the Popeye Express. The characters Wimpy and Sappo appear on the tunnel with lettering that reads "Hamburgers". The M-10000 train now has a red roof, blue windows, and cream sides. There is no airplane. Lettering on the station reads "Glendale" and the bridge is black.

Variations of the 1936 Honeymoon Express have the same train, "Glendale" station, and black bridge. Two variations have pebble-patterned tunnels. One of these came with an airplane, and the other did not. Other variations have green-tinted, tunnels lithographed with rocks and shrubs. Both of these variations came with or without the airplane.

Without airplane	75	125
With airplane	125	175

1937: The 1937 Honeymoon Express toys also have the "Glendale" station, which would appear on most of the later

The 1937 Honeymoon Express came in a variation with an airplane. A similar version without an airplane has red tunnels. W. Maeder Collection. R. Grubb photograph.

express toys. The M-10000 train has a red roof and blue windows. Two variations have the two green-tinted tunnels with rocks and shrubs and a blue bridge. The variations came with and without an airplane. Another variation has red tunnels and a blue bridge, but does not have a plane.

The base now illustrates an M-10000 Streamliner and has the Marx logo. Express toys produced previously have the Marx name and lettering that reads "Trade Mark" on the base.

Without airplane	50	100
With airplane	100	150

1938: In 1938, there were two variations of the Honeymoon Express. Both have a station marked "Glendale"; an M-10000 with a red roof, blue windows, and cream sides; and green-tinted tunnels with rocks and shrubs. The copper bridge was the new feature that year. One of the variations has an airplane, and the other does not.

Without airplane	50	100
With airplane	100	150

1939: With the exception of the new silver bridge, the toy remained the same and was still marketed both with and without a plane.

Without airplane	100	150
With airplane	150	200

1940: Two 1940s variations have the same green rock and shrub tunnels and the station marked "Glendale". But the train now has a red roof, black windows, and yellow sides, and

the bridge is red. These variations also came with and without a plane.

Two other variations have blue-tinted, rock and shrub tunnels and red bridges. One of these has a white and brown station and a red-roofed M-10000 with black windows and yellow sides, but does not have an airplane. The other variation has a red station, a solid yellow M-10000 train without lithography, and an airplane.

Without airplane	25	50
With airplane	75	100

HONEYMOON EXPRESS PROTOTYPE: 1940. This hand-painted prototype named Joy Line Express is pear-shaped due to the addition of a large station and surrounding surface which juts off the edge of the 9-1/2" diameter track.[2] The station, actually built over one of the regular express tunnels, measures 4-1/2" long x 2-1/2" wide x 3" high and lettering reads "Grand Central Station". Another tunnel has a brake, a small crossing gate, and one black bridge.

The small station of the standard Honeymoon Express still appears in the center and lettering reads "Power House". A toy has a streamline passenger train which is also lithographed on the base of the prototype in a scene with houses and animals. The style of the lithography is similar to the later Honeymoon Express toys. Lettering on the bottom of the base reads "Erie, #2008, 1/23/40, returned 2/5/40". Additional markings on the bottom of the base appear as follows:

This Honeymoon Express prototype, made in 1940, has a large station built over one of the regular tunnels. Dr. M. Kates Collection. R. Grubb photograph.

N.A.C.A. — With Tower
N.F.C.A. — Without Tower
N.L.N.A. — No Tower — Old Plane
N.A.E.L. — Without Plane

Marx did not produce a Honeymoon Express from this prototype.

1941: Two 1941 variations have red stations, tunnels with green-tinted rock and shrub design, yellow bridges, and M-10000 trains with red roofs, black windows, and yellow sides. As before, one variation came with an airplane, and the other did not.

A third 1941 variation has a white station; an M-10000 with red roof, black windows, and yellow sides; blue-tinted rock and shrub tunnels; and a yellow bridge, but does not have an airplane.

Without airplane	25	50
With airplane	75	100

1942: Both 1942 variations have white and brown stations; M-10000s with red roofs, black windows, and yellow sides; green-tinted tunnels with lithographed rocks and shrubs; and white bridges. One variation has an airplane, and the other does not.

Without airplane	25	50
With airplane	75	100

1946: After World War II, Marx resumed toy manufacture in 1946. The Honeymoon Express train was changed to a number 6 Great Northern Streamline Passenger Train colored red, yellow, and black. Two 1946 variations have the same white and brown station and the same green-tinted tunnels with lithographed rocks and shrubs as used previously. But the

bridge is colored red and yellow. Like the earlier toys, one variation has an airplane, and the other does not.

All sets produced after the war have an enclosed metal base to protect children from the motor mechanism and the sharp edges of the base. The color of the metal bottoms varies and includes red and black.

There is reason to believe that the Honeymoon Express toys made before World War II, even as early as 1936, were produced with cardboard bottoms. Bases with some pieces of cardboard on them have been reported to exist. The Marx "Busy Miners" toy also has a cardboard base. (See Miscellaneous Toys chapter, Volume II.)

Without airplane	35	60
With airplane	65	90

1948 TO EARLY 1950s: From approximately 1948 to 1952, Marx produced two variations of the Honeymoon Express that resembled the previous ones. He always offered the toy with and without the airplane. But the latest expresses have a freight train with a number 4127 Lumar Lines Caboose. (Marx used the Lumar name on various trains and toys.) The tunnels are only two tones of green and white. In 1952, the Honeymoon Express sold for 98 cents.

Without airplane	50	100
With airplane	100	150

MICKEY MOUSE EXPRESS: c. 1952. Plastic was introduced on both the Mickey Mouse Express and the Subway Express listed below. Although catalog information about the toys has not been found, it is possible that the Mickey Mouse Express was produced before the Subway Express because the former toy has fewer plastic parts.

The 1948 Honeymoon Express (left) also came in a variation without an airplane. Notice the two differently-colored tunnels of the 1936 variation (right). The 1936 express also came in a variation with an airplane. J. Fox Collection. G. Stern photograph.

Mickey Mouse Express was manufactured c. 1952. The same tunnels are also on a later, standard Honeymoon Express. J. Newbraugh Collection. G. Stern photograph.

The 1954 Subway Express is the only express toy with a plastic tunnel. W. Maeder Collection. R. Grubb photograph.

The colorful Mickey Mouse Express has various Disney characters associated with Mickey Mouse printed all over it, including the station, tunnels, and base. Mickey Mouse is lithographed on one tunnel, and Donald Duck is on the other. Like the other expresses of the time, the bridge is red and yellow. The toy has a number 6 Great Northern Streamliner colored red, yellow, and black. The station, marked "Disneyville", has a shingled roof. Mickey's head is plastic and frequently missing from the red airplane.

While some speculate that Marx may have never received permission from Disney to manufacture a Mickey Mouse toy, later toys such as the Mickey Mouse Express and the Mickey Mouse Dipsy Car (see Eccentric Car section, Automobiles chapter, Volume II) suggest otherwise.

The Mickey Mouse Express came in an attractive box which illustrates Mickey with outstretched arms and a suitcase at his side, waiting for the oncoming train. The toy has climbed sharply in price over the years. The June 1977 **PB 84** catalog lists 149 as the catalog number for this toy.   **200   450**

1953: The standard 1953 Honeymoon Express has the same tunnels as the Mickey Mouse Express, but the red, yellow, and black number 6 Great Northern Streamline Train; red and yellow bridge; and "Glendale" station are the same as those on the 1946 version. The 1953 express does not have an airplane.

75   100

SUBWAY EXPRESS: c. 1954. A transparent, plastic tunnel encircles the entire diameter of the toy to represent a subway. The toy still has the red-roofed station, but lettering reads "42nd St." on one side and "52nd St." on the other. Automobiles are lithographed near the station. A lithographed scroll that reads "Subway Express" and a cityscape illustrates the base. The toy has a number 6 Great Northern Streamline Passenger Train in red, yellow, and black. The red, yellow, black, and white illustrated box for the toy emphasizes the plastic tunnel.

The June 1977 **PB 84** catalog lists 161 as the catalog number for this toy. The Subway Express can still be purchased at an affordable price.

The 1927 Pinched measures approximately 10" square and 3" high. The car speeds around the track until the motorcycle policeman rushes out to stop (pinch) him. Dr. M. Kates Collection. R. Grubb photograph.

According to Richard Carver, a former design foreman and model maker for Louis Marx & Company, the Subway Express was not very successful. Although it is a handsome, multicolored toy, perhaps interest in the long-running Honeymoon Express toys was finally beginning to decline. **150 300**

1955: Two 1955 variations of the Honeymoon Express toys have red, yellow, and black number 6 Great Northern Streamline Trains and red and yellow bridges and tunnels with rock and shrub designs. One variation has a "Glendale" station, but does not have a plane. The other variation has a stop lever in place of the station. **NRS**

RELATED CIRCLE TOYS

PINCHED: 1927. 10" long x 10" wide x 3" high. The square-based Pinched is an amusing and whimsical toy with fine lithography. An automobile, like that of the 1927 Main St. toy, drives along an open circular track like that of the Honeymoon Express. The same building with the winding key is in the center of the toy. Except for its green roof, the building is lithographed like the early Honeymoon Express station with a store, a clock above the door, and lettering on a sign that reads "Richmond". Another building is situated so that the roadster is able to drive through it. The Pinched toy has only one tunnel, taller than those on the Honeymoon Expresses, but with a similar brick and shrub design. Two V-shaped pedestrian bridges span the roadway.

Pinched has one policeman figure seated on the motorcycle and another standing near a Stop/Go sign which moves when the car rides by. Two figures from the Main St. toy, with

different lithography, stand on the pedestrian bridges. It was typical for Marx to use pieces from one toy for another.

Comical illustrations decorate the base. Three policemen are shown chasing a speeding roadster on the base center. On the base side, a policeman is stopping a car. The most amusing scene, however, shows a judge sentencing a man in front of a jury—all of whom appear to be baldheaded.

An ad in the 1927 Fall/Winter **Sears** catalog describes the toy as follows: "See the speedy little roadster shoot round and round, through the bridges and tunnels, and all of a sudden the motorcycle cop shoots out from behind the station, stops him and 'pinches' him. When cop is pushed back behind station again, the auto starts away automatically, only to be 'pinched' over and over again." The toy sold for 98 cents.

Two patents resemble the Pinched toy. Number 1,625,326, filed June 9, 1926, shows a similar toy that has four tunnels and lacks the motorcycle policeman. The policeman standing near the Stop/Go sign is shown but with a moving arm.

The second patent, number 1,630,091, filed July 19, 1926, has a similar drawing with the addition of the motorcycle policeman and a flagman who appears to stand on the roof of the building. The standing policeman is not included and only three tunnels are shown. (See Patents appendix.)

The appearance of Pinched at toy meets is less frequent than in earlier years.

A foreign toy, possibly German, similar to Pinched is called "Safety First". It was sold in 1926 and, like Pinched, Safety First is square with a similar automobile that drives around the track. "Safety First" has a different house in the center,

The 1930 Coast Defense measures 9" in diameter and came in a second variation with an airplane but without the back wall. The Zeppelin is missing from the toy shown. W. Maeder Collection. R. Grubb photograph.

figures, and, instead of tunnels, arches similar to the Marx Main St. and Big Parade toys.   **200   375**

STOP, LOOK AND LISTEN: 1927. 14" long x 7-1/2" wide x 3-1/2" high. Like the Honeymoon Express, Stop, Look and Listen has a station building on the inside of the track and a train moving through a tunnel and around a circular track. A second circular track next to the train track allows an automobile to cross a bridge and pass a stop gate.

Several 1927 ads appear in different catalogs for this toy. The 1927 **Edw. K. Tryon Company** catalog describes the toy as follows: "...a railroad crossing with the Stop, Look and Listen sign...seen all over the country. The trains (only one appears in the ad) travels in circles as does the car. At the crossing the car stops at the gate to permit the trains to go by and then proceeds when the trains pass through." The toy sold for $1.15.

Two patents are similar to the Stop, Look and Listen toy. The earlier one, number 1,663,379, most closely resembles the toy and was filed on December 1, 1926. The patent drawing lacks the Stop, Look and Listen sign shown in the advertisement.

The later patent, filed April 15, 1927, bears an earlier patent number, 1,660,716. The patent drawing has two signs. In comparison to the earlier patent, the later one shows a different type of bridge and reverses the sides on which the train and car appear.   **150   350**

COAST DEFENSE: 1930. 9" diameter. The Coast Defense is a circular toy with an airplane or zeppelin instead of a train. The aircraft is suspended from a wire that is connected to the roof of a building. Though no longer in the center of the toy, the same red-roofed building has the winding key and lettering that now reads "Coast Defense" on the roof and "Insert Aero Here" and "Pat. Pending". "Louis Marx & Co." is on one side of the building, and "Start and Stop" is next to a lever on the other. A flat metal piece rests against the front of the building and is slightly larger than it. The tan and green base has a red brick design which covers the edge of the toy.

As its name implies, Coast Defense is a military toy. An advertisement in the December 1930 **Butler Brothers** catalog describes the details of the toy as follows: "9" diameter metal platform representing fort with three 3" disappearing guns, seven 1-1/8" soldiers, 2-1/2" hangar with 2-1/4" revolving airplane (or zeppelin), all metal construction, bright color litho, (coast artillery) guns move back and forward, rise and disappear, airplane circles above fort." The toy sold for 59 cents.

The flat, stationary soldiers are of two types. One type is the figure used in the Main St. toy as the lady and vendor, but the soldier has different lithography. The other type is the same soldier as in the Big Parade toy which shows only the side view of the marching soldiers. Two of these have been attached to the same piece. All wear red and blue uniforms.

The Coast Defense toy came in at least two variations. The more common variation has a flat wall curved around the back part of the toy. The wall, lithographed in orange, white, and blue, shows military barracks with zeppelins and airplanes in the sky. A zeppelin circles this variation of the toy. The other, less common variation lacks the wall and has a circling airplane instead. Various catalog illustrations clearly show both variations.

It is thought that the Coast Defense toy, like the Popeye Express, came with a cardboard insert. Although advertisements which support this belief have not been found, it is possible that the toy did come with an insert.

In 1941, Keystone Mfg. Company produced a toy with the same theme called "Coast Defense Fort". An ad in the March 1941 **Playthings** shows that the toy is oblong and includes extra features such as a boat.   **180 350**

---

[1] Eric Matzke, **Greenberg's Guide to Marx Trains,** (Sykesville, MD: Greenberg Publishing Company, 1985), p. 46.

[2] Joy Line was the name of Marx trains until 1935, when the Marx name was used instead.

CHAPTER XIV: SOLDIERS OF FORTUNE

Soldiers of Fortune sets were manufactured circa 1940. The size of the soldiers vary from 3" to 4-1/4" high. Sets came with different numbers of soldiers and one or a combination of guns and cannons. W. Maeder Collection. R. Grubb photograph.

INTRODUCTION

The Soldiers of Fortune toys are flat, tin soldiers that were produced in the early 1940s to 1950s. The different branches of the armed forces are represented in the Soldiers of Fortune sets including the Army Air Corps, Army, Marines, and Navy. Some sets came with a standing cowboy, a cowboy seated on a horse, an Indian, or a Nurse. The soldiers vary in size from 3" to 4-1/4" high and are scaled, either consciously or coincidentally, to the large tin tanks that were manufactured at the same time. They have a colorful appearance, and the back of each is lithographed in a solid color.

Made from one piece of tin, the base is formed by bending back the bottom part of the toy. A point value, the rank of the soldier, and a descriptive phrase appear on the base. The number of points depends upon the rank and firearm of the soldier. The printing on the soldiers' bases varies in style. The newer Marx logo is on some of the bases.

The soldiers of fortune were lithographed in about 50 different poses on one of five tin shapes, an excellent example of Marx's cost-cutting philosophy. The problem with the soldiers, therefore, is that the lithography is not always properly matched to the tin shape. The inaccuracy is the result of a variety of soldiers being cut from only a few dies. For example, the same tin shape was used for a soldier with an anti-aircraft gun and for a mounted cavalry soldier. As a result, part of a helmet or arm is sometimes cut away.

Space on the tin shape which was not taken up by the soldier was sometimes left blank (as on the foreign soldiers, cowboys, and Indians) and, at other times, was filled with lithographed context clues such as tufts of grass, clouds of dust, boulders, or other "props." Other manufacturers often had similar accompaniment in the form of green-painted bases suggesting grass or context clues such as the camouflage which became part of the Manoil camouflage sharpshooter M87.[1] The Marx tin soldiers differ from the cast toy soldiers because, despite their two-dimensional form, their lithographed context includes objects in the distance. For instance, the captain commanding the battleship has features of a battleship in the distance. The tank commander has a WW I tank in the background, and the 3" anti-aircraft gunner has a black night sky pierced by searchlight beams.[2]

The soldiers came in sets of 8, 24, 36, and 40 pieces with one or a combination of guns and cannons. One set came with 12 soldiers, a military train, station, 2 planes, a tent, and flag. Some of the soldiers were sold in the Marx Army Train sets. Extra soldiers could be purchased separately.

The set boxes were usually designed to be made into a fort. One box is green, yellow, gray, and white. On the front of the box lettering reads "Soldiers of Fortune" with the later Marx logo. The soldiers fighting in battle are illustrated. A stone fortress or barracks is shown on the sides of the box.

Later, Marx made many plastic military figures of different types and sizes. Besides the soldiers mounted to the elongated traffic toys, the Soldiers of Fortune are the only tin military figures that the company made.

SOLDIERS OF FORTUNE SET GUNS
ANTI-AIRCRAFT GUN.
CANNON: 8" long x 2-3/4" wide x 2-3/4" high. The cannon is lithographed in olive drab and fires wooden projectile shells. It has the same wheels as the Marx "Jumpin Jeep" and "Jolly Joe Jeep" eccentric cars, although the lithographed hubs are red.   **35   60**

A variation of the cannon is shorter with a barrel that is 3/4" wider. It came in silver or olive drab with black wheels and fires larger wooden shells.   **NRS**

POP-GUN: The pop-gun shoots corks and is believed to have been made by the Daisy Manufacturing Company in Michigan which produces BB and pop guns. The gun, a carbine type, is 13-1/2" long. It has a steel barrel and a wooden stock. Richard Carver, a Marx model maker, believes that the Daisy company regularly made guns for the Soldiers of Fortune sets.
                                                                        NRS

THE SOLDIERS
CAVALRY SOLDIERS: Lettering on base reads: "Mounted Soldier of the U.S. Army."   **1.50   5**

INFANTRY COMMAND:
(A) Infantry First Lieutenant: Lettering on base reads: "Commands platoon of 36 men. Insignia one Silver Bar on shoulder."   **1.50   5**
(B) Infantry Captain: Lettering on base reads: "Commanding a company of 162 men. Insignia two Silver Bars on shoulder."   **1.50   5**

INFANTRY PRIVATE: The majority of the soldiers in the army set, for example 13 in a set of 24, are privates in the infantry. Infantry soldiers from different sets represented various nations such as America, France, Germany, and Russia. The infantry figures have the following poses: standing at attention, marching, charging, carrying a rifle, and kneeling with guns.
(A) Standing or Marching: Lettering on the base reads: "Infantry—Private. The foot soldier is the backbone of the army."   **1.50   5**
(B) Charging: Soldier shown charging directly at viewer or to the right. Lettering on the base reads: "Charges by infantry furnish many of history's brightest spots."   **1.50   5**
(C) Carrying a Rifle: Soldier carries the new Garand Rifle. Lettering on the base reads: "This rifle is the finest military rifle in the world. Fires thirty shots a minute with great accuracy."   **1.50   5**
(D) Kneeling with Machine Gun: Lettering on the base reads: "Machine Gun Unit-Private with 30 Cal. Heavy Machine Gun. This is standard for machine gun unit. It fires two miles."   **1.50   5**
(E) Kneeling with Anti-Aircraft Gun: 3" gun. Lettering on base reads: "Fires 13-lb. shell — 25 to 30 shots per minute. Range of 6 miles."   **2.00   5**
(F) With Howitzer: Lettering on base reads: "Fires on curved trajectory. Hits objects hidden from ordinary flat fire."   **1.50   5**
(G) Sharpshooter with Rifle: Lettering on base reads: "Sharpshooter"; "Qualified Rifle Expert. Shown here with new Garand Rifle."   **1.50   5**

NOTE: Gene Parker has compiled a comprehensive listing of the Soldiers of Fortune which appears in the excellent book, **Collecting Toys** by Richard O'Brien.[3] The following infantry soldiers are included in the list: American "Doughboy", Private lying with fixed bayonet, Private with automatic rifle, and Sergeant.

Mr. Parker also mentions the following:
Anti-Tank set with soldiers and exploding tanks (See Tanks chapter, Volume II of Greenberg's Marx Toys guide), Bandit on horse, Captain commanding battleship, Chief Petty Officer, Fireman sold with fire truck, Flame Thrower, General, Marine Corps Officer, Marine Corps Private, Mechanic, Motorcycle Messenger, Navy Signalman, Officer in full dress uniform, Parachute Trooper, Pilot adjusting gloves, Pilot with papers, Radio Operator, Seaman equipped for landing force, Ski Trooper, camouflaged Sniper, standing Tank Commander, Wounded Soldier, 50 Cal. Machine Gun.

Foreign soldiers listed by Mr. Parker are: Gordon Highlander, Indian Sikh, Italian Bersaglieri, King Royal Rifle Corps, Royal Scots Greys, and Prussion Cavalry Soldier with lance.

[1] Richard O'Brien, **Collecting Toys,** 3rd ed., (Alabama: Books Americana, 1982), p. 191.

[2] Information provided by John Ritter, a knowledgeable Marx Toy collector.

[3] O'Brien, pp. 335-37.

CHAPTER XV: TYPEWRITER TOYS

The 1930s Dial typewriter and Super Dial typewriter measure 11" long x 6" high. The regular Dial has a flat keyboard while the Super Dial keyboard inclines in steps. W. Maeder Collection. R. Grubb photograph.

INTRODUCTION

Early Dial Typewriters measure 11-1/2" long x 5-3/4" wide x 6-1/8" high. 1930s. Generally, the early typewriters are black, red, and white, with a large dial on the top of the machine. The Marx logo appears in the center of the dial with lettering that reads "Dial Typewriter". The dial is edged with lithographed capital letters and numbers on some variations. The capital letters appear on a flat keyboard with lithographed keys. Other keyboards are lithographed with only a decorative design on the corners. Still others have step-like inclines. Variations with lower case letters may also exist. Later typewriters are more realistic with actual keys and space bars.

Behind the dial is a rotating circular disc with stamped letters and numbers. In order to "type," the dial is turned to the desired letter or number and a lever pushed to print the character and advance the carriage to the next space. A space key advances the carriage without printing to allow spacing between words.

Advertisements for the dial typewriters began to appear about 1933. An ad in the 1933 Fall/Winter **Sears** catalog reads "Famous Marx Dial Typewriter for Boys and Girls!" and describes the typewriter as follows: "(uses) regular office size letter paper. Dial has 40 metal characters, including alphabet, numerals, and punctuation marks. Carriage slides back and forth!...lithographed metal construction." The typewriter sold for $1.39.

REGULAR DIAL TYPEWRITER: The regular typewriter, advertised next to the De-Luxe Typewriter, sold for only $1.39. According to an ad in the 1934 **Sears** Christmas catalog, the regular typewriter was just as practical as the De-Luxe version, but is smaller, less realistic, and has no warning bell. Eventually, extra paper rolls could be purchased for this typewriter as well. The ad states that the measurements are 11" wide x 5-3/4" long x 6-1/8" high. **50 125**

DE-LUXE DIAL TYPEWRITER: 11" long x 7" wide x 8" high. Manufactured in 1934, the De-Luxe Typewriter has a

The 1934 De-Luxe Typewriter measures 11" long x 7" wide x 8" high. The toy can actually type a letter and has a warning bell. T. Riley Collection. C. Myers photograph.

black body and yellow QWERTY keyboard. The simulated keys are lithographed in red-orange with black outline. A single center lever allows the letter to be typed and a bell rings at the end of a line. The red, yellow, black, and white dial mechanism has the key faces mounted to the tread of the wheel.[1] In addition to the typewriter name and the letters and numbers, the dial has a lithographed figure typing.

According to a **Sears** advertisement, the De-Luxe Typewriter is a big improvement to the regular Marx Dial Typewriter. Both were advertised together. The De-Luxe Typewriter, priced at $1.89, was described as being able to type a legible letter. Three extra typewriter paper rolls could be purchased for ten cents.   **75   150**

JUNIOR DIAL TYPEWRITER.   **35   50**

SUPER DIAL TYPEWRITER: The keys are lithographed on a platform with step-like rows.   **45   65**

LATER TYPEWRITER DEVELOPMENT

In 1935, two years after the first typewriter advertisement, the Marx typewriter was still being sold for $1.39. Three extra ink rolls could be purchased for ten cents. The 1936 typewriters, the price of which dropped to 98 cents, are described as having type that is securely fastened to the dial.

In the 1937 **Sears** Christmas catalog, Marx advertised the De-Luxe Typewriter with 232 pieces of supplies: 140 sheets of paper, 50 envelopes, 4 sheets of carbon paper, 1 notebook with 144 pages, 1 pad with 35 pages, 1 pencil, and 1 eraser. According to the ad, the typewriter has a space and shift key and is self-inking and spacing. The set sold for $1.79. In 1939,

the De-Luxe Typewriter was sold with 257 pieces of office supplies.

232-piece set.   **NRS**
257-piece set.   **NRS**

In the 1939 Fall/Winter **Sears** catalog, Marx sold the typewriter in a smaller set with 106 pieces of office supplies. For $1.19, the typewriter came with 80 sheets of regular-sized paper, 25 envelopes, and 1 eraser. The "realistic" keyboard has red and yellow letters and numbers. The extra ink rolls still sold for ten cents. In 1942, the price for the set was $1.45.

106-piece set.   **NRS**

In the late 1940s, dial typewriters not identified as Marx's cost about $3.50. Simplex, American Flyer, and Unique Art were among those that manufactured the typewriters. Unique Art produced a competitive typewriter that Marx undersold by having his toy typewriters produced less expensively in the Orient.[2] The Marx company still made toy typewriters as late as the mid-1970s. With actual keys, these plastic typewriters are much more similar to office typewriters.

The Marx toy typewriters are easy to find.

---

[1] Information from Trip Riley, a well-known Marx Toy collector.

[2] Eric Matzke, **Greenberg's Guide to Marx Trains** (Sykesville, MD: Greenberg Publishing Company, 1985), p.86.

CHAPTER XVI: LARGE WALKERS

INTRODUCTION

The large walkers have been organized into a chapter all their own because they were produced from one die. As might be expected, these tin lithographed windups are similar to each other in appearance, size, and action. They move from side to side on big feet and measure 11" high. The large walkers are considerably taller than other Marx walkers, and quite different in appearance.

The large walkers were produced with flimsy arms which are frequently missing from the toys today. While some collectors will not buy the walker without its original arms, replacement arms are obtainable at modest prices.

AMOS 'N' ANDY: 1930. 11" high. The Amos 'n' Andy walkers, modeled from the characters of the "Amos 'n' Andy" radio show of the late 1920s and 1930s, are among the most desirable Marx toys. The radio pair, Freeman Gosden who played Amos and Charles Correll who played Andy, appeared in the film "Check and Double Check" in 1930. In the 1950s, the show appeared on television, but lasted only a short while.

Many advertisements mention the fact that Andy is slightly taller than Amos. Andy, with his ever-present cigar, wears either a blue or pink coat, a brown-banded derby with a crease in it, a checked vest, and striped pants. He carries a cane in his right hand.

Amos's red porter's cap reads "Taxi". A badge on the cap reads "Fresh Air Taxicab Company of America Incorpolated (sic)". He is dressed in a red- and white-striped vest and spotted shirt. His left pant leg is patched. Unlike Andy, he does not wear a tie; his shirt is open at the collar.

Lettering on Andy's back reads "Original and Genuine Authorized Andy". Amos has similar lettering. [1] Both figures wear badges with their names and the initials "F.A.T.C." which stand for Fresh Air Taxicab Company. Lettering on Andy's badge reads "President", while that on Amos' badge reads "Driver".

Marx's Amos 'n' Andy walkers came in a number of variations. One version of the walkers has eyes that move up and down while another variation has stationary, painted eyes. Andy's coat is usually blue, but a less common variation exists in pink. Apparently it was thought that the skin tones were too dark, so a pair with lighter skin color was made. The difference between the light and dark skin tone is quite noticeable, making it more difficult for collectors to obtain a matching pair.

Amos 'n' Andy walkers are advertised in the December 1930 **Butler Brothers** wholesale catalog in both moving and stationary eye variations. Sold in one dozen pairs, the walkers with moving eyes are priced at $12.00, while those with painted eyes are priced at only $7.50. The catalog also advertises an Amos 'n' Andy Window Display for 75 cents. The display illustrates the highlights of the Amos 'n' Andy radio broadcasts.

There are minor differences in the Butler ad illustrations for the toy with moving eyes and the one with stationary eyes. In the former, Andy wears a darker coat, darker shoes, and a lighter, unpatterned hatband. The Amos with the moving eyes wears a striped cap, whereas for the toy with painted eyes, the cap is unstriped. These differences have been observed only in ad illustrations and not on the actual toys. Reader assistance is requested to substantiate the above comparison.

Apparently Amos 'n' Andy was packaged several different ways. In his outstanding and witty book, **A Celebration of Comic Art and Memorabilia**, Robert Lesser describes the original Amos 'n' Andy box as having grossly exaggerated illustrations of the pair. Eventually, the toys were packaged in a box with their movie title "Check and Double Check". [2] In the 1930 Fall/Winter **Sears** catalog, the ad mentions yet another version of the packaging: "...in a novel display box with cutout feature-forming theatre background." According to the ad, both toys sold for $1.39 and were authorized by Correll and Gosden.

The design patents for the toys, number 87,969 for Amos and number 87,970 for Andy, were filed March 12, 1931, several months after the appearance of the catalog ads for the toys (see Patents appendix). The patent drawings substantially resemble the toys except that there is no lettering on the badges.

Other toys connected with Amos 'n' Andy are the "Amos 'n' Andy Fresh Air Taxicab" (see Film, Radio, and Television Toys chapter) and the "Amosandra" doll (see Miscellaneous chapter, Volume II).

Add $400 to the price of the toy with box.   **700 1600**

FUNNY FACE (HAROLD LLOYD): 1928. 11" high. The Funny Face toy is dressed in a navy coat, green-checked pants, red and white shoes, red bow tie, and red-banded hat. He has very rosy cheeks.

Although "Harold Lloyd" is not mentioned in any of the ads for this toy, it is believed that the toy is a representation of this well-known comedian of silent films and later of talkies. But the box for the toy merely reads "Funny Face" and shows pictures of the character with several expressions.

The most ingenious feature of this toy is its ability to change expressions. This is accomplished by a moving tin cutout of the midsection of the toy's face. His eyes, ears, and part of his mouth are on the moving piece which slides under the character's eyeglasses and nose. When pushed up, the eyes narrow and the mouth opens into a toothy smile. When moved down, the eyes widen and the mouth closes, hiding the smile. Powered by a windup spring, the toy repeats this action as it walks.

Funny Face is advertised in the 1928 Fall/Winter **Sears** catalog where it sold for 53 cents. The figure in the ad holds a cane in his right hand. The 1928 Fall/Winter **Montgomery Ward** catalog advertised the toy as the "Funny Feller." It sold for 49 cents, considered a substantially lower price at that time. In the Montgomery Ward ad, the toy does not hold a cane. The missing cane could account for the lower price or the illustration could have been rendered without a cane. Reader

The 11" high Funny Face walker, manufactured in 1928, is believed to be the film comedian Harold LLoyd. His changeable face can show both a serious and smiling expression. W. Maeder Collection. R. Grubb photograph.

Like the Harold Lloyd toy, the 11" high Mammy's Boy, manufactured in 1929, has changeable expressions. Dr. M. Kates Collection. R. Grubb photograph.

assistance is requested to determine the existence of a variation without a cane.

Apparently, Marx considered making other versions of the Funny Face toy because two patents resemble it. Patent number 1,764,330, published June 17, 1930, shows the character holding a chicken and smiling incongruously while a dog bites the seat of his pants (see Patents appendix). Without the chicken and dog, the drawing is similar to the Funny Face toy and is quite possibly the patent for it. The chicken and dog were used on a different toy, "Hey Hey The Chicken Snatcher" (see the Black Toys chapter). The second patent, number 1,782,786, published November 26, 1930, shows the toy's face with moving features made into a horn.

Other manufacturers also made toys with moving features. There is a German bell toy as well as a Japanese copy of

Marx's Funny Face toy with different lithography. Neither toy was copyrighted with the Harold Lloyd name. [3]

Add $75 to the price of the toy with box.   **100   300**

JOE PENNER: See Film, Radio, and Television Toys chapter.

MAMMY'S BOY: 1929. 11" high. Mammy's Boy is a black toy and, similar to the Funny Face toy, it has moving facial features. He is dressed in a red, two-button jacket with black lapels, a striped tie, yellow pants with black stripes, and red and white shoes. Mammy's Boy wears the same hat as Funny Face, but unlike him, grips a cane in both hands. The toy's skin color is quite dark and its red mouth is edged in white.

In 1929, both Sears and Montgomery Ward sold this toy for 57 cents. The 1929 Fall/Winter **Sears** catalog shows the toy as described above. But in the 1929 Fall/Winter **Montgomery Ward** catalog, the toy is dressed in a six-button coat with different lapels and a bow tie. It is unknown whether the toy actually came lithographed as shown in the Montgomery Ward ad. The Mammy's Boy toy is rare.

Add $10 to the price of the toy with box.   **100   180**

WALKING CLANCY: 1931. 11" high. Like the Funny Face and Mammy's Boy toys, the Walking Clancy has a moving expression as it walks. The mustached Walking Clancy is dressed in a policeman's uniform with a high collar, a badge on his chest numbered "666", and a badge on his hat that reads "P.D." He has three stripes on his uniform, indicating his rank as sergeant. His hands grip a night stick instead of a cane.

The Walking Clancy appears in the 1931 Fall/Winter **Sears** catalog and sold for 48 cents. Advertised in catalogs later than the other walkers, the Walking Clancy was probably the last of the large walker toys.

Add $100 to the price of the toy with box.   **250   500**

1 David Longest, **Character Toys and Collectibles,** (Kentucky: Collector Books, 1984), p. 25.

2 Robert Lesser, **A Celebration of Comic Art and Memorabilia,** (New York: Hawthorne Books, Inc., 1975), p. 79.

3 Gerritt Beverwyk, **Marx Toy Collector Newsletter,** Vol. 2, No. 5, p. 11.

The study of patents is fascinating and informative. The breadth of Marx toy patents is a written record of the company's creative energy. Some patents record toy ideas that were never produced. The toy's manufacture proved too costly, or perhaps other ideas held greater appeal. Sometimes, applications for patents were submitted in order to protect the company's ideas for possible future use or to stop other manufacturers from copying them.

The patents from which actual toys were made sometimes show additional ideas that were dropped when the toy was produced. For example, the patent for the Main Street toy, number 1,674,293, shows airplanes and zeppelins attached to a loop at the top of the toy. The airplanes and zeppelins, and consequently the loop, do not exist on the actual toy.

Patents are important in the research of toys, sometimes establishing a connection between a toy and a manufacturer when no identifying mark exists on the toy. The Jigger toy listed in the Black Toys chapter, for example, is believed to be connected to the Marx company because of its resemblance to the Marx patent, number 1,538,541, "Mechanically Operated Dancing Toy."

While patents sometimes help in determining the date of a toy, patent dates can be misleading as well. For example, while the patent used for the Marx Dapper Dan toys (see Black Toys chapter), number 959,009, was published on May 24, 1910, actually the toy was not manufactured until 1921. In addition, some toys were made before the patent date and are marked patent pending.

Information about patents for specific toys can be found in the listing for that toy. Following are several patents of interest reprinted from the **Official Gazette** of the U. S. Patent Office.

The patents are generally listed in the order in which the toys made from them appear in the book.

ROLL-OVER CAT and FIGARO:

INVENTOR
RAYMOND J. LOHR
RICHARD NELSON CARVER
BY
ATTORNEY

2,189,759
REVERSING ROLL-OVER TOY

Raymond J. Lohr and Richard Nelson Carver, Erie, Pa., assignors to Louis Marx & Company, Inc., New York, N. Y., a corporation of New York. Application June 3, 1939, Serial No. 277,222. 18 Claims. (Cl. 46—104)

A toy comprising a toy body, a reaction member outside said body and connected to a shaft which projects from the body, a motor in said body for rotating said shaft to cause the reaction member to bear against the floor and thereby cause the body to roll over on the floor, and means between said motor and said shaft for periodically reversing the direction of rotation of the shaft so that the body rolls over one way and then the other.

SNAPPY THE MIRACLE DOG:

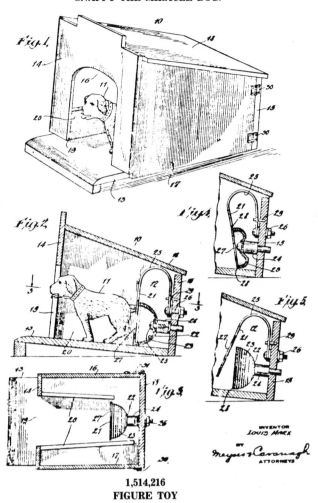

1,514,216
FIGURE TOY

Louis Marx, New York, N. Y. Filed Jan. 5, 1924. Serial No. 684,536. 5 Claims, (Cl. 46—40).

A toy comprising a housing having a front wall opening, the said housing defining a compartment in which a toy figure is positionable for expulsion through said opening, ejecting means within the housing for expelling the toy figure, and pneumatic means operative for restraining action of said ejecting means and for releasing the same to permit figure expelling action thereof.

BALKY MULE:

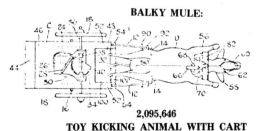

2,095,646
TOY KICKING ANIMAL WITH CART

Raymond Lohr, Erie, Pa., assignor to Louis Marx & Company, Inc., New York, N. Y., a corporation of New York. Application November 28, 1936, Serial No. 113,149. 20 Claims. (Cl.46—101)

A toy comprising a simulated animal and a simulated cart, the forward end of the cart being pivotally connected to the rear end of the animal, means at the forelegs of the animal adapted to move along the floor, a motor on the cart, means including automatically reversing mechanism gearing said motor to a wheel of the cart in order to drive the cart forwardly and rearwardly in alternation, the toy being so arranged that on forward movement of the cart the resistance to movement at the forelegs of the animal is such that the animal rears upwardly and simulatedly dumps the cart.

WEE RUNNING SCOTTIE:

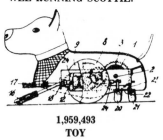

1,959,493
TOY

Heinrich Muller, Nuremberg, Germany. Application January 26, 1933, Serial No. 653,638. In Germany August 27, 1932. 2 Claims. (Cl. 46—45)

In a toy comprising a hollow body representing the body of a quadruped, legs extending forth from said body, cranks to which said feet are hinged, and means for rotating said cranks, in combination with the said feet, a stationary member having slots through which the feet extend and which give them a reciprocation motion in a vertical direction while they are reciprocated in a horizontal direction by the said cranks so as to produce the appearance of the quadruped running on its feet when the toy is in operation.

RUNNING SCOTTIE:

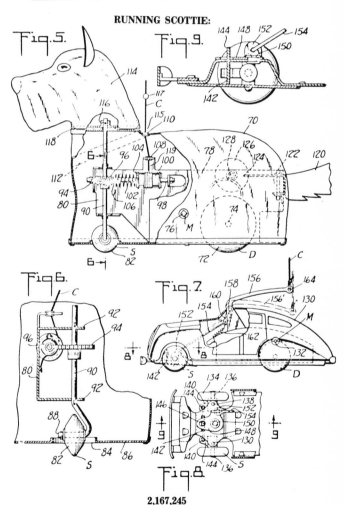

2,167,245
WHEELED TOY STEERED BY REMOTE CONTROL

Raymond Lohr and Richard Nelson Carver, Erie, Pa., assignors to Louis Marx & Company, Inc., New York, N. Y., a corporation of New Yrok. Application January 3, 1938, Serial No. 183,070. 18 Claims. (Cl. 46—210)

A wheeled toy comprising steering means, normally lightly biasing the steering means in one direction, a non-resilient, highly flexible fibrous string extending from the toy, said string being operatively connected to said steering means in such manner that pull tension applied to the string turns the steering means in the opposite direction.

GOLDEN GOOSE:

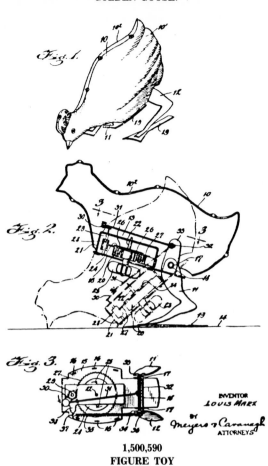

1,500,590
FIGURE TOY

Louis Marx, New York, N. Y. Filed Dec. 19, 1923. Serial No. 681,611. 4 Claims. (Cl. 46—40)

A toy fowl comprising a body member formed in representation of a fowl, a plurality of leg members, the said body member being mounted on the leg members for oscillation movement thereon between a substantially horizontal or normal body position and a downwardly inclined position with the beak of the fowl adjacent a support such as the ground on which the toy is placed, and mechanism carried by the body member and connected to the leg members for oscillation the body member relatively to the leg members in simulation of an eating or pecking action.

MERRYMAKERS:

69,559
TOY

Samuel Berger, Newark, N. J. Filed May 17, 1924. Serial No. 9,635. Term of patent 14 years.

The ornamental design for a toy as shown.

CHICKEN SNATCHER:

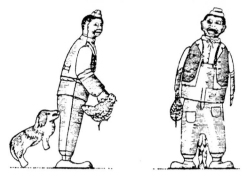

69,900
FIGURE TOY

Louis Marx, Brooklyn, N. Y., Filed Feb. 20, 1926. Serial No. 16,618. Term of patent 3-1/2 years.

The ornamental design for a figure toy, as shown.

BLACK TOYS:

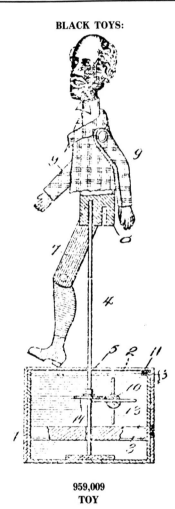

959,009
TOY

Walter S. Hendren, Nicholasville, Ky., assignor of one-fourth to Charles A. Knight, Nicholasville, Ky. Filed Feb. 4, 1910. Serial No. 542,014

A toy comprising a platform, a figure located above the platform and having its body portion formed to provide vertical passages of different lengths, a vertical support slidable through the platform and having its upper extremity interchangeably engaged in the said passage, a horizontal disk carried by said support, a revolubly mounted shaft beneath the platform, and radial pins extending from the shaft and adapted upon rotation of the said shaft to engage the disk to impart vertical reciprocatory motion to the said support and to impart dance-like movements to the figure.

SPIC COON DRUMMER:

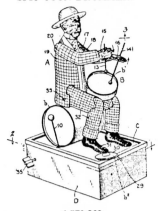

1,570,268
FIGURE TOY

Louis Marx, New York, N. Y. Filed Mar. 21, 1923. Serial No. 626,535. 19 Claims. (Cl. 46—40)

In a toy amusement device simulating a drummer in action, a support, a representation of a bass drum on the support, a figure representing a drummer arranged in sitting position on the drum, means independent of said figure for beating said drum, a simulated snare drum associated with the figure, means for beating the snare drum operated by movement of the figure, and mechanism for setting the figure in motion and for operating the first mentioned means in synchronization therewith to produce a simulated beating of the drums.

GANG BUSTERS CAR:

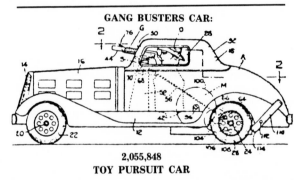

2,055,848
TOY PURSUIT CAR

Louis Marx, New York, N. Y. Application October 11, 1935, Serial No. 44,484. 12 Claims. (Cl. 46—112)

A toy comprising a wheeled toy automobile the body of which is provided with a window opening, a simulated machine gun the barrel of which projects through the window opening, a friction wheel rotatably mounted inside said automobile body beneath and partially housed by the gun, said wheel being so disposed as to be substantially concealed by the automobile and machine gun bodies, a flint engaging said wheel, and means gearing said wheel to the automobile wheels.

AMOS 'N' ANDY FRESH AIR TAXICAB:

82,440
VEHICLE TOY

Louis Marx, New York, N. Y., assignor to Charles J. Correll and Freeman F. Gosden, Chicago, Ill. Filed Mar. 31, 1930. Serial No. 35,075. Term of patent 3-1/2 years.

The ornamental design for a vehicle toy, substantially as shown an described.

ELECTRIC QUESTION AND ANSWER TOY:

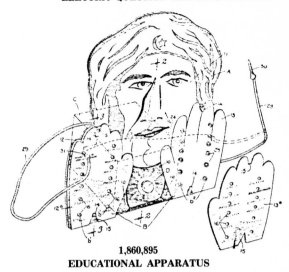

1,860,895
EDUCATIONAL APPARATUS

Louis Marx, New York, N. Y. Filed May 2, 1928. Serial No. 274,385. 8 Claims. (Cl. 35—12)

An educational apparatus comprising a plate having over its single front face two sets of electrical contacts, a unitary question card applicable to one set of contacts, a unitary answer card applicable to the other set of contacts, a stand support for said plate attached to the lower rear face thereof, a battery of the flash-light type housed by said stand support, electrical circuit means interconnecting the contacts in said two sets of contacts and including contact terminals adapted to be selectively contacted with said sets of contacts for completing an electric circuit between the questions and the corresponding answers associated therewith, and a signal lamp for said circuit means mounted over the front of said plate and extending therethrough and into direct engagement with said battery.

SWINGING ARM TARGET GAME:

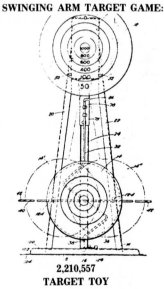

2,210,557
TARGET TOY

Anthony Schillace and William J. Daily, Girard, Pa., assignors to Louis Marx & Company, Inc., New York, N. Y., a corporation of New York. Application March 30, 1938, Serial No. 198,886. 10 Claims. (Cl. 273—105.2)

A target toy comprising a stationarily located target, a motor behind said target, a base, legs supporting said motor a substantial distance above the base, a pendulum-like swinging target suspended below said stationarily located target, mechanism so connecting said motor and swinging target that the motor causes oscillation of the swinging target, and elongated stationary support means mounted on the aforesaid legs and extending immediately behind the path of movement of the swinging target, said support means being adapted to take the reaction of said swinging target when struck by a dart.

MACHINE GUN AND TARGET TOY:

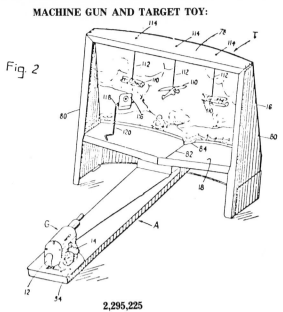

Fig. 2

2,295,225
MACHINE GUN AND TARGET TOY

Raymond J. Lohr and Richard Nelson Carver, Erie, Pa., assignors to Louis Marx & Company, Inc., New York, N. Y., a corporation of New York. Application December 27, 1939, Serial No. 311,224. 6 Claims. (Cl. 273—101)

A machine gun and target toy comprising an open target, a gun having a bottom feed, an arm extending from said gun to said target and secured rigidly to the target, said arm sloping downwardly from the target to a lower portion of the gun and containing a concealed trough-like magazine for returning shot from the target to the gun through the bottom feed, said gun being pivotally mounted on said arm for universal movement, means to limit the angular movement of the gun both in elevation and in traverse to an amount which confines the projectiles discharged therefrom to the target area, said target comprising a background wall, and top, bottom and side walls surrounding said background wall, said background wall being disposed at an angle which deflects the projectiles hitting said wall downwardly onto said bottom wall, and said bottom wall sloping downwardly to a discharge point leading into the aforesaid return trough-like magazine, whereby all shot fired from the gun is continuously returned to the gun.

FLASH GORDON SIGNAL PISTOL:

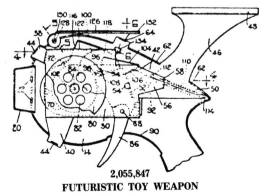

2,055,847
FUTURISTIC TOY WEAPON

Louis Marx, New York, N. Y. Application February 26, 1935, Serial No. 8,254. 12 Claims. (Cl. 46—10)

A futuristic toy weapon comprising a body made of two opppositely convexed pieces of sheet metal placed in edge to edge relation to form a bulbous body portion and contiguous handle portion, a frame in said body, said frame comprising spaced side plates and support arms extending outwardly therefrom and secured between the meeting edges of the sides of the body, a trigger pivoted in said frame and depending through a slot in said body, and mechanism mounted in said frame and arranged for acutation by said trigger.

HONEYMOON SPECIAL:

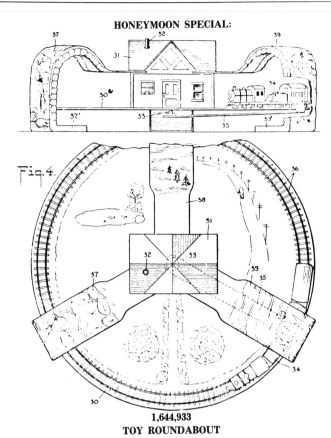

Fig. 4.

1,644,933
TOY ROUNDABOUT

Louis Marx, Brooklyn, N. Y. Filed Apr. 10, 1925. Serial No. 22,015. 4 Claims. (Cl. 272—31.)

A mechanically operated toy comprising a circular platform having an outer free periphery or rim, a toy figure arranged to travel on said platform in a circular path or orbit spaced inwardly of the periphery or rim of the platform, a motor carried by and arranged centrally of said platform, means connecting said motor with said figure for causing the figure to travel in its orbit when the motor is in an energized state, said connecting means extending underneath the platform from the motor to the rim of the platform and then upwardly and inwardly about the rim of the platform to the toy figure, and means for suspendedly supporting the platform and the parts carried thereby, the said last mentioned supporting means comprising a plurality of arch-shaped legs connected to the upper side of said platform.

PINCHED:

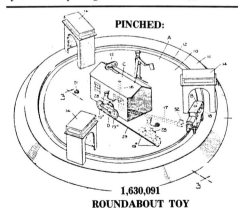

1,630,091
ROUNDABOUT TOY

Louis Marx, Brooklyn, N. Y. Filed July 19, 1926. Serial No. 123,288. 14 Claims. (Cl. 272—31)

In a device of the class described, a vehicle movable in a predetermined path, a motor operating said vehicle, a figure normally held in a retracted position and movable into a position adjacent the path of movement of said vehicle, mechanism for stopping the movement of said vehicle and means operable for releasing said figure and causing the same to move into cooperation with said vehicle and for simultaneously actuating the stop mechanism to stop the movement of said vehicle.

AMOS LARGE WALKER:

ANDY LARGE WALKER:

87,969
FIGURE TOY

Louis Marx, New York, N. Y., assignor to Charles J. Correll and Freeman F. Gosden, Chicago, Ill. Filed Mar. 12, 1931. Serial No. 39,040. Term of patent 14 years.

The ornamental design for a figure toy, substantially as shown.

87,970
FIGURE TOY

Louis Marx, New York, N. Y., assignor to Charles J. Correll and Freeman F. Gosden, Chicago, Ill. Filed Mar. 12, 1931. Serial No. 39-041. Term of patent 14 years.

The ornamental design for a figure toy, substantially as shown.

FUNNY FACE (HAROLD LLOYD):

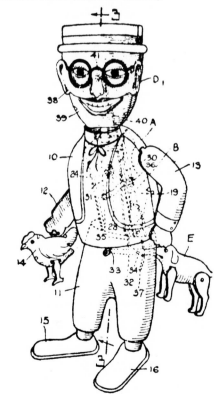

1,764,330
WALKING MANIKIN

Louis Marx, New York, N. Y. Filed Jan. 6, 1928. Serial No. 244,810. 8 Claims. (Cl. 46—40)

In combination, a manikin figure having relatively movable body sections, motor mechanism carried by the figure operative for relatively moving said body sections so as to impart a walking movement to the manikin in simulation of a figure in flight, a second figure simulating an animal in pursuit movable attached to said manikin figure, and means connecting the animal figure with said motor mechanism operative for imparting movement to said animal figure during the walking movement of the manikin.

INDEX

Note: Toys shown in color photographs are indicated with (C).